I0819490

Against the American Grain

Gary Paul Nabhan

AGAINST the AMERICAN GRAIN

A Borderlands History of Resistance

High Road Books Albuquerque

 Published 2024

Printed in the United States of America

ISBN 978-0-8263-6697-9 (cloth)
ISBN 978-0-8263-6698-6 (ePub)

Library of Congress Cataloging-in-Publication data is on file with the Library of Congress.

Founded in 1889, the University of New Mexico sits on the traditional homelands of the Pueblo of Sandia. The original peoples of New Mexico—Pueblo, Navajo, and Apache—since time immemorial have deep connections to the land and have made significant contributions to the broader community statewide. We honor the land itself and those who remain stewards of this land throughout the generations and also acknowledge our committed relationship to Indigenous peoples. We gratefully recognize our history.

Cover illustration: Adapted from Photo by Andrés Sans on Unsplash

Designed by Isaac Morris

Composed in Athelas, Albertran Pro, Circ Slab, and Fenwick

Contents

Introduction

In 1925, New Directions released poet William Carlos Williams's essays *In the American Grain*, which D. H. Lawrence immediately lauded as an unparalleled piece of historic writing with a literary bent.

Like other American classics such as *Moby-Dick*, *Leaves of Grass*, and *Sand County Almanac*, it was largely ignored in the first two decades following its publication. Immediately after World War II, and again in the 1960s, its readership and fame skyrocketed.

Since that time, its reputation as essential reading regarding the American experience has been sustained. As critic Yvor Winter once affirmed, the engagement of Williams's poetic voice in the quirky fabric of American history created a work "superior in all likelihood to nearly any other prose of our time and to most of the verse."

Williams's gift was that he reimagined the context in which familiar figures such as Ponce de León, Cotton Mather, Daniel Boone, and Sam Houston explored the continent and shaped our cultural identity. He set scenes so vivid and revealed actions of such continuing relevance that most early readers were stunned to find that American history could come alive in such a manner.

Unlike other Modernist writers such as Pound, Joyce, and Eliot, Williams's imagination hunkered down on the continent of North America. He broodingly reflected upon America's flawed and fanatical pioneers, our diverse roots, and the tragic collisions among cultures that generated economic, political, and social consequences for centuries afterward.

Such characters and historic settings in the New World were overlooked if not intentionally dismissed by most of the Modernist literati and academic historians of Dr. Williams's era. The good doctor's project was of even less interest to postmodern deconstructionists, and recognition of its elegance withered on the vine of the Ivory Tower.

Brilliantly, Williams implored his readers to use their own imaginations to see America afresh and to recognize the evanescence of "this homemade world" of vernacular constructions that had largely escaped conventionally trained historians up until then.

And yet, due to the social context of his era—more than to any limitations of his own poetic imagination—Williams's protagonists in the book were largely white males who descended upon the "unknown" continent from western Europe.

Only four of the two dozen characters he explored spoke Spanish; only three were women (two of whom were declared "witches" by their peers); just two were Indigenous; and the only African American characters were generically portrayed. Most of these characters were chosen to remind us of the horrible enslavement of their people, but Williams's all-too-brief renderings revealed little agency or intellectual capacity on their parts.

In contrast to the white males who were front and center in many of the essays, most of these additional characters were "tragic victims" whose mistreatment by the dominant society exposed the rapaciousness, greed, and outright insanity of many of the early explorers, political leaders, and ministers.

That his book echoed certain biases of his time while shattering others should not surprise us. Even for a physician as compassionate as Dr. Williams, much of America's ethnic diversity during his era remained muted and masked, if not gagged.

Seven generations of US citizens had been trained or lulled into thinking that North America was settled from east to west, thanks to "Manifest Destiny" and to the obsession with "land development" found among entrepreneurial immigrants from western Europe.

They contended that America was "pristine" and its First Peoples "primitive," rather than recognizing the fifty-five hundred years of agriculture, management of fire and water, and artistic engineering of gigantic earthen mounds and temples across the continent.

There were delightful exceptions. Even among the earlier generations of "settlers" that failed to appreciate the sophisticated storytelling skills of Indigenous cultures, there were some newcomers who recognized their sophisticated literatures writ on canyon walls, stone outcrops, wood bark, paperlike fibers, and wind in what is now the United States, southern Canada, or north-central México.

Many classically trained US historians have only belatedly and often begrudgingly recognized the extraordinary contributions Asian and Pacific Islanders made when they arrived on the western rather than the eastern shores of the Americas. To this day, few museums adequately cover the early influences of Filipinos, Japanese, and Chinese on the history of the Pacific coast, from Victoria, BC, down to Oaxaca City. One might guess that for centuries, American history texts were formally screened and constructed by the Daughters of the American Revolution only to reify the grandfathers!

Thankfully, most contemporary historians now "get" all of that. And yet relatively few—like Kelly Lytle Hernández, Paco Ignacio Taibo II, and Carrie Gibson—have fully recognized the persistent countercurrent and resistance to such rapacious extraction exhibited by Indigenous, African American, and "criollo/mestizo" communities. Such cultural resistance was initially anchored in the Indigenous cultures of the continent, but then embraced by a wide variety of marginalized individuals or clans who "took shelter" among these First Nations. Together, they resisted, repelled, revised, reformed, or rebelled against the fundamental principles of Westward Ho! domination.

As Carrie Gibson elaborated in *El Norte: The Epic and Forgotten History of Hispanic North America*, some of the most evocative but often cryptic American movements of the last five centuries have been south to north, not east to west. This theme is echoed and refined in a more recent history by Kelly Lytle Hernandez, *Bad Mexicans*, which dramatically documents just how much "unrest" south of the border spilled over into the United States to change the perspectives of both American institutions and citizens.

The contrarian Christian, Crypto-Jewish, Crypto-Muslim, Naturalist, and Indigenous individuals who ventured up from the tropics and deserts of the Americas and the Caribbean have continued to resist and defy the dominating forces from Europe who settled inward from the Atlantic seaboard of the United States. Most were propelled not only by sociological facts about disparity and domination but also by apocalyptic visions that gave them a sense that they were part of "holy alliances" to defend, reclaim, and restore sacred lands and waters. Spirit, not just hard facts or mathematical probabilities, moved them.

In a sense, that is the theme of this book, for it is a spiritual, not secular, history of resistance movements that arose from the desert borderlands, since I doubt that purely materialistic explanations by Marxists or capitalists can fully explain the "whys" and "hows" of the world we live within today.

As cultural creatives joined forces with other charismatic leaders and strategists in long-standing resistance movements within and beyond Native Nations, they fought to undermine, subvert, repel, or rewrite the laws imposed upon them, their economic structures, and their secular mindsets.

A largely hidden element of these resistance movements was that they have frequently been *cross-cultural collaborations*. More often than not, they included "renegades" from the dominant culture who served in subsidiary roles as backroom strategists, publicists, legal counsels, and spiritual allies.

Most of the stories here celebrate the hybridity and cross-cultural improvisation that has emerged from the desert borderlands over the past five centuries. Rather than buying into outdated notions of racial purity and narrowly defined tribal sovereignty on the basis of blood quantum criteria, the characters presented here cherished their family members and allies from other cultures and walks of life.

These rebels, resisters, and reformers have forged much of the solid footing that modern American social justice movements have built upon. Their songs, stories, and celebrations of resistance defend and deliver the true riches of this continent: its many land-based cultures and unique landscapes.

Approaching the hundredth anniversary of William Carlos

Williams's beautiful and prophetic collection of essays called *In the American Grain*, I offer you a glimpse into a deeper and often dismissed history of North America: one shaped not only by Indigenous cultures but also by their alliances with outcasts and mystics from the "Old World."

For the most part, they are not much like the conquistadors, commanders, politicians, and Bible beaters whom Williams profiled. Instead, they are nomads, street preachers, migrant farmworkers, wayward songsters, rabble-rousers, bilocators, and hunger strikers forged from another set of the varied languages and cultures.

Many of them first emerged from the deserts and other drought-stricken zones of "the South"—the Southwest borderlands and the Caribbean—to resist dominant paradigms and reshape the cultural dynamics on the rest of the continent.

Their instincts, ethics, aesthetics, tendencies toward magical realism, and strategies for resistance were first discovered, honed, and field-tested as they ran "against the American grain." Their disruptive behavior spread like wildfire, challenging the outdated and dubiously ethical paradigms of the dominant societies that had taken control of other regions of North America.

One only needs to consider the sanctuary movement of the 1980s, which emerged where I live between Tucson, Arizona, and Nogales, Sonora, in 1982, before it exploded onto the national scene.

As you will read about later, more than eight hundred congregations of faith offered sanctuary to tens of thousands of Guatemalans and Salvadorans who "illegally" entered the United States seeking political refuge. As a young man who milked goats and gardened with one of the sanctuary movement's founders, Jim Corbett, and was later blessed in my marriage to my wife, Laurie, by the other founder, John Fife, I had but an inkling of recognition that history was being made by my colleagues at that time.

What was also hidden from my view was the robust Underground Railroad across the border. Few of us who hosted refugees in our homes knew of the collaboration that Jim and John had with Padre Ramón Dagoberto Quiñones and Doña Maria del Socorro Pardo de Aguilar, on the other side of that border in Nogales, Sonora.

Our hearts and faith guided us when our heads could hardly comprehend all the risks involved in what has come to be known as "spiritual defiance." But my modest involvement in a movement that offered sanctuary to fifty thousand marginalized individuals is but one story among hundreds of thousands of others.

Collectively, these humble, scattered efforts somehow congealed into something larger. It changed the way Americans of all stripes treated the so-called other; in this case, "dangerous aliens" from beyond our borders. I was one of many who simply offered a way station for three generations of Guatemalan women who were escaping violence in their distant homeland.

What each of the stories has in common with the others in this volume is that the protagonists were forced by challenging circumstances to change the way the dominant cultures of this continent go about their business. Curiously, many of them were motivated by apocalyptic visions, dreams, or miracles which give their stories an air of magical realism.

Most were not inherently inclined nor trained to be activists or charismatic catalysts of social change. It was "the spirit" that awakened, altered, and animated them, so much so that any purely logical-positivist explanation of their lives is bound to be lamely academic. They took on those roles in the toughest of situations—in the hottest, driest, most remote communities in North America—because they were "called" to do so. Their spiritual charisma was what took their communities beyond what they could have previously imagined.

Often, they explicitly took inspiration from earlier spiritually motivated prophets who had risen out of the same dry land decades or centuries prior to their own emergence. How these threads became woven together across decades and centuries into one unifying story of cultural resistance has never fully been expressed in American letters.

Some of these desert saints remain nameless, or at least poorly known to mainstream historians. Others, such as Dolores Huerta, César Chávez, Woody Guthrie, or Teresita de Cábora, have achieved global fame but encountered plenty of obstacles and adversaries to overcome when they initiated their journeys.

In contrast to Carrie Gibson's *El Norte*, these essays aim to hold true to the tone and texture of Williams's original work. In poetic language, they focus on the charismatic individuals who changed the course of Western history through little acts of resistance or quixotic gestures of contrarian thinking, away from the political capitals, financial capitals, and military command centers that most historians dwell upon.

It is their hoarse, gravely voices and prayerful whispers I wish you to hear; their sunburnt faces and their dusty hands that I wish for you to see. It is their sweat and subtle but sacred fragrances that I wish you to smell.

Together, they have woven a fabulous patchwork quilt out of the grisly fibers, resplendent colors, and harsh textures found in vernacular American storytelling. Since I first heard of many of these "actors" in the "street theaters" of the desert borderlands, I have tried to carry along as much of that orality as I can.

Because I wanted to focus tightly on the interweaving of these mythic stories, with staggering coincidences and hallucinogenic visions imbedded in them, you will see no footnotes, only suggested readings of sources used for each chapter, to point you back to the many fine primary sources. Most of the characters in this book had a magical thread that spun through their lives. This luminous quality that is best to warmly reflect upon rather than to coldly analyze.

And so I leave you with stories—not formal histories—to help *re-story* and restore the spirit of communities and lands that have been neglected or undervalued as elements of the American experience. May their dreams and voices shock and unsettle you, enough so that you may be *re-settled* into a more raucous, cacophonous, and spirit-filled sense of where we live on Planet Desert.

A Note (or Apology) about Changing Names, Dialects, and Local Idioms

Lest you think I am intentionally changing the names of each character every few pages in an attempt to emulate Dostoevsky, Pasternak, or Solzhenitsyn, my intent may be different than that of these fine novelists. Some of these characters underwent events during their lifetimes that changed not just their names but behaviors and countenances. The boy who was called a Black-Tailed Jackrabbit by the Comcaac or Seri on San Esteban Island later became known to the world as Coyote Iguana. The saint of Cábora, Sonora, has been formally called Teresa or Teresita in most English accounts of her life, but Teresista by her playmates and family. Doc Ricketts affectionately wrote letters to Steinbeck addressed to Jon, not John. César Chavez was given at least two nicknames as terms of endearment before he began his activism, one for the herbal tea that calmed him and the other for his love of bicycles when the zoot suiters his age preferred hot rods. It is likely that Lalo Guerrero first met César Chavez at his musical events while he was still called by one of those nicknames, and only later realized that the famous farmworker organizer named César Chavez was the same young man he had chatted with in ballrooms on multiple occasions. All of these *apodos*, motes, nicknames, and *sobrenombres* remind us that many of these characters underwent the spiritual process of metanoia just as monarch butterflies go through metamorphosis.

As for my use of terms from Indigenous languages, they remind us that some terms—particularly desert place names and spiritual concepts—have no equivalent in Spanish or English. But these words both color and anchor the narrative with a place-based sensibility that would be absent from these stories if they were exclusively told in English. And like the rare plants and animals of the desert themselves, this place-based lexicon is now endangered by the very same forces that many of the protagonists in these sagas attempted to resist. Amen.

CHAPTER ONE

Resistance

Indigenous Elders Walking the Line

THE LEADERS of the sacred religious society of the Yaqui or *Yoemem* must have somehow known that alien forces were on the way toward their desert homeland. Was it just an acrid smell in the air, dust on the horizon, or disturbing images in their dreams?

The religious society's leadership called Ya'ura may have smelled a sultry, sulfurous wind that blew up from the tropics. It wilted wildflowers and forced the ocotillo and palo santo to drop their leaves. After smoking their sacred *makuchi* tobacco, some of the Ya'ura dreamed they were flying over their homelands to spot exactly where the intruders were camped.

This prompted them to get ready to go out to "Sing the Boundary" of their homelands. They began to prepare for their first encounter with the other kind, a race that had been described to them as pale, odd-looking, sharp-smelling foreigners. Perhaps they had already heard that these aliens had been capturing the Native neighbors and kin of the Yaqui to sell in the slave markets of Guadalajara and the City of Mexico.

It is probable that their partners in trade to the south alerted the leaders in the dozens of Yaqui pueblos that trouble was on its way. Their trade in macaws, peyote, turkeys, and turquoise had already been disrupted by these voracious strangers.

Perhaps scouts or shamans of their neighbors or of the Yaqui themselves had witnessed from their mountain lookouts the stream of thousands of soldiers coming up the plains along the Pacific coast. They moved like leaf-cutter ants along the plains, using their machetes to chop away the spiny, subtropical vegetation before them, burning and pillaging their way from one ranchería to the next.

All the smoke to the south may have prompted fear among desert tribes like the Yaqui, who sensed that these intruders would try to wrest control of the lands that these Indigenous dwellers regarded as their enchanted homelands.

.ღ.

Later, historians would call those northern landscapes Aztlán or the Gran Chichimeca, for they were not only part of the ancient trade corridors of the Nahuatl-speaking Aztecs but were reputed to live close to the presumed Nahuatl place of emergence.

But there were other means by which the Yaqui may have known of the potential perils they might face. Perhaps their pueblos had been alerted to the imminent danger by the divinations of their own medicine women and men. Perhaps these spiritual leaders listened to the Kuta Nokame—the Talking Tree—to foretell the future.

Perhaps their leaders could transform themselves into owls as the medicine women and men of other desert tribes could do. The makuchi tobacco could simply help with that transformation, so that they could fly low over their adversaries' camps during the night, endeavoring to assess the magnitude of the perils that would soon face them.

And if a crisis or threat appeared imminent, the elders affectionately called Yoyo'otukan would accompany the Ya'ura religious society leaders as they walked the 375-mile margins of their homeland.

As caretakers or *susuame* of the sacred territory of the Yoemem community, they were called to "Sing the Boundary" of 650 square miles of their lands. Their sacred territory stretched from the seashore of the Gulf of California inland, to the Sierra Bacatete rising 2,100 feet above the desert floor.

Their *Surem* ancestors may have first walked and sung the boundary of their historic homelands after the Great Flood in the year 707 (CE); once more in 1414, and again in 1519, when they initially heard of the fall of Moctezuma and conversion of Malinché from her native Nahua spirituality.

And now, in 1533, they were prepared to do it again should a threat from the south materialize as their divinations said it would.

These Yaqui leaders recognized that at any time, existential threats could arise, creating sudden crises whenever forces from afar arrived to push their pueblos off balance. They also knew that such threats could also be quelled by well-hewn acts of defiance or internal resistance. Their ancestors had repeatedly fended off various threats, and they could too. But the leaders in 1533 would need to mobilize all those who truly cared about safekeeping their lands, its waters, its fauna, and its crops, to *Sing the Boundary together*.

Such solidarity would be essential if they were to resist this new onslaught. The many songs and prayers, *gritos* and curses that have surged up during such moments of defiance in the past still echoed across the ages. They would soon see if their collective voices echoed loud enough to awaken and enliven enough of their people to rigorously repel what seemed to be an unprecedented threat emanating from distant kingdoms.

Of course, there was no way they could have known that they had begun a litany of resistance to the forces attempting to overtake their homelands, a litany that would be sung by their descendants many more times over the next five centuries.

On October 4, 1533, hundreds of Spanish conquistadors had directed thousands of their indentured foot soldiers of Nahuatl, Purépecha, and Tlaxcalan blood to cross into the Sonoran Desert for the first time. At that time in the villages, the fiery red *chiltepines* were still on their bushes, the *péchita* pods were still on mesquite trees, and the green-striped cushaw squashes were ripe enough to carve them into curlicues to dry as *bichicoris*. Even from across the river, the sweat of these mercenaries stank with anxiety, for they had not yet captured all the slaves that Nuño Beltrán de Guzmán had demanded. He would not settle for less.

That brutal conquistador was the one who had instigated and

brought the funding to their slave-trading expedition. He mandated that the expedition take into captivity thousands of Natives to serve as slaves in his fiefdom of Nueva Galicia, or to be sold into Nueva España.

But as the Spanish soldiers of fortune peered into an opening in the dense and thorny desert scrublands way ahead of them, they were perplexed by what they saw. The mercenary soldiers began to argue among themselves, unsure whether they were seeing a living fence of towering columnar cacti armed with spines, or a wall of warriors armed with bows and arrows in their hands, standing frozen at the edges of the clearing on a floodplain that spread out below the foothills that flanked the Sierra Madre Occidental.

As the Spanish troops approached the banks of the Río Yaqui in what we now call southern Sonora, they realized they were beholding a sight beyond their comprehension. It seemed more like a mirage or dream than any scene they had witnessed during earlier moments of their lives.

Later, an astonished Captain Jorge Robledo described this scene in a letter he sent anonymously to Beltrán. By Robledo's account, the Spaniards could simply not believe their eyes:

> Those who went ahead returned to tell us that there were warriors waiting for us that were gathered near the river. So we equipped ourselves with gear and guns, then split our forces into a vanguard and a rearguard. We marched toward the native warriors, who were assembled on the other side of the river, in a large opening in the desert that stretched out for more than a league. When they saw us, they began to slowly dance toward us very boldly, throwing fistfuls of flowers, leaves, and red dust into the air, flexing their bows and fiercely grimacing.

Those flowers and leaves represented the Sewa Ania—the sacred Flower World—that could bring any enemies to their knees.

According to Robledo, he and the other captain present—Beltrán de Guzmán's nephew, Diego—caught sight of a wizened old Yaqui maestro. He stood at the midpoint of the front line, where his appearance captured their attention. They deemed him to be:

> more distinguished than the others, for he wore a black robe tied around his shoulders, one that was studded with pearls . . . and he was *surrounded by what were either wild coyotes or trained dogs, birds, deer, and many other beings*. And since it was barely morning, as the first sunlight of the day dawned upon the elderly leader, he glowed brilliantly like silver or gold. With his bow and arrow in one hand, he carried a wooden staff with an elaborately carved handle in the other. He was in complete control of all his people and of the many animals who accompanied him in the arena.

As both Spanish documents and Yaqui oral histories later attested, the maestro went out in front of the troops to draw a line in the desert sand with his staff. According to some accounts, hummingbirds, silk moths, monarch butterflies, white-winged doves, white-tailed deer, and nectar-feeding bats accompanied him. Collectively, these beings offered up a simple but forceful message to the slave traders.

They affirmed that this was their Wilderness World, the truly Enchanted World. It is a world filled with sacred but potent flowers, which will repel all evil so that those with bad intentions will not be allowed to enter. For them, the Sewa flowers embodied a kind of peace, just as Hesu Krihto did when he walked among them.

That's why the Yaqui of many generations have pledged to adhere to and protect in their Yoemem Testamento—a land covenant that has been handed down over the ages—so that any intruder who attempts to take control or defile their sacred places will be resisted or expelled.

The Spaniards were not amused by this show of force. They could not understand the old man's dialect, but they surmised that he had demanded that they leave immediately. And so they commenced to fire cannons, muskets, and pistols at the Yaqui *nasuareo* warriors and the desert creatures who shuffled forward to the slow beat of flutes and drums.

With their very first glimpse of that amazing mass of animal and human resistance, the conquistadors' foot soldiers—especially the conscripted Indigenous fighters within their ranks—began to flee in fear.

It appeared that nearly every able-bodied individual of the thirty to fifty thousand Yoemem alive at that time were defiantly dancing to the slow but forceful rhythm of some ancient anthem of resistance.

The children and old women tossed baskets of cottonwood leaves and flowers up into the air to obscure the soldiers' visibility. The leaves and flowers raining down on the intruders vanquished the evil they carried with them.

This rattled the Spaniards, who suddenly seemed impotent as a force. Had they been emasculated by some preternatural force that they had no way to describe nor divert, let alone defeat?

The older Yaqui men then pelted the Spanish troops with handfuls of red hematite dust mixed with chile powder. This dust cloud burned their eyes and made them weep. The strongest Yaqui warriors lunged toward the Spaniards with lances or flung arrows whose tips were soaked with the poisonous sap of *hierba de la flecha*.

Hierba de la flecha was a powerful plant they used as an arrow poison, but its toxic juices could also stun fish and water snakes. It also harbored the silk moth cocoons the Yaqui made into the hundreds of rattles they wrapped around their legs.

When shaken, each palm seed placed inside a cocoon rattled like a snake as men with deer antlers on their heads shuffled forward. With each syncopated step, tens of thousands of *tenebari* leg rattles resonated with a thunderous drone akin to a storm of locusts.

Within no time, the troops led by Diego de Guzmán and Jorge Robledo were routed.

Guzmán and Robledo were so baffled by what had happened that they chose not to venture any farther into the Yaqui territories in the Sonoran Desert. They turned around and made a hasty return toward Guadalajara, where they knew that Beltrán would be furious to hear that "his" mass capture of potential slaves had failed.

For another seven decades, no Spanish troops tried to enter Yaqui territory. When a conditional entry of priests was later allowed by Yoemem leaders, it was on the terms the Yaqui community dictated, not those of the Spaniards. The few pioneering priests who were granted safe passage through the southern reaches of the Sonoran Desert were just as impressed by the ferocity of the Yaqui as Captain Robledo had been.

Their initial expressions of resistance had not only proved effective but had sent a larger message to the conquistadors: There will be long-term consequences if you ever try to cross the line and defile our homelands while we are on watch.

Nearly five centuries have passed since Beltrán's slave traders were thwarted at the desert's edge. But from the time of the Yoemem resistance to Beltrán, through to the times of Juan de Banderas in the 1820s, Joaquín Murrieta in the 1850s, Teresita de Cábora in the 1890s, and to the present, that deep instinct of resistance has periodically reemerged among Yaqui descendants.

Each year on October 4 at the Feast of Saint Francis in Magdalena, Sonora, the presence of thousands of Indigenous peoples—Yaqui, Mayo, O'odham, Opata, Cúcupa, Cora, Huichol, and Guarijio—echoes elements of that encounter on October 4, 1533.

Families of desert dwellers still make a pilgrimage by foot, train, or pickup truck to celebrate their collective survival across the centuries.

There at the Magdalena festival grounds, the most crowded plaza is the one where Yaqui deer dancers continue to shuffle and step boldly into an arena with the antlers of tiny white-tailed deer mounted on their heads. As the gourds gripped in their hands shake and the cocoons on their legs hiss like rattlesnakes, onlookers forget that it is men who are dancing before them.

For the past fifty years of the Gloria celebrations on both sides of the border, I have been one of those lucky onlookers, awestruck by what I have seen.

As hundreds of Yaqui families gather around them to watch, they see their kin become the deer that accompanied their ancestors who drew a line in the sand.

Six months later, on Holy Saturday of Easter Week, dozens of deer dancers begin to emerge from hiding, at least two or three in every Yaqui pueblo. They stand, stoic, alongside elderly women and excited children adorned with flowers and ribbons.

They are poised at lines in the sand in front of each of their sacred sanctuaries, repelling evil forces from entering their churches.

As hundreds of masked soldiers and *fariseos* with swords charge toward them, the women and children shower them with thousands of confetti flowers and bushels of cottonwood leaves. The deer dancers leap forward to defend the line in the sand, the steady sound of their cocoon leggings and gourd rattles rising above the clamor and the chaos.

These rituals echo the resistance that their ancestors described long ago in their Testamento, a living covenant of faith that has survived centuries of attempted genocide, armed intrusions, racial violence, land grabs, and water usurpments.

No one can recall the name of that wizened old man who drew the line in the sand in 1533. And just who were the original authors of the Testamento? That, too, is obscured by the passage of time. What has not been obscured is the simple fact that the Yoemem successfully resisted domination by the Spanish military from the day that line was drawn in the sand in 1533, to their last armed battle with the Mexican government in October of 1927.

Four hundred years of Indigenous resistance guided by an oral testament—a tribal covenant—is perhaps a human feat that surpasses in tenacity all the collaboration that went into the first US landing on the moon, which lasted only two and a half hours.

Decades after the Testamento was passed on by word of mouth, some elderly Yaqui maestros transcribed it onto paper in a mix of archaic Spanish and their idiomatic Cahitan language. Since then, other maestros with names like Rabbi Kauwuamea, Alfonso Florez Leyva, Juan Maehto Uhyolime'a, and Juan Valenzuela have kept it alive.

During Holy Week, dozens of the young Yaqui boys and girls stand next to their grandmothers and deer dancers in defense of the Enchanted World, and in resistance to anyone who might think they can mess with it.

How many consciously understand the nuances of the histories they are reenacting, ones that may have set the stage for four more centuries of resistance? Whatever the answer, their throats and their hearts still shout out to the rest of the planet an affirmation that is simultaneously defiant and hopeful. They remind us in so many ways that they are still *here*: inside the sacred boundary their elders have sung up for centuries. They are here, inside the Enchanted World that continues to nurture and protect them.

To this day, they still join forces to protect the Huya Ania—the Wilderness World—and the Sewa Ania, the Flower World. To this day, the Yoemem—who now reside in a string of Yaqui pueblos that span political boundaries—remain unvanquished.

For at least half a millennium, they have resisted all manner of insults, intrusions, and invasions. Over the centuries, the power of their commitment to the Wilderness World—the Fragrant Flower World—has periodically spilled out of the Río Yaqui watershed. It has flooded northward, out of the present-day Republic of Mexico, to both rile and enrich other cultures as much as 750 miles north of where the Ya'ura religious society leadership of the Yoemem first drew a line in the sand.

CHAPTER TWO

Metamorphosis

Mustafa al-Zemmouri and Cabeza de Vaca

IF WE look over our shoulders, whom might we glimpse lurking in the shadows of most American histories? How many of these individuals have walked far ahead of us, centuries before us, with a stamina that surpasses ours, as they shaped our collective destiny?

How many Black histories of America begin with African slaves arriving in Jamestown in 1619, as if African influences only flowed through English-settled harbors on the Eastern Seaboard?

What about the *older* African influences in North America, documented at least as early as 1528? These influences swept northward, southward, *and* westward across the continent from present-day Florida, Alabama, Mississippi, Louisiana, Texas, Tamaulipas, Nuevo Leon, Coahuila, Chihuahua, and Sonora, then later into Arizona and New Mexico.

Demographic histories have recently confirmed that there were far more Blacks than Europeans in Mexico and (what is now) the southern United States during the three centuries of exploration and colonialization from 1519 to 1821. It is likely than many Indigenous peoples in Mexico have some Black admixture within them. The reason for this is that many Africans mixed, mated, and married with Native peoples. These zambo populations later dispersed throughout what came to be known as New Spain, a vast expanse of land that stretched up to at least thirty-two degrees latitude in the present-day United States.

While Mustafa's traveling companion Nuñez Cabeza de Vaca told of their peregrinations together twice in print, no written interviews with the Moor were recorded for posterity. It is likely that the Spaniard sugar-coated his own interactions with Indigenous inhabitants of America, while downplaying or even appropriating heroic events in which his companion Mustafa al-Zemmouri played a more luminous role.

And so the voice of Mustafa al-Zemmouri—the Black African polyglot—is mute in most history books. If historians of the Conquest refer to him at all, they are like to call him Estevanico el Moro or simply "the Negro." They tend to overlook his more lasting influence on both Spanish and Indigenous cultures in the Americas, which seems to have been rooted in a stunning capacity to learn from and to heal others from many cultures.

As the first person born in the Old World to take two long treks through the deserts of the New, one might think he would loom large in our contemporary quest for a more inclusive history of the Americas.

And yet, such a long-standing omission seems less surprising when we remember that he was born as a poor Black man on the desert coast of North Africa, and his companions were blue-blooded white men born into the royal families of Spain. Our belated interest in him cannot fully correct that initial inequity and injustice.

The only apocryphal words attributed to coming from his own mouth come from a dubiously credible source—Pedro de Castañeda de Nágera—but they conjure up a prophetic moment. Those cryptic words were far too few to tell us much about his manner of speech, but they tell us much about his imaginative reach.

They were spoken a few days before his death in the pueblo of Hawikuh. There he boasted to the assembled Zuni Rain priests that he was a harbinger of something bigger. He came to them to announce that "a group of white men were being sent by a great lord . . . they were coming to instruct them about things divine."

That is it. Less than two dozen words survive as artifacts of the eleven years he spent in the American Deserta.

That said, just how did this brown-skinned Muslim from

coastal Morocco become the most barrier-breaking, wayfaring stranger and healer ever to set foot in American Deserta? Why have few Americans even heard him called by his birth name, a name that reflects his Muslim heritage and his place of origin?

It is Mustafa al-Zemmouri, the "Chosen One" of Azemmour. Today, peoples of various nations shower him with a litany of the other names he accumulated over four decades: Esteban de Dorantes, Estevanico el Moro, Estabancito el Negro. His fellow traveler Cabeza de Vaca introduced him in print as "*un negro alárabe, natural de Azamor*" (an Arabized black, native to Azemmour), but only referred to him as "el negro" the seven other times in his account that he is mentioned at all.

Others have insisted that Mustafa's skin was a lighter, coffee-brown hue. It is curious that the term *azemmour* also means a tawny-brown wild olive in the Dajira patois of the Amazigh or Berber people of coastal and montane Morocco. He was also called Little Stephen and the Valiant Moor, as well as many other names in Indigenous dialects.

That is fitting, because this child of lowly means somehow became a speaker of Amazigh (Berber), Maghrebi Arabic, Darija, Mozarabic, Portuguese, and Castilian Spanish before he crossed the Atlantic.

He then learned no less than five Native American languages while wandering by foot across three thousand linear miles of coastal scrub, mesquite grasslands, pecan forests, and desert.

For our purposes, we will call him by his birth name, Mustafa, to remind us of his desert roots, his Islamic roots, his African roots, his rural roots. He was born on the margins, and he would die on the margins of what was then known as the "rim of Christendom," a convenient tagline to mask the rapacious and mercenary underbelly of Western civilization.

We can now look to see whether it was being back in a desert that unleashed Mustafa's original sensibilities and skills. Those gifts were no doubt nurtured during his childhood in Morocco, but when he reached the deserts of North America, they seemed to rise and flourish in ways that could either resist oppression or heal others.

Let us go back there—to his origins—before we cover his triumphs and tragedies in the land so strange that he and his Spanish companions were dumbfounded by what they discovered on the other side of the ocean.

·ᘓ·

During my own stay in Azemmour, Morocco, I suffered a persistent cough, as winds from the Sahara deposited all manner of sand and talc-like dust all around the harbor on the desert coast, in the place where Mustafa was born. To be sure, there was greenery along the wadis or washes flowing down to the sea, but the coastal landscape was more a mélange of muted brown, burnt sienna, and pale gray.

As an infant and adolescent, Mustafa lived close enough to the African shores of the Atlantic to walk there whenever he wished. On the days when Saharan dust storms did not pelt him with sand, he played in the fields bordering the intermittent wash or wadi that meandered toward the ocean.

He was less than fifty miles southwest of Casablanca, though he never ventured far from the coast. He slept in a scrappy settlement on the left banks of a wadi now called Oed Oum Er-Rbia, The Mother of Springtime.

Back at the time of Mustafa's birth around 1503, it was still called Asif n Isaffen, The River of Rivers, for it was the second-largest watercourse in Morocco. After storms, it forcefully flowed out of the Central Atlas Mountains for 340 miles before flowing into the ocean at Azemmour. In that watershed, Mustafa may have become familiar with the towering dragon trees and columnar euphorbia succulents that look much like the soaptree yuccas and organ pipe cacti he would later wander between in the deserts of North America. By the time Mustafa was old enough to work alongside other men, the streamflow in the wadi had trickled to a halt. A lingering drought devastated most of their food crops and their flocks of sheep and goats. The Hahi Berber and Gnawa families on Azemmour's edges had to abandon their little garden plots, for there was no water left in the wadi to divert into their irrigation canals and fields.

For a while, Mustafa's clan was forced to revert to living as hunters, fishers, and gatherers. They took to foraging wild "famine foods" in the tidepools and the desert scrub, digging for clams or catching eels and shad, harvesting dates from the wild palms, sweet pods from carob trees, pungent fruits of spiny shrubs, and Saharan mustard greens that they fried in the oil pressed from seeds of wild melons.

It was likely that his mother and grandmother also showed him which leafy herbs he should use as antiseptic poultices, and which roots could numb pain or induce the purging of toxins. He learned to think like an herbalist, and this talent would be of immeasurable aid to him later in life.

Although Mustafa learned by necessity how to forage, fix, and consume all manner of desert foods and medicines while still a child, the unrelenting drought and famine still stunted his growth.

It appears that poverty and hunger many have forced his family to offer their runt as an indentured servant to Portuguese traders who had stopped in at their harbor. He was not a slave per se, but ostensibly working his way into freedom. These traders were always eager to traffic humans while ostensibly hauling cargo of aromatic herbs, gums, and textiles up the western coast of Africa to the Iberian Peninsula.

The Portuguese may have dropped a few coins into the hands of his parents—who knows? In any case, the trajectory of Mustafa's life was irrevocably changed. He would never again see his family nor his birthplace on the arid coast of Africa.

Fortuitously or not, Mustafa's fate ended up in the hands of Andrés Dorantes de Carranza, a minor nobleman from Extremadura. Young Dorantes had little to inherit, so he was eager to join an expedition to the Americas led by Panfilo de Narvaez.

It was Dorantes who tried to change the skinny Mustafa's name to Estevanico, Little Stevie. Andrés was surprised by how quickly Mustafa added Castilian Spanish and Mozarabic to the patois of Berber and Arabic he had spoken in Moroccan harbors.

It would soon become evident to Dorantes that Mustafa's capacity to rapidly learn other languages might become a lifesaver.

The ships commissioned by the treacherous Pánfilo de Narváez landed on the Floridian peninsula in 1528, when Mustafa was barely in his twenties. From there, Pánfilo's expedition went to hell in a handbasket, first with attacks by the Calusa when they set anchor near the site of present-day Tallahassee, then with a series of hurricane fringe storms off the coasts on either side of the Mississippi.

The crews of the various ships became separated at sea. Many drowned. Perhaps just twenty of the passengers on five small rafts or boats survived long enough to be shipwrecked one last time on or near Galveston Island along the Gulf Coast of Texas.

There they were soon captured by Natives who enslaved Mustafa, his master Andrés, and others. Just a handful of expedition members stayed in touch with one another over the next five years. They had no choice but to dwell in servitude to the original inhabitants of that land.

Under miserable conditions, the Spaniards and lone African spent much of their time chopping wood, digging up roots, harvesting prickly pear fruit, making torches of smoke to stave off the mosquitoes, and getting whipped when they could not comprehend—let alone follow—the never-ending barrage of orders. They were on equal footing now.

It would be absurd to claim that Mustafa was one of the lucky ones who survived, for what he and three of his Spanish companions survived were the most brutal, baffling, and hair-raising of circumstances.

Perhaps the three thrill-seeking Spaniards—Dorantes de Carranza, Cabeza de Vaca, and Castillo Maldonado—suffered more than Mustafa did, for they had already tasted the high life of Spanish nobility. The desires for fame and fortune they had once carried were smashed to bits. Cabeza de Vaca in particular was both humbled and horrified by what life without privilege had to offer. During a hurricane that he and several others suffered through early on in their peregrinations, it is clear that he was already experiencing the *surreal in the hyperreal*:

> We had to walk seven or eight together, locking arms to keep from being blown away. Walking in the woods gave us as much fear as the tumbling houses, for the trees were falling, too, and could have killed us. We wandered all night in this raging tempest. . . . Particularly from midnight on, we heard a great roaring and the sound of many voices, of little bells, also flutes, tambourines, and other instruments, most of which lasted till morning, when the storm ceased.

The Spaniards suffered in ways they could not have imagined just a few years earlier: aching hunger, intestinal infections, skin rashes, insect bites, nervous breakdowns, identity loss, psychic trauma, and horrific persecutions. Nevertheless, their later reminiscences suggest that they were socially and spiritually transformed by traversing through these dark nights of the soul.

In contrast, Mustafa had already been suffering from many of the maladies and humiliations of the marginalized since his childhood. He had survived before by eating almost nothing, for he had little else to lose.

And when the four of them reunited and finally fled from their captors, it appears that it was Mustafa's gut instincts, linguistic talents, healing gifts, and survival skills that kept the group alive. Reading between the lines in their later narratives, the power balance among them had dramatically shifted.

Mustafa embodied the dance of resistance to the most brutal forces at work in the world. He had come to the Americas not as a conquistador but as a survivor who would endure any hardship because of his sheer will to persist. That may have been the charismatic life force that the indigenes of many nations would see in him over the next few years.

Moreover, extraordinary powers seemed to well up in Mustafa once his group had reached the desert landscapes that reminded him of his home. To avoid another round of enslavement, he coached his Christian companions on how to offer their "spiritual gifts" as faith healers, herbal *curanderos*, and shamanistic performers whenever they encountered a new tribe.

What they lacked in clothes and gear, they made up for by carrying medicine bundles, rattles, talismans, and staffs, by chanting and blessing their hosts with the sign of the cross.

Cabeza de Vaca later put into print that the healing power was not theirs but that of the Holy Spirit that did the trick, as if to buffer themselves from criticism back home.

The very sight of Mustafa and the naked Spaniards must have baffled and amused all the Native people. They had never seen such odd hues of skin and strange shapes of lips, such bizarre curls of hair, nor such intensely hungry eyes; they had never heard strange words and chants, with sounds so hoarse and cacophonous compared to their own.

They may have also noticed something in Mustafa that was different from the Spaniards other than the color of his skin—a sensibility from his distant (African) past—that had suddenly reawakened in him.

Mustafa may have tried to share his survival skills and shamanistic instincts as an African healer with his aristocratic European companions. Although Cabeza de Vaca claimed that he was the most earnest in applying Christian folk healing to the Indians who begged for medical care, Mustafa was the only one of the four who grew up in a desert healing tradition.

There can be little doubt that the Europeans were awkward at first in their new roles as healers. They could not tell whether the roots of Mustafa's "magic" were pagan, Muslim, Christian, a natural-born gift, or straight from the mouth of Satan. But that did not matter much to the Moor nor to the Natives, so long as they made it through another night without hunger, torture, enslavement, or insanity further encroaching upon their bodies, hearts, and minds.

Now recognized as if he were a noted shaman, or regarded almost as a foreign god, Mustafa sometimes had two to three thousand Indigenous people gathering around him or guiding him down ancient trade routes to the next encampment of sympathetic souls.

Barely over thirty, Mustafa's personality and physique may have intrigued the Indigenous women and men whom he camped among. Some historians and novelists have idly speculated that a few of the women may have had no qualms about sleeping with such an unusual and arresting figure. And yet it remains nothing more than conjecture.

No matter whether they slept together or not, there is little doubt that this charming man may have opened their horizons when he appeared "out of nowhere." Intriguing stories about him and his three Spanish companions persisted in Indigenous communities for generations. Reciprocally, Indigenous women and men almost certainly opened other worlds for him.

Whether Mustafa or the Spaniards left any progeny behind has been a topic for idle speculation over the centuries. Influence and wonder, yes; descendants, who knows? But there are indeed hints of Mustafa and his traveling companions in oral histories retained by Indigenous communities for decades if not centuries around

Cerralvo (Tamaulipas); around the Cañon Blanco (east of present-day Lubbock) on the Texas panhandle near the New Mexico border; near Redford (Texas) and Ojinaga (Chihuahua); and near the Zuni pueblos on the New Mexico–Arizona border.

The four refugees were the subjects of attraction—and perhaps of alarm as well—wherever they appeared. These reactions presaged the interactions that Jumanos leaders such as Captain Tuerto and Juan Sabeata engaged in with foreigners over the following decades and centuries. Both Tuerto and Sabeata clearly knew of earlier encounters with individuals from the Old World, and for reasons not fully revealed in the written record were favorably disposed to making alliances with them. Mustafa and his fellow pilgrims blazed trails through Jumanos territory that were later traveled by Maria de Ágreda, Teresita de Cábora, Lauro Aguirre, Woody Guthrie, and perhaps the Chihuahuan grandparents of César Chávez.

From La Junta de los Rios onward, Jumanos traders and hunters—who had mastered extensive trail networks across the Chihuahuan Desert and up into Sierra Madre Occidental—may have guided the four pilgrims. They began to eat better, move faster, and complain less about their travails than they had on the first stretch of their journey, through Texas and adjacent Mexican states.

Mustafa's participation in a second expedition—this one to the Colorado Plateau, without Dorantes de Carranza or Cabeza de Vaca—likely resulted in lingering effects on the Indigenous communities during their pilgrimage route in search of the Seven Cities of Cibola.

In the Zuni, Hopi, Jemez, and Western Keresan (Acoma and Laguna) pueblos, there is a ceremonial "black ogre" *katsina* figure called Chakwaina, Tcakwaina, or Tsa'kwayna, who is depicted with a black mask, yellow eyes, and black goatee. Some claim that this is a depiction inspired by Indigenous oral histories about Mustafa al-Zemmouri, given that he was the first non-Native "Black" man to appear in these pueblos.

For Indigenous observers, Mustafa must have been a sight to behold.

For his own crew and for subsequent Spanish speakers in the desert borderlands, Mustafa may have played a pivotal role in conferring common names to all the plants and animals they witnessed, harvested, and consumed. He became the person who gave some of the most important food and medicinal plants in American deserts their "Spanish" names, most of which were Arabic, Berber, or Mozarabic terms for analogous plants in the Old World.

As soon as he recognized prickly pear fruit as an edible analog to figs, he called the cultures dependent upon them the Fig People, using the archaic Arabic term *tiin*, from which the Spanish *tuna* and *acetuna* derived. The Arabic term *al-jarub* for carob pods was applied to sweet mesquite bean pods and became *algarroba* in Latin American Spanish. And so on. These terms may have already been used in Al-Andalus in decades prior to the Conquest, but not necessarily among the elite. They were unlikely to have reached the deserts of North America prior to Mustafa's entry.

Once Mustafa made these analogies, he began to show his highbrow Spanish companions how to process the New World foods just as his family had done with their Old World equivalents.

Of course, we will never know for sure whether Mustafa was the exclusive source for these terms and practices that leapfrogged across the ocean from arid North African landscapes to the deserts of New Spain (Mexico). His own memories of the odyssey were never recorded, but Mozarabic and Darija terms clearly "jumped the pond."

Ironically, the first Spanish speakers the survivors encountered when they reached the desert coast of Sonora and Sinaloa included some of the same soldiers of fortune that the Yaqui had repelled just four years earlier. They had once again come north from Nueva Spain to capture more Indigenous slaves, aiming to complete what Nuño Beltrán de Guzmán had hoped to do a few years before. Try as they might, the mercenary troops of the conquistadors were never able to defeat nor dissuade the Yoemem leaders from evicting the Spanish from their sacred homelands.

But Beltrán de Guzmán himself had been recently overthrown,

discredited, arrested, divested of his powers, and shackled in 1536 for his cruel mistreatment of thousands of Indigenous souls. The slave trader had made too many enemies, conquistador Hernán Cortés, Viceroy Antonio de Mendoza, and Bishop Juan de Zumárraga being prominent among his detractors.

Beltrán de Guzmán would be sent in fetters to Spain in 1537 and held in the Castle of Torrejón prison for another year, until he was given petty employment as a bodyguard in Madrid. The former conquistador of Nueva Galicia, president of New Spain's first *audencia*, and governor of Pánuco died in relative poverty a quarter century after failing to dominate the Yaqui Nation.

This time, when the slave traders spotted three white men and one Black man—all naked, with long beards, gourd drums, feathered headdresses, and plenty of scars that testified to their years of trials, tribulations, and occasional torture—the Europeans were speechless, especially when the castaways cried out in Spanish.

Just who were these four feral men who spoke their language but had arrived "naked and ashamed"? The slave traders were so surprised when they heard Cabeza de Vaca speak his name that they offered immediate assistance to the four Spanish-speaking survivors. It would not be unusual if the Spaniard sugar-coated his own interactions with Indigenous inhabitants of America, while either downplaying or appropriating heroic events in which his companion Mustafa al-Zemmouri played a more significant role.

Nevertheless, Nuñez realized that he owed his life to both the Moor and the inhabitants of hot, dry lands many times over, and he underwent a change of heart. By that time, Cabeza de Vaca had been humbled enough to show his immense gratitude to Indigenous peoples throughout the Americas, so much so that to his final days, he tried to ban the enslaving, raping, robbing, and torture of Indigenous men, women, and children under his protection.

When the traders tried to enslave the Indian entourage that had accompanied him, it was Cabeza de Vaca who firmly dissuaded them from doing so. He had abandoned his mindset as a conquistador. All Indigenous allies of the four motley faith healers were allowed to flee northward without any further harassment.

Ironically, as the four vagabonds left their Indigenous allies behind, they were escorted southward to Compostela, Nayarit, where they were graciously hosted by none other than Nuño Beltrán de Guzmán—not yet imprisoned and expelled—who was intrigued by the stamina and stories of the four survivors. Oddly, he treated Mustafa not as if he were a slave or indentured servant but a guest who was welcomed into Guzmán's palace, while the three Spaniards slept elsewhere. It is during this moment in his life that Cabeza de Vaca exhibited the most gratitude for surviving the 3,500-mile ordeal over eight disorienting years. But rather than thanking Mustafa for saving his neck so many times, his thoughts ascended into the heavens.

Cabeza de Vaca credited God alone for "opening roads for us through a land so deserted, bringing us people where many times there were none, and liberating us from so many dangers and not permitting us to be killed, and sustaining us through so much hunger, and inspiring these people to treat us well."

For one moment, Mustafa was no longer reduced to a slave, just an oddity. He adorned himself with the feathers of the spiritually powerful great horned owl and carried a curandero's gourd rattle for singing songs of healing wherever he went.

By the time he reached the streets of Mexico City, he had become the leading edge among the survivors whenever they were strutted out at public events as the latest sensations. At a high-profile reception at the cathedral, he and his fellow pilgrims wore nothing but deerskins to cover their genitals. They confessed to their sponsors that they felt uncomfortable wearing street clothes or sleeping anywhere except upon the earth itself.

For several weeks in Mexico City, Mustafa was seen stepping

out in the evening to party with his new admirers. Some say he was adorned in turquoise and feathers, but others claim that he was still clad in so little clothing that he could exhibit his three decades of muscular masculinity and deep scars for all to see.

His reprieve from slavery was fleeting. While he was still in Mexico City in September of 1537, the city's disgruntled African slaves crowned their own king and initiated a rebellion against the Spaniards. Because slaves of African and Indigenous ancestry vastly outnumbered the Spanish bourgeoisie at the time, the first viceroy of Spain, Don Antonio de Mendoza, had five of the Black insurgents arrested. To frighten the rest into submission, he had ordered his protégé, Francisco Vázquez de Coronado, to use his own Indigenous slaves to execute the Africans.

Nevertheless, Viceroy Mendoza had met Mustafa earlier and had admired his resilience and charisma. He therefore wanted to keep Mustafa isolated from the rabble-rousers in Mexico City, lest he become their poster child. In short order, Mustafa was commodified as a "servant" once more, as Andrés Dorantes ceded the destiny of Mustafa the faith healer to Viceroy Mendoza. Nevertheless, Mendoza granted Mustafa the capacity to work hand in hand with Friar Marcos de Niza in guiding an expedition northward, one that Francisco Vázquez de Coronado would logistically manage.

As the viceroy's employee and the friar's colleague, Mustafa became the first African servant to be mentioned by name—albeit as Esteban, a Christian name—in a letter to the king of Spain.

Even as Mendoza stopped all further arrivals of African slaves to Mexico, he quickly dispatched Coronado and de Niza to initiate a well-funded expedition northward into the deserts. Their hope was that Mustafa's knowledge of the desert and its peoples could assure the success of the adventure.

And so Mustafa consented—or was enlisted—to embark on another field adventure, in part following the same route that traders had taken several years before when the Yaqui rebuffed them. This time, he resisted de Niza's many attempts to control his movements and functioned as a free agent, not as a vassal of the Crown. In many ways, Mustafa had ascended to a leadership role, but it cost the Moor his own life. Whatever collaborations he had forged earlier with both Indigenous healers and the Spaniards were not enough to keep him from facing another wave of perils.

Centuries-old oral histories still circulating among the Zuni of New Mexico recount their encounter with a "black ogre katsina," or ancestral spirit, wandering up through the deserts to the south of them, probably along the San Pedro River.

But when Estevan sent a messenger to the Zuni announcing he would arrive in their pueblos within a day, a priest at the first pueblo sent the messenger packing. The Zuni priest threatened to kill anyone who came into his village.

Brashly, Estevan ignored this warning, and when his entourage appeared the next day, their trade goods were confiscated by the Zuni. The Zuni held the interlopers overnight without food, water, or dialogue.

The next day in May of 1539, a Native American member of the expedition escaped to hide nearby, but then witnessed the Zuni showering Estevan with arrows. That was the last time he was ever seen by anyone associated with the expedition to find the Seven Cities of Cibola.

Months later, when Coronado arrived at Zuni in August of 1540 and inquired about Estevan, he wrote about the Chosen One of Azemmour that "the death of the negro is perfectly certain because many of the things which he wore have been found."

Although he was officially declared dead by the Spaniards, rumors of his survival—in the flesh or in spirit—persisted at Zuni and elsewhere.

To this day, at the annual Nuestra Senora de Los Angeles Fiesta de Los Persingula in Jemez Pueblo every August 2, a katsina dancer who appears to be this first African arrives with his face painted black and curly sheep pelts atop his head to represent his nappy head of hair. At least four other pueblos in New Mexico and Arizona also bring out a dark-haired, brown-skinned katsina that elders claim are linked to oral histories about Estevan el Moro.

And yet, historians' interpretations of these oral histories vary tremendously in what they say about Estevan's (or Mustafa's) ultimate relationship with the Indigenous peoples he encountered near the end of his life. On little if any tangible evidence, some accounts note that Zuni priests were incensed by "this bad man," claiming that he tried to force himself on tribal women and girls. Another account suggests that the Zuni were so supportive of him that they feigned his death and kept him in seclusion until he could move on without detection by Coronado's envoys and troops. We will never know . . .

Still others speculate that Zuni priests condemned him as a false shaman and were outraged that he carried sacred paraphernalia of a holy man with him. Another account posits that Estevan bragged that heavily armed troops would soon be following him to Zuni, and that his warning that "a group of white men were being sent by a great lord . . . to instruct them about things divine" presumed that the Zuni priests themselves had no direct access to the divine.

Both his intentions and his death in the spring of 1539 became shrouded in myth and mystery as disruptive as the droughts and sandstorms that initially drove him from his African home on the desert coast.

·~·

The fragments of Mustafa's life that we have glimpsed linger like pieces of an incomplete puzzle. Meanwhile, Cabeza de Vaca has been cast as the hero of at least two feature films and books too numerous to count. A hero Nuñez may have been, but Mustafa was simply never allowed to tell his own story for posterity's sake, while his traveling companions were given ample opportunity to do.

Although his oral storytelling and chanting may have soothed or healed hundreds of Indigenous people, the words of slaves had no currency on paper during the colonial era. But what other person of his era succeeded in serving as the guiding light for two distinct groups of Spaniards lost in the driest reaches of the North American continent?

Mustafa repeatedly navigated, connived, or magically guided their way out of physical and existential danger. He did so with virtually no privilege, wealth, or formal education, more than two centuries before the United States became a nation.

While his three Spanish companions could hardly admit on paper that they survived by virtue of Mustafa's spiritual healing powers and street smarts in the desert, the oral record of his impression on Indigenous communities has persisted for five hundred years. Mustafa had become an icon of ancestral healing and a spirit with unique charisma among several Native desert peoples and was highly regarded despite any possible hedonistic urges and moral flaws. It is clear that at least Indigenous healers and priests recognized that his powers eclipsed those of Cabeza de Vaca and the other so-called conquistadors.

The iconic image of a brown-skinned Moor transmogrified into a Black Tsakwayna katsina persists in ceremonies of the pueblos in the desert borderlands, while the Spaniards who accompanied him did not gain a memorable place in their imaginations. Instead, they are captured only in history books, statues, and superficial biopics or documentary films.

There is an iconic black butterfly in the arid landscapes that Mustafa al-Zemmouri crossed during his five to six years in the American Deserta. It is known as the pipevine swallowtail, for its larvae are hosted by the chemically potent pipevine plant, which the caterpillars feed upon. When the butterflies themselves emerge from the chrysalis during their terrific metamorphosis, they enter a new world where they occasionally imbibe the nectar of the very same plants whose leaves fed their larva.

Through many stages in their metamorphosis, the pipevine swallowtails shed one identity after another on their journey through life.

So it was with Mustafa's metanoia, which led him to transformed into a slave for the Portuguese, a Christianized ladino commodity, an indentured sailor/servant for the Spanish elite, a shipwrecked Black Mexican, a cross-cultural herbalist and faith healer, a charismatic shaman, a street celebrity in Mexico City, an expedition leader, and a black ogre katsina whose memory lives on among a half-dozen Indigenous pueblos.

Yes, it may be true that Cabeza de Vaca and the other Spaniards were also remade by the journey through the desert from one ocean to another. And yet it would be hard to argue that they went through as many psychic and physical shifts as their indentured slave from Morocco must have suffered.

In a world where hybridity and shape shifting might have more survival value than sticking to more static, essentialist stances, Mustafa al-Zemmouri may have charted a new path for dwellers in the arid West.

He became the original changeling of the American Deserta.

CHAPTER THREE

Volition

María de Ágreda, Jumanos Captain Tuerto, and Enrique Madrid

MARÍA CORONEL traveled far from her birthplace in Ágreda, Spain, in a manner that we still do not rationally understand.

Sometimes, her family and friends just didn't know what to do with her. When young María Fernández Coronel y de Arana showed the other Franciscan nuns of Ágreda, Spain, the altar cloth she had embroidered, they were speechless. As they gazed at the imagery, they realized they could not identify any of strange plants or animals in the austere landscape she had stitched into existence.

For good reason. The flora and fauna that María had conjured up were dead ringers for the yuccas, roadrunners, barrel cacti, ocotillos, and scissor-tailed flycatchers on the high, dry plains and deserts of the New World. The nuns had no idea where these imaginaries had come from, and only later were they told of rumors that María had "materialized" in faraway lands.

Rather than delighting her sisters, María's imagery from strange lands made most of them feel apprehensive. There was something in the way she quietly spoke about these landscapes that hinted she had been there.

That was puzzling to the nuns, because their abbess—who had taken the name of María de Jesús—had hardly ever left the grounds of their convent, the Monastery of the Immaculate Conception in Ágreda.

According to her mother, who was also a nun, the women in their family had never traveled together beyond the Spanish province of Soria since the time of María's birth. And yet there were mystical machinations and apparitions all around Ágreda in that moment of history: In the generation before her, Teresa of Ávila and Saint John of the Cross had aroused the imaginations of Catholics from their "perches" just forty-five miles away, while Sephardic Jews infused the mystic traditions of the Ashkenazi Kabbalah with new fervor, and Sufi poetry inspired the Muslim Moors in her region.

And then there was the fragrance that some of her associates said she emitted every time she came back from one of her "travels." It was a heady scent, one reminiscent of the fragrances of wild culinary and medicinal herbs. Perhaps it emanated from the aromatic leaves of some desert shrub in a distant land.

Could it be that this dreamy aroma came from a small gray bush named *mariola*? Was it one of the fragrances that she had carried back with her in one of her dreams or trances?

Even if those close to her in Ágreda had never known the flower itself, one of the older nuns in the convent may have known that word mariola, for it was common use on the Iberian Peninsula. Mariola—like the word *angel*—meant messenger. In some cases, it was used to describe a holy messenger sent from the Virgin Mary.

Centuries later, the Franciscans learned of an aromatic shrub in the Chihuahuan Desert that is indeed called mariola. It has been used medicinally by a dozen desert tribes whose lands stretch from near present-day Tucson, Arizona, across southern New Mexico, down into the Big Bend and the Edwards Plateau near San Angelo, Texas. It was given the scientific name *Parthenium incanum*. *Incanum* means "something so gray and hoary that it inspires veneration." The plant's gray leaves are coated with a half dozen aromatic oils that are said to smell like the "hope for rain."

The abbess's uncanny prescience and fragrance also baffled, embarrassed, and at times worried the Catholic hierarchy in Spain. María had begun to speak eloquently and pray fervently by the age of four. A family friend, Bishop José Jiménez y Samaniego, recalled that even as an adolescent María experienced ecstatic visions and prophecies in which she felt that God was warning her of the sinfulness rampant in society and the material world. It has been claimed that when she was barely seven years of age, she had become entranced by the tragicomic play by Lope de Vega called *El Nuevo Mundo Descubierto por Cristóbal Colón*, for it explored faraway lands where virtuous Natives displayed their love while villainous Spaniards displayed their greed.

Could that have prompted little María to side with the forces of resistance among Indigenous peoples when she grew older, repulsed by the more rapacious behaviors of colonizing Europeans?

Perhaps discussions of that play about a New World triggered some spiritual yearning in her to seek out other cultures, other places, other ways of being. In his own versions of their conversations, her confessor claimed that she had participated in curious encounters with unusual plants, animals, and peoples that she could describe in extraordinary detail. And she could see, smell, and feel them for hours after she had awakened from her dreams.

Before she had reached the age of five, María caught the attention of Bishop Don Diego de Yepes of Tarazona, a relative of Saint John of the Cross and the last confessor of Teresa of Ávila. He recognized something special in her and asked her parents to reserve a special place for her in their house where she could pray and study the mystics and saints.

Well before her parents had adopted monastic religious life and converted their former home into the convent for Concepcionistas, her precocious grasp of the contemplative life of a mystic had become evident to those around her. As she wrote later on:

"From the age of nine or ten, [my parents had me and their other] children pray in constant devotions. . . . [They] had us engage in mental prayer. . . . Ever since [then], it seems the Lord filled my inner life with light."

But such constant devotion seemed to take its toll on her health and maturation. By the time she turned thirteen, she suffered from an illness for six months that pushed her into the throes of death. She received the final Sacrament of Extreme Unction, and her parents prepared for her funeral and entombment.

But then her condition flipped as she identified with the suffering of Jesus, a shift that she said "eroded the hardness of my heart," bringing her happiness and light: "It was like placing a little girl at the start of an exceedingly straight path. . . . Ever since, I found that when I focused my attention within, I would enter a state of exceedingly quiet prayer."

At age fifteen she erupted with a vision of a journey to a New World, which she called her journey across the face of the earth. As *The Face of the Earth* poured out of her dreamlike trance, she transcribed it into fifteen chapters, which she later linked to a still-unpublished cartographic work, *The Map of the Spheres*. The peoples she met along the way in her journey had a geographic orientation "entirely opposite of ours." But, she cautioned, "We should not judge based on our own situation who is right side up. The truth is that we are all right side up! There is a great diversity in human appearances and a variety of social customs . . . [but through] the diversity of their outer appearances, one cannot know their inner qualities."

The revelations received by such a young girl threatened to upset the apple cart of the male-dominated Catholic Church in Spain, so much so that it prompted visits to María by official inquisitors. And yet she welcomed them without expressing much fear, for she was already under the protection of the king of Spain, who frequently asked her for both spiritual and moral advice over the coming decades.

Her confessors, guardians, and perhaps even her sisters would listen, marveling at her storytelling. As is natural, some were secretly concerned by how distracting it was to kneel and pray next to María de Jesús. With little notice, she would become overwhelmed by her *exterioridades*—trances, visions, dream travels, and levitations—in a manner that made not just a few of them secretly envious.

CHAPTER THREE

It was in 1620 that María's visions took another, deeper, more focused but inexplicable turn. At the age of eighteen, while still cloistered in her Concepcionista convent, she gained the capacity for what has perhaps been erroneously called "bilocation" or "flight" to a specific region, the deserts of North America. Several Indigenous tribes in the deserts of North America began to report visitations by someone who in many ways fit her description. Although the "Flying Nun" misnomer has been difficult to shake, there was a sense that she had begun to converse with Indigenous populations in the American Deserta. Franciscan officials in New Mexico who had heard of these reports asked if it would be possible to interview nuns in Spain to confirm or deny the veracity of these claims. It fell upon Franciscan padre Alonso de Benavides—a *custos* or head cleric—stationed near the Río Grande in New Mexico to return to the Iberian Peninsula to evaluate these claims.

During that era in Europe, acts of bilocation and "out of body" materialization somewhere else were not categorically dismissed as disappearing acts, as if they were sleight-of-hand parlor tricks. Instead, "rematerializing somewhere else" was regarded as the consummate expression of the spiritual acumen of any mystic. Several other mystics—from the Virgin Mary herself, to Saint Francis Xavier, Saint Martin of Porres, and Saint Joseph of Cupertino—were gifted with this spiritual capacity.

That prompted the Catholic hierarchy in Spain to invite the cleric Benavides back from New Mexico to investigate the claims and reconcile the reports from Ágreda with those from the Río Grande. The ambitious but sympathetic Franciscan was hoping to draw more attention—and perhaps favor—to the remote desert region where he had been laboring. What he found both thrilled and stunned him.

For his part, Benavides reported that her call had indeed been heard by Indigenous inhabitants of the lands we now refer to as Arizona, New Mexico, and Texas. Most curiously, a Jumanos leader known to the Spanish as Tuerto—the One-Eyed Captain—encouraged thousands of his tribal members to flock from the Indigenous territory she called Tixtlas toward the Río Grande in Nuevo México to receive baptism.

Oddly, these were the same Jumanos that Estevan el Negro and Cabeza de Vaca had encountered a century before in the Chihuahuan Desert near the Big Bend of the Río Grande. Cabeza de Vaca affectionately remembered them as "the finest persons of any culture we ever encountered."

Numbering perhaps as many as sixty thousand tribal members in New Mexico, the Big Bend of west Texas, Chihuahua, and adjacent Coahuila, the Jumanos were consummate traders of salt and turquoise, as well as irrigation farmers, bison hunters, and harvesters of mesquite pods, pecans, and the hallucinogenic "buttons" or buds of the peyote cactus.

They were nicknamed the Rayados or Striped Face people, due to their tattoos that spread across their faces like the rays of the sun. The men cut their hair in a bowl-like sphere but kept one long lock to which they attached a "topknot" of feathers, much like desert quail. Many Jumanos spoke multiple languages and had well-honed skills in cross-cultural communications, having maintained trade relations with at least thirty-six other Indigenous cultures from the Chiricahua Mountains just west of the Great Divide clear to the Louisiana bayous.

Conceivably, they may have congealed into a "hybrid" trading culture that engaged members of several Indigenous language groups as a confederation. They were intellectually if not spiritually curious about strangers and were open to the artistic expressions and spiritual pursuits of others.

It is not surprising that the nun's focused attention on the Jumanos tribe confounded her Franciscan guardian, because to his knowledge, Sor María de Jesús de Ágreda had never been known to physically travel *anywhere*. And yet, between 1620 and 1623—and perhaps at late as 1630—she claimed she had wandered among the Jumanos in the Americas at least five hundred times, conversing with them and exchanging ideas with complete comprehension, even though they spoke different languages.

She also admitted that she had been martyred twice during these dangerous journeys but had been resurrected through the grace of God and the discipline of her faith.

Benavides's reports to other Franciscans in the Church created a sensation among Catholics of that time, for they were largely inclined to favor a direct, mystical way of engaging with the Creator throughout Creation. Spanish missionaries heading off to Mexico took the news of her trance-mediated visions to the Americas, where they triggered astonished attentiveness to missionaries already residing in the desert of New Mexico.

Indigenous elders matter-of-factly reported that they had been having dialogue with a young woman in blue habit for some time. She had encouraged the Jumanos and other tribes to seek out priests who could baptize them, teach them the rosary, provide them with blessed crucifixes, and protect them from the depredations of marauding Apache and Comanche bands that had been challenging the social stability and economy of the entire region.

Benavides had become the "broker" and "editor" of accounts from the Indigenous peoples of Nuevo México and Tixtlas about meeting a lady in blue. He asserted that they continued to desire to be reunited with this beloved friend and fine teacher. Jumanos families who lived along the Río Pecos, Río Grande, and Río Conchos claimed that she would appear out of thin air to cure their sickness, to scare off the devil who had dried up all the local water, or to teach them of Jesus and Mary.

Cures attributed to María were like those attributed to another blue nun in Spain: Mother Luisa de Carrión. There were reports that Mother Luisa had mystically appeared to miraculously heal the children of the Hopi (Moqui), the Zuni, and the Nde (Apaches de Navajo) to the west of the Río Grande.

Jumanos leaders claimed they knew the younger sister very well, from numerous conversations and shared travel. Because of her visits, the Jumanos whom Benavides interviewed already knew how to venerate crucifixes and statues of Jesus as an infant.

The Jumanos nonchalantly affirmed that they had been worshipping as Christians for some time, thanks to the guidance of the Blue Nun. Inevitably, she would wander off toward the blue mountains on the edge of the desert in an equally blue cape that covered her coarse earth-colored sackcloth habit.

When Benavides showed the Jumanos a painting of the elderly Mother Luisa from the Sisters of Saint Clare in Spain, they said that their own spiritual guide dressed in the same manner but was younger and more beautiful.

Not long afterward, other reports of a lady in blue came in from Ohlone Indians along the central California coast near Carmel, the Hopi up on the mesas and sand dunes in present-day Arizona, and the O'odham near Tucson.

In visiting these places hoping to find out more about the Indigenous people whom Sor María and Madre Luisa reputedly visited, I did not encounter any additional verbal confirmations that the Blue Nuns are remembered today, as they are among the Jumanos.

And yet I could sometimes inhale a lingering *presence*—perhaps just a *fragrance*—in these places that offered me a sense of familiarity. It may simply have been my imagination, but imaginations are not always simplistic. Sometimes they bring to attention something palpable that has been deeply buried in our collective subconscious, what Kiowa storyteller Scott Momaday referred to as racial or cultural memory.

Could these sensations have come from encounters with the same Sister of Saint Clare dressed in a blue cloak? Were some of the apparitions of Mother Luisa de Carrión instead, or of other Franciscans who wore a blue cape or smock over their habits?

Benavides's interviews with the Jumanos did not answer many questions, but instead opened many others. In his role as the head cleric of New Mexico, he became more than convinced that there was sufficient evidence of Indigenous interest in collaborating with those who had "arrived" as messengers of the Catholic faith. He urged that he and other Franciscans amply support efforts to respond to the needs of Jumanos and their neighbors, and to protect one another through mutual aid.

María eventually burned her journals that referred to her visits to Nuevo México, but she remained comfortable noting how she had developed a deep friendship with a leader of the Jumanos when she was younger. He was the one who could see with just one of his eyes, a disability that afflicted one of his children as well.

Benavides had been particularly intrigued by this, since the priests at Ysleta Pueblo had introduced him to an Indian leader from west Texas called Captain Tuerto, the same Jumano who had encouraged mass conversions. Benavides confirmed to her that Tuerto had come looking for her on multiple occasions, and that he had brought thousands of his tribesmen and women to be baptized and healed.

María was delighted to be remembered by this tattooed man with short, brightly painted hair, who seemed to be wise about the world in so many ways. Like the other men of his community, he had one long lock of hair that was tied with the absurdly long and colorful feathers of the scissor-tailed flycatchers and macaws that had ceremonial importance to many tribes.

Captain Tuerto wore tegua sandals tanned from the buckskins of deer or antelope, long leggings, and a colorful cape to protect him from the cold winds of winter. What he lacked in eyesight he made up for with his keen sense of hearing and his capacity to form alliances.

He forged his disability into a gift. And he ensured temporary protection of his people against Comanche and Apache raiders by using the Spanish as a buffer against his Indigenous adversaries.

But had María already been alerting her friend to the perils of dealing with some of her fellow Spaniards, recalling the tragicomedy by Lope de Vega that had disturbed her so much as a seven-year-old? Was she quietly urging the Jumanos to prepare their resistance against the Conquest?

Knowing of her interest in "spiritual geography," Benavides plied her for more details about her travels in Nuevo México. She aptly noted that Ysleta Pueblo—where Tiwa was spoken—was farther up the Río Grande than most Jumanos settlements. She precisely placed it near where the river rises out of the yucca-studded desert into the piñon-juniper woodlands and ponderosa forests of the Sangre de Cristo Mountains.

María briefly described how she had traveled across the high plains of eastern Nuevo México and western Tixtlas, before descending into a fissure in the earth now called Palo Duro Canyon, where tribes frequently gathered for ceremonies, to hunt bison, and to trade. She also painted a verbal picture of La Junta de los Rios—where the Río Grande and Río Conchos converge.

That's where many Jumanos descendants still dwell to this day, keeping elements of their ancient culture alive. That's also where I feel that palpable sense of familiarity whenever I stop to see friends along the floodplain of the Río Grande and look across to the farms of Jumanos descendants on the other side of the river.

In María's time, the Jumanos lived in clusters of huts that were scattered along the rimrock just above the floodplain, where they grew the same maize, beans, squashes, and chiles that the

Tarahumara and Mountain Pima cultivated farther west in the sierras. They capably irrigated with water from springs or streams. From the secluded canyons along the three rivers, they ventured out into the Chihuahuan Desert, whose topography they knew like the veins and wrinkles on their own hands.

Benavides was impressed by the precision of details he claimed she had offered to him without hesitation. He concluded that her descriptions of the peoples, deserts, plains, and watered canyons of North America "were so exact, that a person who had been there for many years and had traveled over that entire country could not have answered with more truth and sincerity."

Once, when Benavides had asked María for her own explanation of how her appearances in remote areas could have possibly occurred, she reiterated the impetus for her journey:

"The Lord filled my inner life with light, and it was like placing a little girl at the start of an exceedingly straight path, telling me to walk without deviating from your goal or turning aside. . . . I found that when I focused my attention within, I found I could enter a state of exceedingly quiet prayer" that took her places she would not have otherwise imagined.

Years later, Sor María humbly offered a briefer but nondualistic way of accepting her capacity for bilocation without any urge to overanalyze it:

"It is difficult to interpret such elevated intellectual and spiritual processes in terms of matter alone."

But then she added, "[But] I can assure you beyond any doubt [that my visits] did in fact happen. [Yet] I was [still a teenager when this happened] and inexperienced [and] whether or not I really and truly went in my body is something about which I cannot be certain."

.~.

No one can doubt that Sor María's original intent was sincere, and there was no reason to enter into something sensationalistic: *To work on behalf of those whom her Creator's compassion was most inclined to favor*: the poor, the marginalized, and the imperiled Natives of a remote place.

Is that what Captain Tuerto sensed in her? Someone whose compassion could help guide his people to stay out of harm's way? Someone who treated him as an equal? That alone was an expression of resistance, worthy of prompting an inquisition.

Judging from her elaborately embroidered *paisajes de plantas, pajaros, y pueblos*, the blue lady of the blue deserts had found a home away from home, perhaps to prepare her friends in the Jumanos communities for the challenges that lay before them.

·~·

Of the first several hundred European and African immigrants who set foot on the sands and stony ground of North American deserts, nearly all were men.

The voices of the few women—Native or immigrant—were hardly ever recorded in accounts from that era. The voices of women who resisted the pressures of military and ecclesiastical forces of their time were far fewer.

Was María de Ágreda some surrogate, some placeholder for them?

Perhaps her Jumanos confidant Captain Tuerto wondered that aloud:

Just why did it take a cloistered nun from Spain to speak for the voiceless? Is that why she came into the desert to visit us of her own volition? Did this mystic really think she could disrupt the stifling biases of her own colonial culture? Why was this mystic so confident she could help protect us? How was she sure she could make so many cultural, political, and spiritual walls vanish into the crisp, thin, azure-blue air?

·ঌ·

Sixty years after Sor María de Ágreda and Jumanos leader Tuerto had initiated their cross-cultural dialogue, the Pueblo Revolt erupted in 1680. Simultaneous attacks by Indigenous resisters left four hundred Spanish immigrants dead in New Mexico and the future of Indigenous-Spanish collaborations in peril.

All Spanish soldiers and missionaries in New Mexico had retreated as far south as El Paso, and their entire project of colonization along the Upper Río Grande was deemed a failure.

And yet, three years later, a thirty-seven-year-old Jumanos leader appeared in El Paso to offer a hand. His name was Juan Sabeata, and although he had been born at the Jumanos pueblo that Sor María had reputedly visited, he lived downstream of El Paso del Norte, at La Junta de los Rios. As a young man, he had the will and tenacity to make a 250-mile pilgrimage to Hidalgo de Parral in Chihuahua to be baptized.

In 1683, Sabeata invited the Catholic priests who had survived the Pueblo Revolt to move downstream and build churches among his Jumanos people. He not only offered to help the Spanish fend off encroachments by the French from the southeast but informed them that he had already won one battle when a large cross descended from the heavens to protect his Jumanos forces and vanquish their enemies!

In exchange, he requested that the priests help him secure forces from the Spanish military stationed in Mexico to help the Jumanos against the increasingly devastating raids on their rancherías by the Apache.

The priests acquiesced and initially secured a troop of twenty Spanish soldiers led by Captain Juan Domínguez de Mendoza. But it did not take long for Mendoza to lose interest in the collaborative endeavor, for he felt he was not fully in charge. To marginalize Sabeata, Mendoza claimed that the Jumanos leaders had exaggerated the severity of threats the Nde posed for the region and did not have the full support of his own people. History proved otherwise, for, more than any other culture, the Nde overwhelmed Jumanos settlements and gradually absorbed most Jumanos into their ranks as slaves or by marriage.

Although unsuccessful in his dealings with Mendoza, Sabeata struggled to forge stronger alliances with both the Spanish and French until he died around 1692. With the loss of his leadership and his alliances with other cultures, the solidarity that he had developed among Jumanos and neighboring communities was weakened. By 1715, most of the surviving Jumanos were integrated into Lipan and Mezcalero Apache families, or later into Mexican families settling in the Big Bend region.

Almost three centuries later, the Franciscan nuns at the Monastery of the Immaculate Conception in Ágreda were alerted that a delegation of Indigenous people from America had accepted their invitation to visit them. Descendants of the Jumanos whom Benavides had interviewed had decided to make a pilgrimage to Spain to champion the call for sainthood on behalf of Sor María de Ágreda. While other Indigenous nations in the West had no interest in seeing any more priests or nuns of the colonial era "sainted" by the Roman Catholic Church, many Jumanos pledged their support in advancing Sor María's status as a Holy Person.

Some of those Indigenous Americans arriving in Spain had already been making holy pilgrimages to the ruins at the ancient pueblo of Jumanos, now known as Gran Quivira, in Salinas Pueblo Missions National Monument of New Mexico. They had been praying there and at the other historic Jumanos settlements of Abó and Quarai south of Albuquerque to reconnect with "their matron saint."

It seemed that their prayers had been answered.

Whenever I have visited the Jumanos homelands in New

Mexico and Texas—Gran Quivira ruins, the confluence of the Río Conchos with the Río Grande, or the semi-arid plains above Palo Duro Canyon—I have felt a prayerful presence there. Whether it emanates from the ancestral Jumanos buried in the earth, or from a blue nun hovering above us in the dry but fragrant air, I cannot say.

Nevertheless, some palpable, historic bond was being renewed. Something—or someone—was fostering a renewed connection between the Franciscan sisters in blue and the keepers of the Jumanos tribal heritage.

The blue nuns at Sor María's monastery in Ágreda were delighted to be in dialogue with Jumanos descendants from around Redford and El Paso, Texas, as well as those who lived near Ojinaga, Chihuahua, upstream from the Junta de los Rios. They invited them to Ágreda to be the honored guests of the nuns themselves.

One of those from Redford who agreed to travel to Spain was my old friend Enrique Madrid, the official tribal historian for the Jumanos-Apache tribe. To many who have known him, Enrique has earned the status of a national (or trinational) treasure, for he is a culture bearer of the traditions that have enriched the Junta de los Rios for centuries.

And when these communities have been placed at risk by one government or another, it has been Enrique who raised his voice against injustice.

When Esequiel Hernández Jr.—an eighteen-year-old former student of his mother—was killed by the US Marines one mile north of the international boundary along the Río Grande, Enrique was among those who went to Washington, DC, to protest the military buildup along the border. That three marines camouflaged in gillie suits were emboldened to shoot and kill a young US citizen herding goats within US territory became a national outcry.

Hernández grew up among old families of Jumanos descendants who had lived along the Río Grande for centuries. Not only was the Marine Corps forced to pay $1.9 million for the wrongful death of Esequiel, but the secretary of defense halted the deployment of armed forces as antidrug patrols along the border.

Soon Enrique became a consultant in the making of two films by Tommy Lee Jones, the 2005 feature called *The Three Burials of Melquiades Estrada* and the 2007 documentary *The Ballad of Esequiel Hernández*. The latter film, including extensive commentaries by Enrique, won best documentary awards at Film Festivals in Mexico City, El Paso, and Santa Fe.

When I recently visited Enrique and his wife, Ruby, in Redford after visiting a Jumanos and Lipan Apache cemetery in Presidio, he recalled to me his visit with neighbors and cousins "to see María de Ágreda's body in Spain."

He remembered how warmly the nuns treated the Jumanos entourage during their stay in Spain, as they listened intently to the oral histories of María's "travels" to Texas and New Mexico centuries before. They were delighted that the Native Americans would heartily accept rather than reject the efforts to move María de Ágreda toward sainthood. As Enrique noted to the blue nuns and later to me:

"We remain here along the Río Grande today because of her. We would not have survived were it not for her. She suggested that we convert to Catholicism so that the Spaniards would not attempt to kill us but would help protect us. In a way, she has always been our Matron Saint."

Enrique recounted the story of sharing with the Spanish nuns a double-armed pearl crucifix crafted in Spain centuries ago that was much like the ones that Sor María of Ágreda and Mother Luisa de Carrión had distributed among pueblos in Arizona and New Mexico. It had been fortuitously found on the Río Conchos near San Antonio Julimes in an inaccessible part of the watershed upstream from Ojinaga, Chihuahua. Perhaps that portion of the watershed was the famed "River of Pearls" that many of the Spanish frontiersman had sought out. Two Texas towns where Jumanos descendants still reside—Presidio and Redford—are also downstream from San Antonio Julimes, near the site of the pearl beds.

Enrique dryly added his own commentary to this story of reunification:

"For us, the pearls signify anguish or suffering, for the clam suffered much to coalesce its pain into a beautiful pearl. In that matter, the pearls offer us hope in the face of difficult challenges just as the bittersweet aroma of the desert's mariola does."

Enrique Madrid also recalled to me a bit of Texas folklore that remains dear to many living in west Texas today.

"We associate good spring rains and abundant blooms of Texas bluebonnet wildflowers with the blue nun. Perhaps she seeded them when she visited the Jumanos ancestors there, so many centuries before our own time. Her presence lingers uneasily among us, perhaps as a fragrance."

CHAPTER FOUR

Abyss

Francisco Garcés and Salvador Palma

IT WAS in December 1776, the same month that George Washington crossed the frozen waters of the Delaware with his disheveled troops. On the twenty-third of that month, Thomas Paine released the first of his *American Crisis* pamphlets, including this simple declaration:

"These are the times that try men's souls."

Padre Pedro Font's soul was already tried *and* tired. He had left Tubac in "Arizonak" months before to be on the wayward expedition to Alta California led by Lieutenant Colonel Juan Bautista de Anza. Font was charged with keeping a written record of the Anza expedition to establish a harbor town to be named San Francisco up the Pacific coast.

But Anza's caravan was moving far too slowly for Font's liking. Even his closest companion—Francisco Garcés, with whom he had gone through seminary at the Queretero Missionary College north of Mexico City—was getting on Font's nerves. It was *the* Catholic university where scholars and students were most intrigued by the stories of Sor María de Ágreda's feats of bilocation, feats that entranced Garcés, while Font merely groaned and rolled his eyes.

Still—despite his cynical and xenophobic biases—Font begrudgingly admitted that Garcés was better suited to deal with the many daunting conditions of their odyssey than he would ever be:

> [Francisco] is so well-fitted to get along with the Indians and to move about among them that he behaves much like a native himself. He shows in everything he does the cool composure

> and reserve of a native. He squats on the ground with them in the circle, or at night around the fire, he sits cross-legged. There he will sit listening to them and musing over their wisdom for two or three hours or even longer. In such moments, he is so absorbed by their stories that he is oblivious to everything else, conversing with them with much serenity and deliberation. And although the native foods of the Indians are as vulgar and distasteful as these outlandish people themselves, Padre Francisco consumes them with great gusto. He even says that they are soothing to the stomach and appealing to his senses. In short, God has created him, I am sure, for the sole purpose of seeking out and engaging with these hapless, uneducated, rustic people of the earth.

From what is known from others who may have been far less caustic than Font, Francisco Garcés was an athletic, cheerful, sometimes joyous, and always observant immigrant from Aragon, Spain. While crossing long stretches of the desert, he appeared to be able to live on minimal food and water for days by somehow drawing upon his "spiritual reserves." When confronted with conflicts between tribes, or between Indigenous and Spanish warriors, he endeavored to make peace rather than taking sides.

It seemed that Garcés enjoyed going on a good field adventure far more than he enjoyed formal preaching After one of his eighty-day jaunts through the desert, another of his Franciscan colleagues Juan Domingo Arrivicita had this to say of Garcés:

> He had met with daunting difficulties, either because of harsh treatment by the Indians, getting lost on the many paths crossing vast expanses, fearing the fording of streams, the paucity of productivity in those arid lands, the anguish from hunger and thirst, the unpalatability of native foods, or many other dangers that would make anyone else desperate; nevertheless, his high-minded aspirations allowed him to re-emerge from these strange landscapes unscathed.

Unlike most of his cronies, he had not come to the Americas to merely convert and conquer. He seemed far more interested in venturing off the beaten path to find humanity and God's grace in the strangest of places. Strange places he did find, where he could observe and converse with humanity in all its baffling complexity.

But no place that Font and Garcés visited would be as crucial to the settlement of the desert West as the Yuma Crossing, one of the most accessible crossings of the Río Colorado. In a 1771 report, Garcés predicted that the crossing would soon be seen as a gateway for trade and transportation from the rest of North America all the way to Monterrey, the newly developed capital in California. Just eighty years earlier, virtually all Spanish explorers had presumed that California was an island separate from the American continent. Jesuit padre Eusebio Francisco Kino dispelled that myth in 1701 after a map he had made of California as part of New Spain was rejected by the authorities.

But over the centuries following Kino, Font, and Garcés, the majority of settlers coming overland into eastern California had opted for the safe passage of Yuma Crossing to forge the river. These travelers would ultimately include the likes of Joaquín Murrieta, Teresita of Cábora, Lauro Aguirre, Woody Guthrie, César Chávez, and Lalo Guerrero, to name a few. It became one of the five best-known fords or *vados* in the desert Southwest.

But Garcés could not have fathomed that possibility the first time he encountered the Quechan villages just above the floodplain at Yuma Crossing. He could not have predicted that the meandering riverbed would become his deathbed. His mind was elsewhere.

As a thirty-year-old Franciscan with less than five years of shouldering priestly responsibilities, Garcés had been assigned to minister to the Tohono O'odham communities near present-day Tucson, Arizona. And now he was venturing out, away from his core duties to explore the world with cranky old Pedro Font.

At about that same age, I, too, had a work assignment among the Tohono O'odham, not as a missionary but as a field hand for elderly farmers who could not do all their agrarian tasks alone anymore. But one day, when torrential rains kept us from working in the fields, I asked an archivist at the Arizona State Museum if I could see microfilmed images of the letters that Garcés sent back home or to his superiors. Some of the field notes had been written in the Tucson area, while others recounted his journey into the depths of the Grand Canyon. In a humble and readable if not altogether beautiful script, there were Francisco's own words, ones I would ponder over when I, too, chose to descend into the Grand Canyon's shadowy corridors and caves. I sensed that Garcés was somehow accompanying me.

As soon as Garcés had arrived in the desert for duty, the Catholic hierarchy in Central México ordered him to take charge at Mission San Xavier del Bac. It had recently lost its former priests and much of its budget on account of the politically motivated expulsion of all Jesuit priests from México in 1767.

Since the Jesuits' departure, the mission had been crumbling back into the dust of the desert. The Nde or Western Apache had pillaged the place twice after the departure of the Jesuits, badly damaging the mission buildings while robbing their stores of food and other goods.

San Xavier Mission was already revered as "the White Dove of the Sonoran Desert." It was strategically positioned at the northern edge of Mexican Christendom.

Young Garcés was a bit like a white-winged dove himself, flying away on a moment's notice wherever he heard of fruitful opportunities for learning more about the desert and its peoples.

He was also like his namesake Saint Francis, who had heard the command from God to "repair my sacred place, which as you can see, has fallen to ruin." For both of them, it was not merely about rebuilding a chapel or an institution but more about restoring relations with surrounding tribes frightened and dismayed by the land grabs that the Spaniards were mounting.

Perhaps it was the Church itself—not the little church before him—that was once again on the verge of ruin. The Church had forgotten about praying for the poor as it joined with the empire to prey upon them.

That said, Garcés appeared to defy his hierarchy's command to stay at San Xavier until the church was rejuvenated. Instead, he opted for trying to restore confidence among the desert's diverse Indigenous communities. Fortunately for Francisco, the Catholic hierarchy hardly had the capacity to track his movements, let alone evaluate the efficacy of his activities.

Over the next thirteen years of his brief but brilliant life, the peripatetic Garcés set out by foot in five expeditions, spending more time in travel than in residence at the mission. During his dozens of months away from mission that he was charged with physically rebuilding, he instead tried to rebuild the bruised relationships the Church had with the many tribes on the rim of Christendom.

It should come as no surprise to anyone that he ultimately failed at both tasks.

Naively, perhaps, Garcés sought out at least a dozen different tribes on both sides of the Colorado River, trying to renew their *confianza* in engaging with their brusque new neighbors from Europe.

The itinerant Franciscan encountered a hundred thousand unconverted souls on the rim of Christendom along the way.

It remains unclear who was better at converting whom. Once, when he got lost during the torrential floods of the rainy season in the Sonoran Desert, he was put back on his way by a Quechan Indian elder who spoke several languages, including the O'odham language that Garcés had been learning back at San Xavier.

That man—Olleyquotequiebe, or Salvador Palma—informed the affable Franciscan in his gray habit that he was no longer standing along the Gila River. In fact, they had met on the banks of the Colorado, for Garcés had missed the easiest crossing.

Garcés took a liking to Olleyquotequiebe, a curious soul who was affectionately known as The One Who Wheezes. He lived among the three thousand to four thousand Quechan (or Yuma Indians) living along the river at that time.

And yet, the Wheezer had already made peaceful contact with the Spanish several years earlier while visiting Caborca, Sonora, 250 miles to the southeast. As their *kwoxota*—the Quechan's civil and spiritual leader—The One Who Wheezes embodied good will, fended off attacks by marauding Nde, diminished the squabbling between neighboring tribes, and exhibited awe-inspiring dream power (*icama*).

Now, he personally chose to guide Garcés from village to village, where his kin acknowledged the appearance of this lost soul with two days of feasting and dancing.

Over the previous years, Olleyquotequiebe had done much to unite both the Quechan and other neighboring tribes on the Colorado around their common goals. The goals of his pan-Indian union of Colorado River tribes included resolving conflicts between different villages, deflecting armed challenges from the newly arrived Western Apache and other displaced tribes, and skillfully managing the floodwaters of the Colorado River.

As a result of his pact to collaboratively manage the river flows for flood irrigation, most of the tribes were able to grow an enormous diversity of seed crops, from millet and corn to tepary beans and pumpkins on the fertile floodplain below their homes.

Garcés was deeply taken by Olleyquotequiebe's cross-cultural skills, his openness to other ideas, and his spiritual depth. They became such fast friends that they spent hours talking with one another, sometimes with the help of a translator, sometimes without.

In trying to make peace between the church and the seminomadic desert tribes, perhaps Garcés hoped to show the kind of generosity of spirit that Saint Francis himself had modeled in his dialogues with Sultan Malik al-Kamil in desert camps along the Nile during the Crusades.

Gradually, over several visits, Garcés became one of the few priests who gained the respect of Quechan leaders for his capacity to listen rather than judge. In turn, the Franciscan priest promised Olleyquotequiebe military protection from other tribes and skeptics within his own people as they tentatively explored and evaluated the teachings of Christianity.

Despite their hopeful first encounter, the high regard that Garcés and Olleyquotequiebe had for one another would not be enough to override the insatiable drive of the Spanish military and Catholic hierarchy to fully control a path from the mainland into the highly prized Californias. Nor would it fully eliminate the skepticism that Quechan other than Palma had for Spanish intrusions into the Colorado River Valley. There had already been one assassination attempt planned against Anza, but the Palma-Garcés friendship must have dampened the tensions, at least for the moment.

Nevertheless, their naivety that others on each side of the power imbalance would come into the tent with them was a failure to foresee the pressures that would soon be heaped upon both by their respective cultures, which would eventually lead to the murder of the priest and the collapse of Palma's power as a Quechan kwoxota.

I once stood alone at the Yuma Crossing on a hot summer morning, looking upstream to where the Gila River joined the Colorado River from the east. I was not far from where Francisco Hermenegildo Tomás Garcés became the first among Europeans to ever cross the Gila and Colorado Rivers to reach the Californias "on foot."

And yet, as trucks and boats and trains zoomed by me on superhighways, and rivers flowed tamely due to large dams upstream, I had a hard time envisioning how frightening that river crossing must have been for the young man born in Zaragosa six thousand miles to the east of Yuma.

Garcés had never learned to swim back in Europe or Mexico, so his devoted Quechan friends lifted him onto their shoulders and carried him across the river while he donned only his undergarments. He gave the latter river its current name, the Río Colorado, in honor of its bright red mud that stained his skin and his clothes.

Garcés also became the first European to arrive on the Colorado River delta in more than a century, when Hernando de Alarcón and Melchior Diaz had briefly glimpsed this backwater paradise in 1540. But in contrast to those explorers, he invested far more time deeply listening to the Quechan and valuing their own spiritual cosmovision. That may have been what inspired their leader Salvador Palma to encourage his community to reflect on the similarities and differences between Christianity and their own Indigenous spirituality. Palma also worked diligently at peace making and resource sharing among neighboring tribes, aiming for an alliance in some ways similar to what Juan de Banderas would propose later on.

Around that time, Palma—or Olleyquotequiebe—saved the life of a Christianized California Indian named Sebastián Tarabal, who had become lost in the desert between Yuma and his home at the newly constructed Mission San Gabriel.

During this era, San Gabriel was just one of several modest outposts in Alta California. It was situated in the foothills just east of the present-day downtown of Los Angeles, near where a now-dry river spilled into the Pacific Ocean.

In 1773, Olleyquotequiebe personally accompanied Tarabal three hundred miles on foot to place him in the care of Catholic priests in the Altar Valley of Sonora. Olleyquotequiebe later asked for help from Spanish speakers, writing three letters petitioning the viceroy of Spain in Mexico City for further collaboration.

When he received no immediate response, The One Who Wheezes went on foot and horse with three of his tribesmen some 1,500 miles to Mexico City in late October of 1776. He was assisted by Lieutenant Colonel Anza and his expedition members in making the case to Viceroy Bucareli for a Spanish presidio at a strategic crossing on the lower Colorado River, to help his alliance of several tribes repel the marauding Apache.

If all went well, the Spanish would be assured access to California and the sea, while the Quechan would be buffered from the agitations of their adversaries. While the Quechan leader was awaiting a response, he donned a suit and a regal cape while carrying his staff of authority over his people and became formally baptized as a Catholic.

The One Who Wheezes was formally christened in Mexico as Salvador Carlos Antonio Palma on February 13, 1777. Ironically, the priest who "catechized, anointed with oil, and baptized . . . the chief of the Yuma tribe of wild Indians" had been a commissioner key to the Inquisition in Mexico of such "pagans" just four years earlier.

Once again—this time as a fellow Christian—Salvador Palma personally urged Viceroy Bucareli to give protection to—rather than take dominion over—the twenty-three Indigenous communities he had endeavored to unite into one confederation in the Colorado River watershed.

But when the requested help for Palma did not materialize and anxieties heightened in the Quechan villages, Garcés disappeared for six months. He took flight rather than fight. He first escaped to the Joshua Tree forests of the Mohave Desert, and then went far upstream, to peer into the deepest depths of the Grand Canyon. He must have caught the desert lilies right at the peak of flowering in the Mohave Desert, which reminded him of other lilies adorning his birthplace in Zaragosa at Easter time. From there, he struggled to make sense of the immensity and complexity of the Indian nations strung like beads along the Colorado River.

Garcés ended up going deeper into their barrancas and farther into their canyon sanctuaries than any Spaniard had gone since Europeans first arrived there in 1540.

Amazingly, Garcés coursed along the much of the southern rim of the Grand Canyon all alone. Francisco became completely preoccupied by the possibility that he may need to plunge down into some its barrancas, then climb back up their steep stone walls on the other side. Shaken to his bones, he called the Grand Canyon "a horrible abyss," for it was unlike anything for which a childhood in the bucolic countryside of Spain and an education of the altiplano of Central México could have prepared him.

Facing the greatest abyss on the earth's surface, Garcés was stopped in his tracks. He faced an existential crisis.

Alone, like an early day Everett Ruess, hundreds of miles from his "own" mission, he realized that he had virtually no influence on this patch of the world where he stood. He felt humbled, from head to toe. As he looked out across the abyss, he tossed his ego into it.

The humble Franciscan was definitely out on the most remote margins of everything he had ever known, a fourth of the way around the circumference of the earth from where he was born.

Garcés may have been entranced by the beauty and strangeness of the desert, but that alone was not enough to buffer him from looking over the brink at the bottomless depths in the world. At only one place did he venture down into that abyss, climbing a rickety ladder on a well-worn path that took him down to Supai Village in Cataract Canyon, near the western end of the entire Grand Canyon complex.

There he was surprised to see the Havasupai had fields of annual crops and turkeys, but because it was too early in the cropping season for the harvest, they offered him pit-roasted agave to eat and mildly fermented mezcal to drink. He became the first European to break corn bread with the People of the Blue Water.

As he looked up from his campsite on the last day of his stay, it seemed he was still suffering "landscape shock," despite the generosity of the Havasupai in helping him get around. He wrote in his journal that "This canyon is so deep that it is ten o'clock in the day before sunlight begins to descend down upon us."

Francisco was no longer sauntering like an avid explorer through the Southwest, seeking souls to convert. His own mortality, his own adherence to a set of European beliefs, and his own life had been put on the line. His soul kept descending, deeper into the depths of the desert, into the darkness that was held fast by the canyon walls, into an abyss as troublesome to his psyche as anything he could imagine on the face of the earth.

The Havasupai must have sensed that Garcés was suffering from vertigo or acrophobia, unaware how severely his spirit had been shaken. They quickly led him back out of the canyon by a circuitous but less precipitous route.

Their patience with a dramatically disoriented stranger allowed him to avert another potential trauma: climbing straight up into the sky on a rickety wooden ladder lashed together with agave fiber. He grew faint just listening to it wobble and creak with every move whenever one of the agile youths ascended toward a distant horizon that he could hardly see, let alone imagine.

When he arrived up on the rim of the Grand Canyon once again, Garcés humbly confessed in his journal that he had veered completely out of his comfort zone:

"I am astonished by the roughness of this country, *and by the impassable chasm which Nature has placed within it.*"

That singular moment in 1776 was the instant that the soul of Garcés was most irrevocably shaken. He was forever humbled by those moments of peering into the planet's innards. Even as he passed eastward toward the rim of the not-so-little barranca that brings the little Colorado River into the Grand Canyon, his sense of uneasiness stuck with him:

"The bed of the river, as far as the confluence, is a trough of lively but solid bedrock. It [snakes down until it is] very profound and about as wide as a stone's throw. For those reasons, it is impassable for anyone on foot, not just for those on a mule or horse."

The usually cheerful and confident Garcés had glimpsed into a physical manifestation of the dark and wild heart of Earth itself. He had come from verdant valleys and rolling ridges of Aragon, but now he was bearing the brunt of something uncontrollably wild as the Grand Canyon. Was he suffering from cultural vertigo, not just topographic vertigo?

It was his psychic comeuppance, for he had lived much of his life as a generous Franciscan, who, like his patron saint and namesake, believed that Creation itself was largely made up of a benign community of caring brothers and sisters. But the Vishnu schists and the Zoroaster granites in the bottomless barranca did not care a rat's ass about what he thought of them.

His experience of the Grand Canyon did not necessarily ascribe to or align with any narrative he had previously imagined. And soon, he would suffer from another wakeup call: All his human brothers and sisters were not as benign as he had presumed—or at least hoped—them to be.

Perhaps the harshness of the desert and its hardy people were converting Garcés to a wilder but far more uncertain point of view. As Saharan storyteller Nohou Agab once put it:

"The desert is very simple to survive in. You must only admit that there is something larger than you . . . the wind . . . the dryness . . . the distance. . . . You accept that, and everything is fine. . . . The desert will provide. . . . If you do not, the desert will break you."

If the desert itself did not break him, the Hopi had done so by flatly refusing to allow him to preach a single word in their sacred pueblo of Oraibi once he had entered it.

The Hopi had already joined the Pueblo Revolt against Catholic colonialism in 1680, and after brutal retaliation by ecclesiastical and military leaders, they wanted nothing more to do with any Catholic.

Perhaps it was clear to them that a single good-hearted priest from afar could not rectify—let alone reverse—the damage being done by the massive machines called Spanish colonialism and Catholicism.

After he had taken flight from the conflicts brewing in the Yuma Valley, Garcés had put as many as two thousand miles on his sandals before he came back home to San Xavier to find his mission in further ruin.

He could not sleep in the badly damaged clerical quarters there. Instead, he chose to stay on the packed-dirt floors of O'odham family homes nearby. There they would help him fix his deer hide sandals, called teguas, before he would set out on the road again.

Within two years of returning from the Grand Canyon to San Xavier to write up a report on his travels amid the sagging mission, he was given yet another unsettling field assignment, one that would cost him his life.

The new commandant general for the frontier provinces, Teodoro de Croix, tried to coerce Garcés into serving as his pawn in another land grab. The field commander had convinced the king of Spain to allow him to colonize the lower Colorado River, merely using priests to subdue the Natives.

De Croix wished to establish a civilian and military presence of power-hungry Spaniards that could eventually displace the Quechan from their pivotal position at the Yuma Crossing and control access to ports along the Pacific coast.

It appeared that de Croix was hardly competent to organize anything, so after a year of getting nowhere near the Colorado, he assigned Captain Rivera y Moncada and Garcés to help him execute his plans.

Trouble was Rivera y Moncada and Garcés were worlds apart in their ethics toward Indigenous peoples, having already tangled in the past about the military's poor treatment of Native communities.

But now de Croix and his new captain moved ahead with a plan to build two new military outposts and agricultural settlements at choice sites along the Colorado. They had selected the very site that Garcés had already promised to the Quechan as a permanent sanctuary for them and a hub for his nascent alliance of all tribes along the lower Colorado River.

Never had the Spaniards attempted to mix spiritual, military, and commercial activities in a single community so far north. Unfortunately, Garcés found no clear way to disrupt nor resist de Croix's plans.

As a commander general of the area who reported directly to the viceroy, de Croix had built up the largest military force the region had ever seen. In fact, he naively believed he could mediate a far better relationship with the tribes through his friendships with the Palma brothers.

In September of 1780, Garcés issued his last cry of resistance, telling Teodoro de Croix in no uncertain words by letter that the Quechan were "already irritated by so many delays and evil influences. . . . [They] were becoming every day more restless and could not be controlled except by superior force."

Of course, de Croix read those protests simply as a confirmation that he should exert enough force to shock and awe the Quechan into submission. But when de Croix's settlers and military entourage began to confiscate irrigated croplands to pasture their horses where the Natives had been growing crops for their food, Salvador Palma had to put his foot down.

He regretfully reminded Garcés of his promise to offer his people sanctuary, by building a mission for baptisms and bringing horses as well as other goods down to the river for the exclusive use of his tribe, not for the benefit of outsiders.

Garcés, of course, empathized with his old friend, but like many do-gooders of the world, he simply did not see that empathy alone—when facing the triad of brutal military forces, bureaucratic hierarchies, and the monetary interests of greedy colonists—could not be enough to stop such rapaciousness.

Even though Salvador Palma and Francisco Garcés had endeavored to patch things up between their peoples, Salvador's brother, Ygnacio, turned against them.

Worse yet, a younger Quechan and his Apache allies were inspired by Ygnacio's defiant words as well as his sense of betrayal by Garcés, who could no longer buffer them from Spanish intrusions. They took up Ygnacio's cause, choosing to rebel on the very morning when Garcés and another priest had wanted to offer a mass for peace.

They couldn't care less what the priest had promised Salvador. In their first assault, two guards were killed, but an angry youth spared Garcés and most of the others assembled. That restraint by the youth did not stop the Spanish from immediately retaliating by capturing Salvador's brother, Ygnacio, placing him in stocks to sizzle in the hot sun, and then flogging the Quechan youth who had wounded a Spaniard's horse.

Naively, Garcés still believed he could banish misfortune by holding another mass to offer prayers on behalf of all parties. As soon as the mass had begun, the Quechan dissidents allied with a few displaced Apache outliers roared in to disrupt it. Garcés and others fled to hide in the *carrizal* cane breaks along the river. Salvador Palma formed a search party to find Garcés, urging the younger men from his tribe not to put their hands on the priest but to bring him back to safety.

In the stifling heat and humidity of a July day in 1781 along the lower Colorado River, one young Quechan man's temper spilled over like an overtaxed radiator. He rebelled against Salvador's request for peace by clubbing Garcés and three other priests to death. Fearing retaliation from his own people that would cost him his own leadership position, Salvador conceded that he must join forces with his brother and the twenty-three communities in their alliance.

Under his renewed leadership, the Quechan warriors commenced to kill 105 Spanish men, women, and children. They took all survivors captive to sell as slaves to other tribes. They seized and slaughtered nearly 260 head of Spanish livestock and absconded with all the remaining Spanish muskets and pistols.

It became known as the Massacre at the Yuma Crossing, or at least the first phase of a reciprocal massacre.

As the Quechan and their allies pillaged and burned both Spanish settlements, Olleyquotequiebe garnished the shield of Captain Fernando Rivera y Moncada. In actions rather than words, he renounced his Christian identity as Salvador Palma and reaffirmed his position as kwoxota, a Native leader whose power came from dreams and visions, not from external authorities.

Regaining his former status among some of the Quechan and their affiliated tribes, Palma ordered his warriors to gather up all the Christian religious paraphernalia that could be found in or near the church. He then placed all the crosses, gospels, liturgical missals, and rosaries in a wooden box. Palma then heaved the whole holy mess into the dark and sullied waters of the Río de Purisima Concepción.

It was the same river that Garcés had named the Río Colorado in honor of its crimson sediments, but now the river ran red with his own blood.

The brothers once known as Los Hermanos Palma had won a decisive battle against Spanish intrusions, even though it had cost them a former friend.

Their victory set back the empire's economic goals of controlling trade between the Californias and the Mexican mainland for many more decades. No other Franciscan would dare visit the lower Colorado tribes for another century.

The loss of his own men did not stop Teodoro de Croix from retaliating a year later with a horrendous show of force, killing more than one hundred Quechan residents in the Yuma Valley and enslaving eighty-five others. That event became known as the second round of the Massacre at the Yuma Crossing.

Even so, it took the Spanish less than a year to realize that the resistance of the remaining Quechan and their allies was far too much for de Croix to handle. His failure to secure a safe land route to the Californias had infuriated the political leaders in Sonora, the state in which the Yuma Valley was positioned during that era.

Teodoro lost all political and military support in Sonora for his attempt to both dominate the valley and trailblaze trade routes to the Pacific coast. His troops were permanently withdrawn from the Colorado River watershed. His excessive use of force had not won him anything.

He was reassigned from New Spain in the north to Peru in the south. Just as soon as he was recalled, the Spanish settlements near the Colorado River were destroyed, and they were never revived before de Croix's death in Madrid in 1792.

More than two centuries later, Quechan descendants of Olleyquotequiebe remain present in the Yuma Valley, while no descendants of de Croix or Moncada y Rivera remain in the valley, nor among any of those who call the lower Colorado River their home.

The friendship and spiritual bond between Francisco Garcés and Olleyquotequiebe were clearly not enough to prevent the horrific violence that ultimately terminated their collaboration. Their openness to cross-cultural collaboration and hybridity irked the essentialists on either side, who remained stuck in "either/or" attitudes for the rest of their days.

And yet their friendship perhaps served as some kind of model—however cautionary—for others who came after them.

Others who did not think in red or white dualisms.

The Quechan—at the very least—had proposed and temporarily formed an intercultural alliance within a desert watershed. Their collective skillfully managed its key water sources of the Gila and Colorado Rivers for many more decades. It was exactly the kind of watershed council that John Wesley Powell proposed two centuries later as units of governance in the American West, but Powell failed to find a way to enact his modest proposal.

Three centuries later, however, agrarian and environmental activists in several parts of the West initiated such watershed councils as a comparable structure for collaborative conservation and local governance.

·~·

Olleyquotequiebe and Francisco Garcés had joined together for what may have been the first recorded attempt at cross-cultural collaboration in resource management and spiritual dialogue that had ever occurred in their region.

They also attempted (but failed) to do what they could to resist the seemingly inexorable loss of lives and lands—not to mention the demise of Native sovereignty—that characterized their era.

Whether such oppression of the human spirit and degradation of sacred lands was inevitable can be debated. What cannot be debated is that these changes along the Colorado River came at great moral, spiritual, social, and environmental costs.

·~·

It may be too easy to dismiss the friendship between Francisco Garcés and Olleyquotequiebe as an abject failure. They believed they could achieve something better together—through a watershed-wide alliance—than what the warfare of their era offered either of their peoples. Although a laudable goal, it simply could not be achieved at that point in time when the disparity in power between the Spaniards and the Quechan was so great.

But Olleyquotequiebe's vision of multiple cultures working together as a confederacy to conserve and frugally use water to the benefit of all may be one of the highest goals that desert peoples can aspire to. Some political scientists worry that wars over water—rather than over gold or oil—will dominate future centuries if stronger guardrails against abuse and overuse are not put into place.

Today, with water wars and climate change wreaking havoc in the lower Colorado River basin once again, many citizens of this binational watershed are coming back around to propose some of the same structural solutions that Olleyquotequiebe—The One Who Wheezes—proposed two and a half centuries ago. In fact, just downstream from where the Palma clan lived at Yuma Crossing, a unique partnership called Raise the River involves six US and Mexican nongovernmental organizations and many volunteers.

It has come not a minute too soon, for the entire Colorado River water system is now in peril, and the river may never flow again to the sea for more than just a few weeks a year. But the coalition is undaunted and has found multiple ways to restore vegetation, wildlife, and satisfying jobs back to the Colorado River delta. Upstream for the Yuma Crossing, tribes, farmers, wildlife conservationists, and recreationist are trying to "save" the Colorado River by increasing on-farm water use efficiency and reducing the waste of river water. The verdict is out on whether these efforts will prevent major crises for those who live and drink in the Colorado River watershed, but they would do well to take Salvador Palma into their hearts as they proceed with such courageous efforts.

CHAPTER FIVE

Indigenous Nationhood

Juan de Banderas and Padre Pedro Leyva

WHAT ARE the options that a people may muster when their place-based traditions, lands, and waters are suddenly overwhelmed by intrusions generated from afar? What alternatives do they see before them when they realize they must resist the dominating forces that are diminishing the quality and integrity of their lives and their communities?

The first public record documenting the incipient acts of resistance by the Yaqui flag bearer Juan Ignacio Jusacamea appeared in 1825, less than four years after Mexican independence from Spain. Federal authorities reported that Juan had to be thrown in jail for physically resisting soldiers and federal land commissioners who had come into his hometown, the Yaqui pueblo of Rahum.

Rahum has always been a small but significant village on the fertile soils of the Río Yaqui floodplain, where monsoon rains in late summer overflow river banks, inundating its fields and isolating its farmers for weeks. But in the dry months, drought can harden and crack the soil into fissures in the fields there, giving Rahum its name as "standing on hard ground." The community learned to be self-sufficient, materially, spiritually, and at times politically. The petty bureaucrats in the land commission and the soldiers of the *exercito* apparently did not know whom or what they were messing with. Rahum was one of the original eight sacred towns of the Yoemem, which were collectively known as the Wohnaiki Pueplem. The Rahum community also supported a trading outpost of the same name in southern Arizona, so its sphere of influence was extensive. All the eight sacred pueblos and their outposts were always ready at a moment's notice to repel or evict those who did not respect their traditional spiritual, political, and military leaders.

At that time, Juan held the position of *alferez*—"a bearer of banners"—so that he could devote his time to rallying the community around the flag of the Rahum community militia should any conflicts occur with intruders.

This may explain the "secular" roots of his nickname, Juan de Banderas.

And yet it was the second record of John the Standard Bearer that was far more revealing with regard to the kind of man he was. While jailed, he began having visions, ones in which he was saved by the Virgin of Guadalupe, who commanded him to rediscover and recover the "crown" and "flag" of Moctezuma to Indigenous peoples.

As a *cuentacuento* of his own prophetic visions, Juan began to use storytelling and a small flag to challenge and subvert the oppressive federal and state bureaucracies, not through open dissent but through infectious expressions of solidarity within the Yoemem community and among neighboring tribes as well.

The first detailed accounts of Juan's visions were probably transcribed and translated by his friend Padre Pedro Leyva. Leyva resided not far from Rahum in the neighboring Yaqui pueblo of Cocorit (Ko'oko'im). It became clear to anyone who heard or read of his visions that Juan's view of the world was mystical, apocalyptic, radical, and expansive.

While behind bars, Juan had fallen into a trance so deep that he lost consciousness for a full day and was pronounced dead. But just then he was transported out into the desert, where he fasted for three days until the holy people began to appear before him.

Juan's guests in prison included the Virgin Mary, her son, Jesus (who some say had emerged from a flower), Saint John, and Saint Bartholomew, as well as flocks of angels and wild animals. He was commanded to prepare a feast for these prophets or holy ones, which he did. It was clear to all who attended the feast that Juan felt that building *spiritual* solidarity among Indigenous people could ultimately overcome the materialistic, secular world view of the Mexican military and bureaucracy.

While fettered in prison, it was revealed to Juan that certain iconic forms of wildlife—birds and mammals—had been willing to offer their power to him. He took on the spirit power of *mata'e* (*matupari*) and *choparao*—the kit fox and raccoon—so that he could lead his people into a new era.

At the same time, the Virgin had asked Juan *de la Cruz* Banderas to unite all Indigenous nations in Mexico under the same flag, hence the spiritual underpinnings of his nickname. He would launch his resistance movement with nine Native communities living in the present-day states of Sinaloa, Sonora, and southern Arizona northward to the Gila River.

Together, their Indigenous homelands made up the bulk of the land area in the recently designated (but short-lived) state of El Occidente. At that time, these Indigenous communities included the Yoemem or Yaqui; the Yoremem or Mayos; the Opatas or Eudeves; the O'odham or Pimas and Papagos; the Comcaac or Seris; and the Piatos, who may have been some of the Pima who later moved up to the Gila River.

In the first written accounts that Padre Pedro Leyva transcribed, Juan declared that these Indigenous nations would evict all *gachupines*, the Spanish oligarchs who had historically controlled much of the land in New Spain.

The greed of the gachupines and their grip on Indigenous lands in the south began to decline during the eleven years of civil war that led to Mexico's independence in 1821. Nevertheless, the wealthy families who had to forfeit their land holdings in central and southern Mexico simply changed their names and moved to the northernmost hinterlands to grab other property, much of it in Indigenous territories.

In later speeches and writings transcribed by Padre Leyva, Juan de Banderas softened his rhetoric. He invited any non-Indians who were disposed to respect Native sovereignty to stay and live under specific conditions that Indigenous people dictated!

In many regards, the vision of Juan de Banderas echoed that of the Iroquois (Haudenosaunee) Confederacy, established between

1570 and 1600. It may have been the first pact to engage five Indigenous nations in a league of intertribal governance. The confederacy was forged by Huron leader Dekanawidah as a peace-making body among Algonkian-speaking tribes. They pledged to join forces to withstand any more invasions by the English or the French in the northeastern woodlands of North America.

While the Haudenosaunee Confederacy has often been praised as one of the first participatory democracies on the planet, few Americans realize that another confederacy was formed on the southern edges of the present-day United States 120 years after the first of such pacts. Perhaps it is because tribes as far north as Canada had little opportunity to hear of efforts parallel to their own by "Native Americans" whose lands became part of Mexico, not the United States and Canada.

The unsolved question is how did a recently incarcerated Yaqui man in his thirties rise to the occasion to forge a new multitribal Indigenous nation in a country where no such thing had ever been recognized?

There were probably five key factors that propelled him:

1. Juan's "God-given" commitment and his charisma as a prophet of a "chosen people" (the Yoemem);
2. His capacity to develop strong rapport with leaders of other tribes that had considerable military expertise as well as weapons;
3. His conviction that if Mexicans could declare and gain independence from Spain, then Indigenous peoples could throw off the yokes of taxation and policing by declaring independence from Mexico;
4. His belief that he was guided and empowered by other prophets; and
5. His collaboration with Padre Pedro Leyva of Cocorit, who may have been a brilliant behind-the-scenes strategist in service to the alliance that Juan de Banderas had envisioned.

The charisma of Juan de Banderas became widely recognized. The English travel writer Robert Hardy penned this about Juan when visiting Sonora in the late 1820s:

"He is said to be small of stature but endowed with a natural flow of eloquence quite extraordinary, and with a talent and activity which have kept up the revolution for two years."

And yet Hardy only glimpsed the onset of Juan de Banderas's campaign. Over a seven-year period, his alliance gained temporary control of roughly 10,000 square miles of what is now northwestern Mexico and southern Arizona. Juan de Banderas's vision mobilized thousands of Indigenous resisters and fighters to join his cause in an area equivalent to Maryland, Massachusetts, or Hawaii.

Juan's nemesis, Ignacio Zuñiga, commandant of Mexican forces at Pitic, begrudgingly wrote of him with some admiration:

> The chief of these last two [uprisings] has been the Indian Banderas, General of the [Indigenous] Nation, a man of genius for directing and enthusing his followers, gifted with a spirited imagination, with eloquence and with a rare talent, with which he could have accomplished many more evils if his plans had been favored. He conceived the plan of crowning himself king and of bringing about a general reconciliation among all the tribes for establishing his monarchy and sustaining the cause of the Indians against the whites. To this end he sent envoys to the other tribes, charging them with artful and flattering messages to invite them to join cause with him. He reminded all of them of that which should move them most, that is to say, the question of the lands: he painted our race as ambitious and dominating, and made use of the [existing] hatreds, grudges, and [desire for] vengeance, passions common to all the Indians, to excite them to agree to the consolidation of his military movements.

Remarkably, there is no evidence at all that Juan de la Cruz Banderas wished to be a king or to take up arms against the gachupines.

Juan carried a flag, not a pistol. He did, however, wish to share the "crown" and "flag" of Moctezuma with other spiritual leaders of participating Indigenous tribes.

Juan did not merely send envoys to visit other tribal leaders. He often went to visit them himself and to assist them in their own struggles.

Perhaps for the lack of any inclination toward military leadership of his own, in 1830, Juan enlisted the friendship and military support of two brilliant Opata commanders, Dolores and Virgen Gutíerrez. The number of Indigenous guerrilleros they collectively led swelled to over two thousand.

Juan did the same with Mayo military commanders, so much so that they took back lands formerly belonging to the Yoremem in Sinaloa, not just in Greater Sonora. Their rebellion against the federal government and the state government of Occidente was so fierce that it forced the state of Occidente to move its capital southward from El Fuerte to Cosalá, some 180 miles! Juan's genius as a prophet was that he could make the impossible seem doable, if not probable. He had posited that if other American peoples who had inherited from their ancestors had refused to have their lands taxed or sold, why couldn't the Indigenous nations of the deserts rebel against taxation without representation? Banderas reasoned that if Mexico had both the right and strength to cut ties with Spain, why couldn't Indigenous nations do the same with this newly formed and weak Republic of Mexico? And if other American peoples refused to have their lands taxed or sold because they had inherited it from their ancestors, why couldn't the Indian nations of the Occidente—present-day Sonora, Sinaloa, and Arizona—do the same?

Juan's birthplace near the Port of Guaymas became the equivalent of Boston Harbor during the Tea Party. It was the hub of resistance against an extractive economy that robbed lands of Indigenous peoples and made money off the sweat-drenched backs of poor men and women.

Like so many other rebels, resisters, prophets, and insurgents—from Captain Tuerto, Juan Sabeata, Coyote Iguana, and Joaquín Murrieta to Teresita Urrea, Reyes Tijerina, César Chávez, and Dolores Huerta—Juan felt that the Creator bestowed upon him a *don*—a talent, gift, or calling—to do the sacred work of social justice. The angels and saints had come down from Heaven to help the Yoemem. Heaven was not a noun serving as place name for a distant place but a verb for sending sacred envoys among the people.

This was not the first time that holy ones from both the Yaqui origin story and from the Bible had appeared in what the Yaqui called the Yo Ania or Enchanted World.

It was said that Jesus and the Virgin Mary had once walked across the Huya Ania or Wilderness World of the Yoemem homelands. Juan was among the many Yoemem who were instructed as children that they were among the many "chosen peoples" and that the lands they lived on were sacred or blessed. He had learned while still a boy that when soldiers came to crucify Jesus, Mary appeared in the Wilderness World to transformed herself into the tree that would be cut down and made into his cross to bear.

It was only when the soldiers nailed Jesus to the Tree-Who-Was-His-Mother that the blood gushing out of his wounds bloomed into the sacred Sewa flowers. Those are the spring wildflowers and cottonwood leaves that Yaqui toss in the way of evil to stop it in its tracks.

In his vision, Juan was charged by the Virgin Mary to stop the evil of the gachupines in its tracks and to restore the sovereignty of Indigenous nations by creating a new kin-dom.

When you believe your personal coach is the Virgin Mary, how can you fail to accept that your *manda* or sacred duty is not only God-given, but completely achievable?

The final but least-discussed factor in Juan de Bandera's success was his collaboration with Padre Pedro Leyva, who tended the flock of Catholics in Cocorit. There are few details of Leyva's personal life that have become known, except that he was once attacked by gachupines for aiding and abetting the Indian nations in their quest for independence. But because people with the surname Leyva have long been known to reside in and near the eight sacred pueblos, it is possible that one or both of his parents were of Yaqui ancestry.

After going away to seminary, he arrived in Sonora to serve as a parish priest and was assigned to the Cocorit community. He soon teamed up with Juan de Banderas both as a transcriber and translator of Juan's five long letters in Spanish that have survived to this day. But there are subtle hints from one letter to the next that he did more than just translate Juan's words; he may have influenced their content through conversations with Juan and added his own rhetorical power as well.

The most probable influence we can detect is the shift from a rigid anti-Spaniard (gachupin) stance in Juan's first letter to a more welcoming invitation to non-Indians willing to endorse, promote, and participate in this modest proposal for Native sovereignty.

That shift allowed Juan to counter Zuñiga's argument that the ultimate goal was to ethically cleanse all Yoris, gapuchines, or Mexicans of "non-Indian" descent from all reaches of Indian country.

Instead, Leyva probably helped to position Juan's goals as a class struggle of the rural, mostly Indigenous poor against the wealthy elite. Those aristocrats were whom the majority of all Mexicans had wished to evict in their quest for independence and self-government. In that way, they checkmated their critics who had argued that the goals of Juan's confederacy were substantively different and even antithetical to the original operating instructions that had guided the establishment of Mexico as a sovereign nation.

The relative weight of Leyva's contributions to the vision of this Indigenous confederacy cannot be measured, but it would be a grave historic mistake to presume that he was nothing more than Juan's transcriber or translator. There was something spiritually lofty but also politically pragmatic that emerged out of their collaboration.

Whether of European or Indigenous ancestry, Pedro Leyva played an underappreciated role in polishing the vision given to Juan de Banderas.

Rather than the letters being dismissed as "unpatriotic" and therefore seditious to the republic, there was an inherent logic to Juan's vision that many outsiders appreciated. Juan (and Pedro) had argued for a multicultural confederacy in Mexico where some fifty local Indigenous leaders per region would have a place at the table to shape the destiny of their cultural patrimony.

In many ways, Juan de Banderas along with Padre Leyva and the Gutíerrez brothers from nearby Opata communities were pioneering a prototype of Indigenous land sovereignty. We might say that it failed for reasons other than its inherent viability. Nevertheless, Juan's vision spilled over to influence the Comcaac or Seri, the Tohono O'odham or Pima, and even the Nde or Western Apache.

It surely raised alarm among those in Mexico's nascent federal government, which was struggling to keep its republic from being chopped into innumerable splinters. The Mexicans in power went after Banderas and his allies with a vengeance, roundly defeating them. That decisive battle occurred in the mining town of Soyopa, far east of the Yaqui pueblos, in the foothills of the Sierra Madre in the final days of 1832.

Less than a month later, Juan de la Cruz Banderas, Dolores Gutíerrez, and eleven others from the confederacy were executed in the former capital of Sonora, Arizpe. Juan's death occurred less than sixty miles south of the present-day border with the United States. Descendants of Banderas and Gutíerrez now live on both sides of that fragile and impermanent boundary line.

Ironically, it was his old arch-enemy Zuñiga who offered the greatest back-handed compliments to Banderas:

> This *caudillo* [chieftain], both outrageous and ambitious, was shot at Arispe. He left a memory among his people which perhaps will contribute strongly to the future development of his doctrines. Thanks to Juan, the seeds have already been sown. Should they be left to germinate, propagate, and grow, will they not produce their fruit?

For sure, the ideologies of this insurgent, as well as the great riches of all kinds which his bandits distributed to all the Indians, will for a long time serve to nourish frequent rebellions and raids. He succeeded in convincing them that they are the legitimate sacred stewards of whatever there is in this holy land.

Juan de Banderas remains known and revered among the Yoemem communities on both sides of a militarized border that did not exist when he was alive. Under Juan's banner, his leadership team engaged Indigenous communities in a confederation that ran northward to the Gila River, covering into 35,000 square miles of the present-day United States. And yet, there is not a single college course on governance in the United States that regularly tells of Juan's acumen, brilliance, and charisma to the 120,000 to 150,000 Native American students enrolled in higher education each year. That simple fact not only impoverishes Indigenous students but it impoverishes us all, for it keeps us from understanding a means of organizing humans for shared goals and dreams other than the flawed ones we have been stuck with for the past 250 years.

CHAPTER SIX

Race

Coyote Iguana and Lola Casanova

WHO KNOWS where his name Coyote Iguana came from, even though it has been used in films, pulp novels, pop histories, posters, and website home pages for well over a century? In the years immediately after his birth on San Esteban Island, this Comcaac (Seri) boy was simply called Teepor (Liebre Alazán, or Black-Tailed Jack Rabbit). That was the name given to him by his sea fishing and foraging clan.

They could not have known then that he had been born in such an auspicious and disruptive moment in their history, and in the history of other Native nations in the American Deserta.

It wasn't that his ears were unusually long; perhaps it was that he was unusually alert to strange sounds and sights. Before the rest of his kin even noticed anything, his ears perked up enough to pick the rustling of unusual movements around the little Comcaac Indian fishing camps strewn along the shores of the desert islands. When he heard something disturbing, he could race away as fast as a hare and disappear at a moment's notice.

The movements of concern on the islands of the gulf were not simply those of wildlife like rattlesnakes, iguanas, and chuckwallas. The Comcaac had begun to see both iron and wooden boats passing off their shores that belonged neither to their relatives on the Sonoran mainland nor to their more distant kin—nicknamed the Cachanillas or "arrowweed people"—who came fishing and turtling from the Baja California peninsula.

When some of their close kin had paddled their kayak-like balsa boats down to the port of Guaymas sixty miles or so the south, they had heard disturbing stories about invaders from some distant lands to the south. Their Yaqui, Pima, and Opata contacts called these intruders the gachupines.

Following Mexican independence, more and more of the gachupines had been coming northward to set up ranches and mines in Indian territory. They had lost their Spanish land grants and haciendas in south and central Mexico during the war. They slipped past their neighbors they had oppressed for decades in the south and moved to where their names and their fortunes would not immediately become known. Most of them had rejected the urge to return to Spain to fight with their brothers and sisters there for their portion of family fortunes.

But by 1832, Yaqui, Opata, Mayo, Pima, and Comcaac guerrilleros had become alarmed—if not entirely fed up—by the pale-skinned intruders. They had lost Juan de Banderas, but he had inspired them to collaborate across tribal lines to evict any troublesome Spanish-speaking settlers from their lands.

The pan-Indian alliance burned their ranches, killed their cattle, and robbed their corrals of their horses. They then slipped back into the desert canyons and mountain barrancas, leaving little trace.

Despite the earlier warnings and military efforts by the slain prophet, Juan de Banderas, fair-haired Spaniards kept arriving in droves to the port of Guaymas, Sonora. These foreigners made headway in taking control of most of the decent harbors, waterholes, gathering grounds, and mining areas for salt along the coast of Sonora, where they became known in Sonoran Spanish as the Yoris, and in the Cmique Iitom language of the Comcaac as the Casopin and Cocsaar.

Within one year alone, the Comcaac or Seri had engaged in armed conflicts with these invading forces to the east, to the south, and to the north of their core aboriginal territory. One occurred in the Pueblo de los Seris in what is now the Sonoran capitol of Hermosillo, another 60 miles to the south at the small harbor of Tastiota, and another more than 150 miles to the northwest of Hermosillo in the Cieneguilla district, not far from where Joaquín Murrieta was born.

·✤·

Then, just to the north of the gulf and the desert gathering grounds of the Comcaac, opportunists in the United States had begun to look for a way to establish a port in the Gulf of California. They desperately wanted access to Pacific trade routes down the Latin American coast.

In late 1845, President Polk sent diplomat John Sidel down to Mexico City to convince President Herrera into selling the United States all the land between Nuevo México and Alta California that was within his jurisdiction. Herrera refused. A war with Mexico began in 1846. It was rudely settled within two years' time.

In the first and perhaps largest attack of the US Navy on any foreign territory up until that time, Commander Samuel DuPont ordered the sloop-of-war to let loose cannon fire on the Guaymas harbor on October 3, 1846. In retaliation, the Mexicans then burned and sank two gunboats that the US Navy had been pursuing. Heavy artillery fire from both sides created a stalemate for weeks, although the Mexican musketry and artillery fire came from a large military force in town, not at sea. DuPont and his crew continued to occupy the harbor for several weeks before tropical hurricanes forced the Yankees to return to San Francisco.

·✤·

The power of the US artillery was no doubt heard if not seen by the Comcaac and the Yoemem or Yaqui in neighboring fish camps. By 1848, Mexico was forced by the United States to sign the Treaty of Guadalupe Hidalgo, ceding half of its land to its greedy neighbor to the north.

Then, with one single swipe of the pen, the state of Sonora—the largest state in Mexico at that time—lost 815,000 acres of its land base, and much of that was occupied by Indigenous communities who played no role at all in the two-year war.

That year alone, five thousand Sonorans who lost their land holdings to the United States left their desert homes for the California Gold Rush. Ironically, three US citizens and three Frenchmen—all of whom had failed to strike it rich in California—began undercover efforts to plan six separate filibustering attempts in the hope of conquering what "little" remained of Sonora.

By the mid-1840s, the Black-Tailed Jackrabbit had been given a Spanish name—Jesus Ávila Sanchez—and had paddled to the mainland in a balsa boat to where his mother's brother lived near Tastiota, just north of Guaymas. He wanted to hear with his own "rabbit" ears and eyes what the trouble was all about. He aimed to arrive at his uncle's camp a bit inland for the beach at Tastiota, where many of her relatives had intermarried with Yaqui.

It became clear that both the Mexican and US governments wanted to get "pesky" Indians like the Seri, Yaqui, and Apache out of the way so that they could fully exploit the waters and minerals of the Sonoran coast.

The mixed communities of Indians at Tastiota were villainized by the Spanish as "infinitely vile and cowardly . . . bandits, assassins, thieves and inhuman brutes" who came at night to ranches to kill livestock so they could eat horsemeat and beef they had not raised.

And so the governor of Sonora instituted a bounty on all Seri through Decree 126. Like his 1837 Decree 122 against the Apache, Governor José de Aguilar put a price on the head of any Seri Indian found in a troublesome situation in Sonora. He offered a reward of 150 pesos for every Seri or Apache male warrior killed or imprisoned, and 50 pesos for every Comcaac woman to be enslaved.

These decrees mandated that any child of Comcaac or Apache heritage under fourteen years of age should be abducted and taken permanently for schooling away from the coast to acculturate them to civilized ways.

The same year (1848), three Mexican land speculators had the audacity to use Sonoran Law 22–29 to legally claim title to parcels of land on the Tiburón Island—the stronghold of the

Comcaac—launching the first attempt by any outsiders to appropriate land within the heart of Seri territory.

If ever there was an explicit attempt to commit genocide against the entire Comcaac population—who are even now considered "an endangered people" with a unique but threatened language—this was one of those moments. And it was the moment in which Jesus Ávila Sanchez—later known as Coyote Iguana—was prompted to become a multicultural icon of resistance in Sonora.

Amid all the turmoil in Sonora in 1848, this young but strong and gifted Seri man arrived at his uncle's hunting and foraging camp in the desert. It was the jackrabbit-like Jesus Ávila, who had recently turned twenty years of age. By that time, he had paddled to the Baja California peninsula and several islands and was deeply interested in what was occurring in the wider world.

Just four years before, in 1844, he ascended into a cave on a rocky hill called Inámx, within the most rugged portion of Tiburón, for his vision quest. Jesus not only underwent a rite of passage into manhood but also gained shamanistic capacities called *ziix haaco icáama*.

At first, Jesus did not recognize what his spiritual power might offer him or his people. But when he met a Seri woman prophet named Tola, she recognized that his supernatural abilities might guide their people though the conflicts and catastrophes of the next few years.

His descendants still claim that Jesus Ávila had gained the capacity to be a shape shifter. Once, while being pursued by Mexican soldiers, he was transformed into a lizard so that he could climb sheer cliff faces to flee the scene of conflict. Another time, when jailed and prepared for execution, he changed himself into a water bug that escaped beneath the gate of the prison so that he could float down the Río Sonora to reach the gulf coast, where he had a balsa boat hidden in the brush. Within hours, he was out to Tiburón Island and considered going farther out to the sea to hide in caves near his birthplace on San Esteban Island.

Within two years of Jesus Ávila's rite of passage, he was married and living with his first wife, a Comcaac woman named Lupe. They moved between her family's fish camp near the small bay of Tastiota and another camp fifty miles to the south, one called Hast Quiijam, in the vicinity of Bahia San Carlos and Miramar.

There they foraged and fished just north of the port of Guaymas. Without a doubt, they must have witnessed ranchers and prospectors grabbing land and generating considerable fear and heartbreak among the Indigenous peoples of the Sonoran coast. Guaymas had become a key entry point for the invasions of both the Spanish and French into his people's lands and waters, and two decades later it became the site where the Yaqui leader Cajeme would fight to evict them.

Around then, an event occurred that not only ruined his first marriage but changed Jesus Ávila's life. It occurred when Jesus and his family were camping at Bahia San Carlos just north of Guaymas. Some of the Yaqui and Seri men camping with them had gone into the port of Guaymas to obtain alcohol, probably to drink.

When they arrived back at the fishing camp, they became inebriated, which led to a drunken brawl. It also led to the murder of Jesus's brother-in-law, the older brother of his wife Lupe. When Lupe ran to find her husband to stop the conflict, she had to awaken Jesus from a deep sleep. He rose in a state of disorientation, grabbed a weapon to protect his family, but ended up killing some of his brother-in-law's assassins.

The community forced him into exile because of the deaths, and he never returned to live with Lupe and his in-laws.

Jesus Ávila was forced into exile, and it seems that he lived for a while among the Yaqui, learning some of their language and their strategies for resistance to the gachupines, while finding mentors and allies among both the Yaqui and the Pima. It may be that during this time he was gifted the name Coyote Iguana by the other tribes, for some Spaniards claimed that the guerrillero by that name was not Seri but Yaqui or Pima.

It is probable that as Jesus Ávila fled southward from Guaymas en route to Empalme and the eight sacred Yaqui pueblos, he would have crossed the ranchlands recently acquired by a Catalan merchant named Don Diego Casanova. We will never know for sure whether Jesus saw or directly interacted with Don Diego Casanova or his daughter, Delores, before the winter of 1850. Most likely, he spent months and maybe years in contact with the Yaqui and Pima, while avoiding further contact with his wife and her family at Tastiota.

What we do know for sure is that there had already been brief hit-and-run guerrillero attacks on the livestock of the gachupines in the Guaymas area. Indigenous foragers and hunters were frustrated with the ranchers for letting their livestock foul the few freshwater holes that their ancestors had always relied upon.

After consultation with Yaqui elders, Jesus Ávila, aka Coyote Iguana, decided to stage an attack on a carriage with twelve passengers and its escorts on February 23, 1850. His Yaqui mentors declined to be part of the confrontation. But they had all watched carriages and buckboards traveling between Guaymas and Hermosillo, and they knew where to stage a surprise attack. The site chosen is now called La Pamita, and it lies only fifteen to twenty-five miles east of Tastiota, where Jesus Ávila had once lived with his in-laws.

The Comcaac still know the exact site where the altercation occurred, calling it Zamij Haap, while Sonorans have proposed three other sites where the conflict took place. It is not all that far from the barranca and rincon called La Pintada, where families from several tribes regularly convened below caves and canyon walls that featured centuries of rock art.

As the carriage was overturned and set on fire, armed conflict ensued. Chaos raged in the smoke and dust for over an hour. Conflicting reports made it back to Guaymas that very same day, making it difficult to precisely determine how many people had died and how many were taken captive. The brother of an eighteen-year-old girl named Dolores Casanova initially reported that he had seen his sister's body on the ground as he fled from the attack.

Within the days, weeks, and months that followed, it became clear the fair-haired Lola Casanova had not been killed at all. According to the Comcaac, she had not been intentionally abducted or kidnapped. They claim that she was rescued after fainting on the edge of the fiery wreckage of her father's carriage, before being taken away from the conflagration by Coyote Iguana.

Nevertheless, rumors swirled around Guaymas. Some suggested that the fair-haired Spaniard had been abducted and raped by an Indigenous warrior named Coyote Iguana. Others reported her dead. To this day, some of the Comcaac insist that Jesus Ávila had moved her out of harm's way and then nursed her back to health. In fact, they claimed she was voluntarily living him as his partner. Other elders concede that while he had kidnapped Lola, she eventually came to accept being in his company. No two Seri elders tell the story in the same exact manner. It continually changes shape amid campfire smoke and flames, and in this way it has been forged into the stuff of legend.

To the gachupines who were already frustrated by the death of Lola's escorts and their horses, the additional insult of an abduction or coercion of a young woman of Spanish descent by any Indian man enraged them. While many Spaniards had taken wives or mistresses from Indigenous communities throughout Mexico, miscegenation of women of Spanish blood with men of Indigenous heritage was still taboo. It may not have been a legal offense but it was certainly a social and religious affront in their minds.

Moreover, the gachupines were repulsed by the notion that Lola may have accepted being a partner or wife of an Indigenous man with a bounty on his head. That they soon were taking care of a "mestizo" child named Victor—no matter whether Lola became pregnant involuntarily or voluntarily—was seen as the ultimate insult to the blue-blooded "purity" of the Iberian race.

Within two months of the attack, the prefect of Guaymas, Caytano Navarro, launched a punitive expedition to take revenge. He told his troops to arrest, interrogate, and, when feasible, kill any Seri who were found at three places on the Sonoran mainland where the captors where rumored to have taken sanctuary.

By April 24 the same year, his forces had killed at least seven Seri at these camps, but found no Lola among them. At one point, they may have had Jesus Ávila in their hands as a captive, but apparently did not know that he was one and the same person as Coyote Iguana.

The Seri individuals related to Coyote Iguana claim to this day that each time he was cornered, Jesus Ávila escaped on his own, transforming himself into a small animal that went unnoticed when he departed from their company. Then, when he turned to encampments of his own people who still knew him as Teepor—the Haaco Caama shaman—he would shift back into human form to join his family and neighbors in their activities.

One time, while working with Seri friends looking for bat caves on Tiburon Island, I was taken to a series of stone-walled sleeping circles at the base of cliffs. It was said to be one of the places from which Coyote Iguana had escaped his pursuers by scaling the cliffs in the form of a spiny lizard. They divulged that Lola had stayed in camp as a decoy, pleading with the troops not to kill him. If they did, she said, she would kill herself rather than being forced to return to her gachupin family and fiancé on the mainland.

When I have visited these historic camps on Isla Tiburón, I have felt that I was being watched by some person or spirit peeking out around the many boulders and giant cacti that surround these secluded sites. At hideaways with water—like Xapij Háx and Pazj Hax—I must say that I got spooked: unnerved by a palpable presence where bare footprints appeared then disappeared; by calls that sounded like human voices turned into the plaintive coos of doves; and by glowing embers in fire rings where no one had come to camp for weeks.

I asked the Comcaac friends who were guiding me if we could return to the shore for the boat that awaited us, because I did not not—under any circumstances—want to remain there after dark.

Unfortunately, the military pressure on the Comcaac to reveal where Coyote Iguana was hidden—and to kill him—was relentless. To this day, many elders lament that many of his tribesmen were killed or jailed as the military pursued him. Some elders I have known blame Lola Casanova herself for this injustice, while others categorically dismiss that she was guilty of inciting the violence against the Comcaac. It had already been going on for decades.

But as the months wore on, Cayetano Navarro's troops caught Coyote Iguana with his back up against a giant cardón cactus at the foot of a sand dune in a place called Xaasj Heeque Ilít Cpoozi, where the shores of Isla Tiburón can be clearly seen across the water. Having heard the soldiers coming, Coyote Iguana quietly butchered a sacred sea turtle that he had just caught and began to roast the meat on coals for his last sacramental meal. He gave his tribesmen some of the meat and dispatched them to leave as quickly as possible. A few minutes later—surrounded by soldiers—he refused to surrender, challenging the soldiers half his age to fight him one on one. He was trying to buy more time so that his terrorized kin on the other side of the sand dune could escape. Fearing that he might try to elude them once again, the soldiers shot him dead.

For at least a dozen more decades, Comcaac families made pilgrimages to the site of his death, leaving offerings and prayers beneath the giant cactus before it, too, fell on the same ground where Coyote Iguana himself had fallen.

Whether Lola went back to live with family members in Hermosillo, Guaymas, Mexico City, or Spain remains hotly debated. That her son, Victor, stayed among the Comcaac is not. He was one of the lucky Seri males who was not murdered. Over the next century, their population dwindled down to fewer than 160 individuals, and one report suggests that fewer than 120 Comcaac adults of reproductive age remained in their homeland, while others were enslaved or taken away to have "the Indian taken out of them."

Some elderly Seri couples claim that decades ago, a family claiming to be Lola's descendants came up from Colonia Roma in

Mexico City to acquaint themselves with their Comcaac relatives in Sonora. Others insist that could not be true, because she was swept off by her fiancé to Spain, where she died of malaria.

One hundred twenty years later, elders in the Comcaac or Seri community can recount every move and every hideaway Coyote Iguana and Lola Casanova used as they scurried away along the coast, then out to the small islet of Alcatraz in Kino Bay, and then to clandestine camps in caves in the heart of Tiburón Island. They remember the foods they subsisted on, the designs that they painted on their faces, and the songs they sang.

They have particularly strong memories of their son and the five generations of his descendants. It is documented that Victor Ávila would occasionally venture out into the wider world, just as his father had done. Even though Victor lived many more decades than his father, Jesus, he never did carry the spirit power that Coyote Iguana was lauded for. It is unclear whether he did not inherit it or whether his abuse of alcohol diminished it.

Late in life—near the end of the nineteenth century—Victor was formally photographed in Nogales, Sonora, while wearing an elegant suit. The caption for the black-and-white photo referred to him as Coyote Iguana II. Given the timing of his visit to the international border, it is plausible that Victor Ávila was hosted by some of the same Yaqui who had protected Teresita of Cábora in Ambos Nogales that same decade. With their help, she had escaped across the border to evade assassination attempts by the *sicarios* who worked for President Porfirio Ordáz.

Since there was no border fence at that time between Nogales, Sonora, and Nogales, Arizona, he may have been free to walk across International Avenue into the United States, perhaps as the first of the Comcaac to do so.

At that time, at least twenty-eight US states and the Territory of Arizona still had miscegenation laws that forbade even consensual relationships between Europeans and Indians. But nothing in that casual moment prevented Victor from walking right up to the border—or even into the United States—in defiance of those laws. *No fence, no wall, no armed border patrol would have stood in his way.* Curiously, the United States was far more recalcitrant in abandoning its miscegenation laws than Mexico, which proudly celebrates the Indigenous roots of most of its population today.

It is worth pondering why the Coyote Iguana and Lola Casanova saga remains so fresh and vivid in the memories of our contemporaries living in the two Comcaac fishing villages on the Gulf of California. They very well know that the fame of these two romanticized characters has spread through film and literature throughout Mexico and the United States, but that is not what interests them.

What seems to matter most to the Comcaac is not outside opinion but the tenacity with which their own families have kept alive the traditions regarding this tragic incident. These community-based traditions are replete with storytelling and songs as well as face-paint designs and embroideries that they associate with Lola Casanova de Ávila.

Perhaps their efforts to keep this saga in front of younger generations for 170 years is illustrative of how acts of defiance undertaken by one generation in an earlier century remain valuable as models for resistance against the diseases and dysfunctions of the dominant society. One hundred seventy years after the altercation involving Lola Casanova and Coyote Iguana, nearly every member of the Comcaac Nation over twenty years of age knows who in their community is a descendant of this Coyote Iguana and Lola Casanova.

When they try to fight land intrusions by ranchers, miners, or developers, their response is immediate and fierce. I witnessed their solidarity when the government did not help them evict one intruder who would not admit he had phony papers to gain rights to their land. I watched as the tribal elders quietly went into the state's Indian affairs office on a Friday afternoon just before closing time to lock themselves into it through the next week, releasing statements to the press every few hours.

In the meantime, their youth activists flew to Mexico City to have a Monday morning press conference with the Committee of One Hundred organized by Homero and Betty Aridjis, calling for the resignations of the state and national directors of INI if the conflict was not resolved swiftly and permanently. By the time they flew back to the state capital of Hermosillo to pick up their elders, the rancher was evicted and the state director was fired.

That legend may guide the options that Comcaac community members consider whenever there is a physical or existential threat from the outside. It metaphorically helps them in selecting which modes of cultural resistance they should reactivate as future perils emerge.

As a persistent people that barely survived genocide, they are as alert today to these looming perils as a black-tailed jackrabbit is to the presence of coyotes or pumas.

CHAPTER SEVEN

Rebellion

Joaquín Murrieta Orozco and Alfredo Acosta Figueroa

WHERE HAVE the great rebels, renegades, resisters and re-visionaries of the Western world come from? Certainly not from the mainstream, not from the elite ranks of the Daughters of the American Revolution, from the Skull and Bones Society at Yale, from the Fox Club, the Porcellian Club, or the Final Club at Harvard.

Instead, many of them have been blown in with the dust from the arid *edges* of America; have crawled from ramshackle lean-tos of mining camps in the sierras; have arisen from the wattle-and-daub jacales and sun-dried adobes of the desert; have fled from the barrios and plywood colonias on the wrong sides of the tracks; and have waded up to shore from the hand-hewn canoes and patched-together houseboats within river deltas near the sea. They emerged from the margins of our society where grinding poverty, horrific violence, shattered families, and the oppression of ethnic or racial diversity had threatened to pull them asunder.

For them to resist the seemingly inexorable forces of uniformity, hegemony, and globalization, they had to remember and treasure what had been essential throughout the ages to their survival, sustenance, and spiritual resilience. Whenever they could sustain those values in the face of adversity, they found ways to palpably commit themselves to protecting what mattered at all costs.

As they raised themselves and their communities up, many of them have struggled against seemingly insurmountable odds.

They ached with the loss of loved ones.

They fought hard to hang onto what their families and pueblos had built out of the scraps thrown to them by the elite.

But as they emerged out of such challenging conditions, they seldom forgot where they came from. They deeply remembered the love and generosity of those who sheltered them when they were children.

·✿·

I have heard so many corridos sung of Joaquín Murrieta and read so many tales told about him over the past half century that he has begun to appear in my dreams. He first appeared not as the hero nor as the supposed scoundrel he became as an adult but as a child born to the desert, trying to find his way through the dryness and darkness of the world. Here are a few fragments of those dreams, as they verged upon turning into nightmares:

Ten-year-old Joaquín Murrieta Orozco awakened, shed the serape that had served as his only cover, and sat up on his petate sleeping mat woven of plaited sotol fiber. He was trying to remember what had startled him out of his slumber.

And then he heard them again: passionate pleas, prayers, slurs, and shouts spilling in from the next room. The adults gathered in his home that night had not yet gone to bed, for he could recognize the voices of his father, uncles, and cousins bantering, arguing, and grieving.

As he listened to those voices in the other room, Joaquín crawled through the darkness along the wall of his room in the pitch-black jacal. He followed the horizontal lines of saguaro cactus ribs that held the mud in the wall, using them to guide him toward the light. He got up on his feet when he finally reached the weighty mesquite plank door of the room, one that opened into the more crowded space where all the racket was coming from.

When he had used all his force to push open the door, little Joaquín was instantly dazzled and disoriented by the bright lights emanating from the big oil lamp on the table and the raging fire in the horno oven in the corner of the adobe walls in the kitchen.

At the first he could not figure out who was who. The bushy hair and beards of the male presents were backlit by the woodfire behind them, while the lamp light cast shadows on parts of their faces.

Slowly, he recognized the distinctive countenance of his father, Juan, who motioned him to come over to sit at his side on the dirt floor. As Joaquín cuddled against his father's hip, Juan affectionately brushed his hand through his son's curly hair and whispered for him to stay silent as the men finished their heated debate.

When I awakened from this dream, I wondered what event Joaquín's family could have possibly been arguing about at that moment in Sonoran history, if there was indeed any shred of historic fact embedded in my out-of-the-blue dream.

Puzzled, I went back through timelines in written histories and in my own notebooks of oral histories recorded from Sonoran families. The only possible matchup was a tragic event that happened at La Ciéneguilla, a placer mining area between Caborca and Tricheras. More significantly, the La Ciéneguilla oasis had once been a trading grounds between Comcaac (Seri) and Tohono O'odham (Desert Papago) territories in the years prior to Joaquín's birth. But it took place at the placer mines, trapiches mills, and watering grounds where many Murrietas have lived and worked over the decades.

I had heard about the event by chance when camping together with both O'odham and Comcaac elders near Caborca, and the trauma embedded in their accounts had brought the elders of both tribes to tears:

At the height of gold fever in northwest Sonora prior to the Gold Rush in California, a wealthy rancher and mine owner had asked an Indian couple—the man an O'odham, his wife of Comcaac heritage—to guard his cattle and mine claim while he and his henchmen went to Hermosillo for supplies. Some of those driving the wagons to Hermosillo were of the Murrieta clan, and they went south with the cowboys to bring back the supplies.

But while they were gone, some nomadic Comcaac families came eastward from the coast, hungry and destitute from a drought that had hit their encampments at Pozo Coyote. They were kin to the woman caretaker at La Ciéneguilla, but before they made contact with the couple, they found a cow stuck in the oasis reservoir. It looked as if it would die, so they killed it and butchered it to roast the meat.

As they all sat around the campfire that night enjoying carne asada and jerking more meat as tasajos to carry away, the rancher's front guard suddenly returned. When the rancher saw the party eating beef that must have been poached from his herd, he ordered his cowboys to kill every Indian within sight. By the time the Murrietas and other wagoneers arrived on the scene, no Seri or Papago was left standing.

When the relatives of the O'odham woman came to visit her a few weeks later, all they found were the corpses of the victims that had been dragged out into the desert, where they were being picked over by vultures. They were told by the rancher's cowboys that "Seri savages" had massacred them all.

From that day on, the O'odham broke off contact with the Comcaac, blaming them for the massacre. But one of the Comcaac witnesses had escaped and survived, returning to his people on the coast to tell them the truth of what had occurred. Despite their efforts to correct the matter with the O'odham, decades went by without any reconciliation.

And yet a dark cloud hung over every family for fifty miles in any direction who had survived that incident, whether Comcaac, O'odham, or part Yaqui like the Murrietas. They all knew that such injustices were buried in their own family histories, and it was up to them to make sure that nothing like that ever happened again.

Sonoran *cronistas* can argue fiercely about what they called "*nuestra historia*," but they frequently tell their stories as if they had happened just the day before. Who could discern whether some of the events they recounted had occurred a few years before or during the era when Jesus walked in the desert? How was a boy like Joaquín going to learn how long ago these things had actually happened?

Whenever I awakened from such dreams, I wondered why the ghost of Joaquín Murrieta has gotten under the skin of so many people from the likes of Cherokee folklorist John Rollin Ridge and Zorro storyteller Johnston McCullen, Chileans such as Pablo Neruda and Isabel Allende, and Chicanos such as Corky Gonzalez and Luis Valdéz. Their works may have become published late in their lives, but these cuentacuentos, *poetas*, and *habladores* grew up on the spoken word, with stories told around campfires and wood-fired ovens, before electric lights crowded out all darkness, mystery, and magic.

I decided to seek out such stories of Joaquín, the ones that have lingered in the dark corners of the desert.

What I have heard from his descendants and distant relatives in Altar, Caborca, Tubatama, and Trincheras is this: Joaquín and his kin lived in a time when placer mining in Sonora was waning, so they temporarily left; but they were born in and died in Sonora. They had sought out greener pastures in California, and yet most of them returned to their motherland south of the border.

As they became teenagers, Joaquín and his brothers and cousins learned that the placer mining at La Ciéneguilla had left the water in many of the wells in their area toxic. Heavy metals in the water troughs killed some of the cattle and sickened the children. Those wells were abandoned and sealed over. Springs were drying up and so the vegetation was increasingly desiccated.

Even as toddlers, Joaquín and the other boys had played at panning for gold. On the rare days when one of them lucked out and found a nugget, their fathers would take it into Caborca to sell, but would not divulge where it came from.

But such a pursuit required stream flows in the arroyos if they were to find nuggets cropping up in the sand that were as large as kernels of corn. And yet the rains came to San Rafael el Alamito less frequently, and the desert washes remained dry for most of the year.

The Murrieta boys also learned how to ride and break horses, to hitch mules to a tahona grindstone to mill corn, wheat, or ore, and to saddle pack trains to gather firewood, cut ramada posts, or harvest wild oregano in the desert.

And yet, as the drought dragged on, even the usually hardy plants like oregano and mesquite began to dry up, dropping their leaves until the next rains came, or slowly dying during the hottest months.

Among the many Murrieta youth, Joaquín seemed particularly clever, agile, and adept at learning many skills. When working for an uncle who managed a livery stable in Caborca, he learned how manage remudas of horses, saddling them, tying their reins to one another, and mounting the lead gelding.

At such livery stables, Joaquín also learned the rudiments of English from the many Californians and Arizonans who were scoping the area to acquire land, either legally or through swindles. Most were carpetbaggers.

Having puzzled for years over the argument he had heard when he was ten, Joaquín was surprised to learn as a teenager that the massacre his father and uncles debated must have happened before 1811. That was at least eighteen years before his birth! By the time he had figured that out, nearly all the gold in La Ciéneguilla's dry placers had been spent, and the other mining operations not far from that desert oasis hardly employed anyone anymore.

That's about the time when Joaquín must have first heard the words Fiebre del Oro and Gold Rush! The fifteen thousand miners who had once lived in Sonora's Golden Triangle—including his older brother, José Jesus Murrieta—picked up and left the Desierto de Altar for good. They began to cross the treacherous Camino del Diablo, first to another gold strike on the eastern edge of the Yuma Valley in Arizona.

I later learned these Sonorans first made camp not far from where César Chávez would be born three-quarters of a century later.

They lingered for a while near the confluence of the Gila River with the Colorado River, placer mining or panning for gold. But the vein was not anywhere near as rich as the Golden Triangle around La Ciéneguilla had been in its glory day, so they forded the Yuma Crossing known to Salvador Palma and Francisco Garcés, crossing into the California territory to seek other opportunities.

In February of 1848, when his brother José Jesús learned that Joaquín had married their neighbor Carmen (or Carmelita) Féliz, he sent a letter back to Trincheras to convince the teenage couple to join him in California.

However rough-hewn the writing was, José Jesús had tried to convey a simple but urgent message, which read something like this:

> There is hardly any gold left in Sonora or near Yuma. But prospectors have discovered a treasure trove of it this January near Sutter's Creek. It's more than six hundred miles north of the Yuma Crossing over the Río Colorado. That may sound far from home, but you might want come to live with me here, where the gold will make us rich. If so, meet me in three weeks at Yuma Crossing of the Río Colorado. As soon as you make it over that *vado*, I will take you from there . . .

By that time, Sonorans like Joaquín and Carmen must have been painfully aware that the war with the United States had crippled Mexico over the two years of fighting and massive annexations. When the Mexican-American War ended, the state of Sonora had to forfeit 13,200 square miles, including a third of its most productive lands.

The state's homegrown economy and trade relations were ruined, and it was no longer regarded as the largest state in the Mexican republic. The carpetbaggers from the north were already staging clandestine operations, positioning themselves to usurp more lands from Sonorans. As late as September 1851, Antonio Urrea of the Desierto de Altar complained to the Sonoran governor that he was plagued by bands of foreigners who had no respect for Mexican authority nor sovereignty.

For Joaquín—who had not even reached twenty years of age—the land grab by gringos and the demise of the Sonoran mines had generated double exposure to destitution and displacement. Abject poverty forced Joaquín and Carmen to leave their desert birthplace.

In the springtime of 1849, the newlyweds left the Desierto de Altar in Sonora with six of Joaquín's brothers and cousins. They headed across 250 miles of the Camino del Diablo, stopping at three different tinajas along the way to rewater their horses and fill their canteens. It was the first of many trips across the Camino that Joaquín and his brothers would take over the next four years, covering thirty miles a day.

Once the newlyweds crossed one of the driest stretches in all of North America, they waded their horses through the muddy red waters at the Yuma Crossing and met Joaquín's brother José Jesús on the other side.

They would ride their horses for another six hundred miles over three more weeks. At first, they were told to head toward a little town along the Pacific coast called Nuestra Señora la Reina de los Ángeles de Porciúncula. They rested their mounts and bought more supplies there in Los Angeles.

Two of the Murrieta brothers then sent a letter back to Trincheras, informing their parents that they had survived the worst. They encouraged Joaquín's parents—Juan and Juana—to consider settling in Los Angeles, which they would do—at least for a while—a few years later.

From there, the newlyweds rode over a coastal range toward the Central Valley and on to the Sierra Nevada foothills, about as far north as San Francisco.

To see so much water, mountains so high, and emerald green forests so immense must have filled the Murrietas with awe. Not far from the Yosemite Valley in present-day Tuolumne County, they finally set up camp. They obtained their supplies in the spanking-new town of Sonora during the very first year it was settled. It was named in 1848 after their home state by other earlier arrivals from the south. It was animated with a nostalgia for the desert that made the Murrietas feel they were part of a community.

Before they reached Sutter's Mill and Sonora Camp, where the Gold Rush was raging, they would have covered at least six hundred miles, half the distance that most Conestoga wagon trains in the north would take to reach California. They were among the ten thousand Sonorans who had gone north immediately after the gold strike in 1848; three hundred thousand Americans from other parts of the continent would soon join them.

It soon became clear that the Murrieta brothers and cousins knew far more about searching for gold than most of the recent arrivals, either from other parts of Mexico, from the eastern United States, or from China. Joaquín and his kin knew how to find accessible veins in the motherlode, to excavate tunnels to extract it, to pan in the streams for it, and to hide their treasure so others could not find it.

It is not surprising that Joaquín staked several claims in his first two years in Alta California, ones that promised great wealth if he could prove them up. While the Murrieta boys were out prospecting, Joaquín's lovely wife, Carmen, cooked up beans and made piles of tortillas, for she had become camp cook for a half-dozen or more hungry and sometimes rowdy young men.

They met Chinos and gringos in camps nearby who watched their every move, hoping to tap into the same veins where *la familia* Murrieta had struck gold. There was the exhilaration of discovery in the air around Sutter's Creek and Sonora that infected anyone who arrived with a shared sense of adventure. But it would not be too long before those sensibilities would become overwhelmed by skullduggery and bigotry. Competition soon drowned out good-natured enthusiasm, as three hundred thousand miners and merchants, swindlers, and scoundrels came to California to make it rich off the Gold Rush.

Joaquín was so good at moving gold from mine and stream to market that his relatives claim he garnered more than $40,000 between late 1848 and 1850. That would be equivalent in purchasing power to about $1.5 million today.

But his visits to the banks with his brothers did not go unnoticed by other, more hapless prospectors nor by California's first wave of greedy and often racist politicians. When California finally achieved statehood on September 9, 1850, among the first statutes the "Know Nothing" Party pushed through the legislature were the Foreign Miner's Tax and Civil Section 394.

The Foreign Miner's Tax was a xenophobic demand for high monthly taxes from Indians, Mexicans, and Chinese, to discourage them from finding any more gold or filing any more mining claims. Civil Section 394 made it illegal for minority "races" to legally accuse whites of European descent of any misdeed, from murder and rape to robbery, claim-jumping, or any other form of plunder.

As Antonio Franco Coronel lamented during that same era, "The reason for most of the antipathy against the Spanish race was that the majority of them were Sonorans, who were men used to gold mining, and consequently they more quickly attained better results." It was as if the California legislature's first significant acts were about establishing structural racism as the official modus operandi in the new state.

Because most Mexicans were legally considered to be of a fourth or more Indian blood by descent, they could not legally challenge any Anglos of any misdeed in court. They, like the Chinese, were mandated to pay $20 a month—the equivalent of $500 today—simply to obtain a license to prospect for and to mine gold.

While that impeded the poorest Mexican-born and Asian-born miners from staking many claims, Section 394 had far worse ramifications. Any Anglo could jump the claim of a Mexican or Chinese prospector without legal recourse for those who had initially discovered the gold. As a result, thousands of gringos either extorted their "foreign" competitors to take over their claims, or they brutally beat and killed them to clear the way for their own dubious claims.

In short order, ten thousand Spanish-speaking miners were driven out of California, most of them back to Sonora. But when gringos started to jump the Murrieta family's mining claims, Joaquín urged his brothers and cousins to resist.

Resist they did, for at least three more years, but at an extraordinary human and economic cost.

One day, while many of the Murrieta brothers were away in town, hoping to resupply Carmen with provisions, a vigilante party of whites mobbed their camp. They accused Joaquín's older brother, José Jesús, of stealing a mule from an Anglo miner, and hung him from a tree.

When Joaquín stumbled upon the scene and tried to stop the lynching, they horsewhipped him until he could hardly breathe or move. They then went after his wife, first trying to force her to disrobe. When Carmen fought back, they tore off her clothes, beat her, and gang-raped her in front of her husband, as Joaquín pleaded with them to let her go.

Some say that Carmen died immediately, while others say she survived a few more days. They note that she was pregnant at the time and bled to death shortly after while suffering from a miscarriage. The vigilantes left Joaquín for dead and disappeared.

A day later, his brothers and cousins arrived to find Joaquín barely able to walk, but he was a changed man. In his pain and delirium, had Joaquín remembered the massacre of the Papago and the Seri woman that had occurred not far from his birthplace?

In any case, Joaquín vowed then and there that he would not let such indignities happen on his watch to any Mexicans or Indians again.

From that point on, the story speeds up and gets murkier. It seems that the Murrietas all chose to dress the same and go by the name of Joaquín. They broke into four gangs and went after Carmen's rapists and those who had lynched José Jesús. They killed the perpetrators of these nightmarish acts, robbed their purses and stores, and burned down their abodes.

With the support of other Mexicans and some native Californians, they then broadened their reach. They ranged far beyond the Sonora mining district to destroy the camps and steal the horses of any other gringos known to have impinged upon mine claims that rightfully belonged to Sonorans, Natives, or Californios from the Baja Peninsula.

The four Murrieta gangs began to drive 300 to 350 horses back to Sonora at a time, each completing as many as twenty drives over La Vereda Caballo "Horse Trail" per year. At best, they could accomplish the round trip down from the Sierra Nevada and across the Camino del Diablo then back again in six weeks' time.

At that rate, it is possible that the Murrieta gangs pulled as many as twenty-four thousand stolen horses out of the California economy in each of their most productive years, while "gifting" or selling them into Sonora and Baja California Norte.

There is simply no way to tell whether Joaquín Murrieta Orozco himself personally took part in any or many of these vengeful thefts and associated murders. He had been beaten so badly the day of the lynching and raping that his own capacities may have been temporarily compromised.

While Joaquín's whereabouts during this period of retaliation remains hotly debated, his kin and his allies had great success scouring out many of the claim-jumping Anglo scoundrels. Two of his cousins—who were also named Joaquín at birth—began to go by the nicknames of Joaquín El Guachipín and Joaquín El Guero. Hit-and-run attacks on Anglo mining camps would simultaneously occur in a half-dozen California counties the same week. To execute this reign of terror, it is plausible that as many as fifty Mexican resisters all donned dashing garb to become clones of Joaquín.

Collectively, they were the precursors of Zorro. Their coordinated efforts to turn over the apple carts and reclaim lands through carefully orchestrated attacks inspired warfare by guerrilleros throughout Latin America over the following century.

Inevitably, the California legislature of interlopers, carpetbaggers, and filibusterers put up a $5,000 bounty for the head of the "real Joaquín," even though many sheriffs in the state were sure that there was more than one fish in the school that they wanted to fry.

To no one's surprise, the scallywags in the legislature then announced to the press that California Rangers had executed and beheaded the "authentic Joaquín" and his sidekick, Three-Finger Jack García. It was nothing more than a publicity stunt to save face. They claimed to have bottled up both Joaquín's head and Jack's hand in a batch of whiskey, as if they were making ceviche.

No matter that there was little resemblance between the pickled head in the bottle and the countenance of Joaquín Murrieta Orozco recognized by everyone who knew him.

With this sleight of hand, California's state legislature declared that the game was over. They had won their little battle but had lost tens of thousands of horses and mules during the brief war with Sonorans.

So where did Joaquín go if he was not actually dismembered by the California Rangers in 1853? Oral histories from family members suggest that he went undercover to find his parents in Los Angeles, but they had returned to Sonora by then. There is some evidence that he took stolen horses down a second trail to Baja California that was called La Vereda Mesteña or Mustang Trail. There, on the other side of the border, Joaquín may have lain low in Tecate, Baja California, with relatives, before clandestinely returning to remote parts of Sonora. After years of trauma, Joaquín apparently avoided public appearances for the rest of his life.

For more than a century, his kin in Trincheras, San Rafael de Alamito, and Altar have repeatedly confirmed that Joaquín Murrieta Orozco lived nearby them until 1908. He was buried without fanfare—head still on his neck!—on the mesa-top cemetery by an old Spanish mission in Cucurpe, Sonora, just eighty miles south of the US-Mexico border. That would have made him almost eighty years old at the time of death, with only five of those years documented as a life lived in California.

For most viewers of Westerns, readers of pulp novels, and singers of corrido ballads, the oral histories of la familia Murrieta haven't mattered as much as the legend itself. Whether Joaquín Murrieta Orozco was much aware of it during his lifetime, his charismatic acts of resistance have been remembered and celebrated in Mexico, Chile, and the United States.

Rather than being disparaged today as he was in decades past as a "gringo eater," he has been hailed as the father of the Chicano resistance movement by many of the great Latinx activists, poets, novelists, and filmmakers of the past century.

No, Joaquín Murrieta did not succeed in repatriating parts of Indigenous Mexico that had been dubiously ceded to the United States. But he did reinforce the deep values of cultural resistance in desert peoples that were being pushed aside by economic globalization. Millions of Americans have heard his name and have listened to the ballads and stories about him. They have become the cultural antibodies to a kind of society-wide disease that has afflicted North Americans off and on for more than four centuries.

As if those cultural instincts of resistance can be passed on from one generation to another like heritable antibodies, they reappeared in a descendent of the Murrieta clan from San Rafael de Alamito, Alfredo Acosta Figueroa, who was born in Blythe, California, in 1934. His great-great-grandmother Teodosa Martínez Murrieta was from the La Ciéneguilla oasis when its placer mines were still in operation. She was a cousin and contemporary of Joaquín Murrieta Orozco.

In addition to his ancestral ties to the Murrietas, Alfredo's mother, Carmen, also lived among her family of Chemahuevi

Indians on the lower Colorado River. In 1905, his father came north from the Río Yaqui of southern Sonora.

Alfredo's father had both Yaqui and Pima ancestry. He spoke the Yaqui language and performed the traditional pascola and matachín dances at community fiestas.

But Alfredo also held to many of the Yaqui or Yoeme expressions of resistance that have been documented in oral and written histories for centuries. Alfredo's father warned his sons—some of whom were baptized not far from where Joaquín Murrieta was buried—that "your biggest enemy will be your boss." Alfredo's uncles and father had come face to face and toe to toe with such enemies while working as miners all across the borderlands.

Alfredo once recalled that his father "was very independent, and when he saw any injustice, he would intervene and protest." When his father was just eighteen, he got hired on as a miner in the border town of Bisbee. When he went on strike with the other men, he witnessed many of his cronies being forcibly evicted and taken away by train to Mexico or Texas. That convinced Alfredo's father to become one of the leaders in strikes at the Sonora Rey Arizona mine.

Alfredo and his brother Mike grew up around the Wobbly sensibilities of his father and other miners who told the children that "this land has been stolen from us." That assertion did not sit well with Alfredo's Anglo schoolteachers.

By the time the brothers were in their twenties, they had begun to hang out with Mexican farmworkers, who told them of the abuses they had suffered in the grape vineyards and lettuce fields. By raising their concerns to officials, Alfredo and Mike got on the bad side of the Blythe police force.

One day in 1963, Alfredo was singing in Spanish to the bartender in the El Serape Café when police officers barged in. They complained that he was disturbing the peace and that he had to leave. When he refused, they threw Alfredo against the bar, then flung him out the door and dragged him over to a police car where they kicked him.

When he shouted, "This will be the last Mexican you'll ever kick," they beat him even more, wedging him into the squad car. That was the last straw for Alfredo, just like the rape of Carmen Féliz was for Joaquín Murrieta.

Knowing that there was a new judge in Blythe, Alfredo and his brother Mike took the risk of suing the police officers involved in the incident. Alfredo became the first Chicano in the United States ever to win a police brutality case against local law enforcement officers.

From that point on, there was nothing that could stop Alfredo Figueroa's quest for social justice. Around 1964, he threw in with César Chávez—whom he had personally known since 1949—in fighting the racism that remained prevalent in the fields of Arizona and California.

Alfredo had already known César's wife, Helen, since she was sister to Alfredo's next-door neighbor. Both César and Alfredo had spent time as adolescents along the shores of the Colorado River and in the fields nearby. When César and Dolores Huerta initiated their new union, Alfredo went out in 1966 to organize the farm-workers he knew. He had been pitching watermelons and cutting lettuce part time since he was ten, and he fully empathized with the braceros and the old-time families of Mexican Americans.

By 1976, he had asserted his Native ancestry in public debates, becoming a key figure in a tribal coalition that successfully halted the Sun Desert nuclear power plant that San Diego Gas and Electric wanted to build in their midst. In 1992, he helped organize another tribal coalition that stopped the plan for a Ward Valley nuclear waste dump in its tracks. He also endeavored to protect sacred desert sites of his people by forming an alliance with famed archaeologist Boma Johnson.

If there ever was a moment to celebrate among the extended Murrieta clan, it was when Alfredo Acosta Figueroa was invited to be a featured singer at the National Folklife Festival held each summer on the Capitol Mall. My old friend Big Jim Griffith remembers the day when he heard the melody of one of his favorite corrido ballads coming from a performer on a stage nearby. As Jim wove his way through the crowd, he spotted old Alfredo, playing his guitar and singing one of the many versions of the enduring *Corrido de Joaquín Murrieta*, written in another century and another place:

Yo no soy americano
Pero comprendo el inglés,
Me lo aprendí con mi hermano
Al derecho y al revés,
A cualquier americano
Lo hago temblar a mis pies. . . .

Yo me pasee en California
Por el año del 50,
En mi montura plateada
Y mi pistola repleta,
Yo soy ese mexicano
De nombre Joaquín Murrieta.

Alfredo—kin and kindred spirit to Joaquín—has kept the family's campfire burning.

CHAPTER EIGHT

Revolution

Teresita de Cábora and Lauro Aguirre

FOR MORE than half my life, I have been both haunted and helped by a woman who lived in the border county where I now live, but well over a century before me. After a terrible tumble from a mule damaged my vision, cognition, and speech, I would lay in pain in bed with my eyes closed. If I opened them, I would see three separate images in the distance, or halos around objects that were up close. There were also aural and visual hallucinations that lasted just a few moments, but sometimes scared the wits out of me, so much so that I would pass out or feel so dizzy I would tumble to the ground. I had to keep my eyes closed for a while before I could resume any activity again.

But on more than one occasion, I would feel someone gently brushing their fingers over the wound on my temple. As I quietly felt that healing touch, I saw an image of a quiet young woman whom I could not identify at first. Her face was partially concealed from me by her long, curly hair that rained down over her shoulders to cover my ears and shoulders as she leaned over me.

As I thought about who I knew with long hair that almost reached to her waist, I remembered an old photo from at least a century before of Santa Teresita de Cábora, a charismatic healer who once lived within twenty miles as the crow flies of where I live today.

Of course, when such a vision comes to any of us who have had traumatic brain injuries, there is no rational way to confirm any of this. But neither could those who were blind during the times of Yeshua of Nazareth or Muhammad of Medina, those who, under the healing spell of these mystics, began to see.

·ঔ·

I once drove four hundred miles southward into Mexico to see the ranchería where "la Santa" had grown up before she had taken refuge in Arizona, Texas, and California. Arriving at the remote desert ranching village of Cábora, Sonora, after hours of driving and years of dreaming, I found it hard to reconcile its modest appearance with the facts that a saint had found her powers there and had helped it become *the* place of cultural resistance that presaged the Mexican Revolution.

I was not so much disappointed by Cábora but humbled: How could it be that this little scatter of rancherías was propelled into a pivotal role in triggering a revolution that changed the course of Mexican and US borderland history more than thirteen decades ago?

Was it simply that it was a bridge between the Sierra Madre and the Pacific coast, and a bit of high ground that escapes inundation every time hellacious floods overtopped the channels of the Río Yaqui and Río Mayo, turning the coastal plains into a six-foot-deep wall of water fifty miles wide?

Marginal even to the vast expanse of fertile, well-watered lands of the Río Mayo, the pueblo of Cábora is nestled between low hills against a small laguna that accumulates most of the meager rains shed within an internally drained basin. Most of its waters and people seem to go nowhere, but stay right there.

Nevertheless, one of the individuals that sprung from this pale Sonoran soil generated cataclysmic impacts on the borderlands that continue to ripple out into the rest of North America to this day. She did so at a time in North American history when industries were first becoming more powerful than governments, and when taking land and water from Indigenous inhabitants had opened up deep wounds in both the United States and Mexico.

·ঔ·

It took me a while to read all this between the lines, for Cábora is now a land of blowing dust where fertile soil once ran deep. And yet, this remote ranchería was the home of the charismatic faith healer and herbalist who unwittingly served as the catalyst for the growth of the global Spiritist movement and the Mexican Revolution.

At her birth, she was named Niña Garcia Nona Maria Rebecca Chávez, but she soon became better known on both sides of the border as Teresista, and later, as Santa Teresita de Cábora. Much later, she became heralded as the queen of America, the best-known Mexican American woman in the world during her time.

Her status at birth was far humbler than any queen. She was conceived out of wedlock, as the "love child" of a fourteen-year-old Tehueco Indian girl, Cayetana Chávez, and a wealthy rancher of Morisco descent, Don Tomás Urrea. To avoid the wrath of the legal wife of Tomás, Cayetana was hidden away in 1873 as soon as her pregnancy became apparent. And so, Teresista was born in a place where there was no doctor, stepsister to thirteen other progeny that her father had sired or one of her "comothers" had carried.

La Niña Garcia Nona Maria Rebecca Chávez was simply dropped out of Cayetana's womb into the arms of a Yaqui midwife kneeling onto the hard-packed dirt floor of a jacal. She was then washed in a ceramic tub or pottery bowl beneath a shade ramada of mesquite and cactus ribs.

The clay dirt and desert herbs that she later used to heal more than forty thousand poor, desperate people in several countries were all around her there in Ocoroni, Sinaloa, and later in Cábora, Sonora, during her childhood. Some of them may have been used on her or her mother in the hours after Cayetana *dio a luz*; she gave birth to a baby, and in doing so, she "turned on the light" in an otherwise darkening world.

La Niña's birthplace was on the banks of a dry arroyo not far from the headquarters of her father's Rancho Santana. No one present there that day had an inkling that the bastard child of a rancher and his servant would amount to anything, especially anything significant enough to change their community's destiny. The newborn was not immediately welcomed in her father's hacienda estate.

But when Tomás moved his entire family and its cadre of servants from the ranch in Ocoroni, Sinaloa, to another in Cábora, Sonora, Cayetana and her precociously bright daughter were "invited" to come along. It was there that a whole cadre of Yaqui and Mayo girls her age began to call her Teresista—an affectionate nickname for Teresa—rather than continuing to refer to her as La Niña.

She remained there for the next decade, halfway between the colonial silver mining town of Alamos and the international port of Guaymas, on the cactus-studded plains, many miles away from any major highway or city.

While permitted on the grounds of a newly constructed hacienda in Cábora, Teresista lived most of the time with her ornery aunt in an inelegant jacal in the nearby ranchería of Aquihuiquichi. She grew up playing with the poor families of Yaqui and Mayo cowboys who spoke a rare dialect akin to her mother's Cahitan tongue.

It was during the first years of her adolescence there that Teresista saw a three-year-old Yaqui girl hung from a tree by a ruthless military commander. That horrifying scene may have seared into Teresista's memory forever. Perhaps that brutal act of injustice was what kindled in her heart a lifelong commitment to help Indigenous peoples in their struggles to reaffirm their dignity and rights to their ancestral lands.

Along the way, Teresista's mother disappeared, never to return to be seen by her daughter again. It appeared that her father simply ignored her presence at Aquihuiquihi until one day in 1888. That's when Teresista, by then a lovely, fair-skinned, bright-eyed child of fourteen, appeared at his doorstep. She politely asked to be taken in as a worker at headquarters to escape her aunt's bellicosity and abuse.

She was immediately spotted by a charismatic Yaqui woman, María Sonora, whose nickname was Huila. As a curandera and cook there at the Aquihuiquihi headquarters, Huila had the authority to accept Teresista as her helper. Her father not only tolerated the girl working as an assistant to Huila; Don Tomás welcomed her presence and gradually began to introduce her to others as his legitimate daughter. Teresista then took on his last name of Urrea, abandoning her mother's surname altogether.

We now know that it was Huila who set Teresista on her path as a healer or curandera, known in Yaqui as *hitebi*. While Huila knew the Yaqui ways and terms for curing, most of the plants, animal parts, and clays she kept in her medicine bundle were widely used by most tribes in northern Mexico and the adjacent United States.

But Huila was also familiar with Spanish-introduced concepts of hot and cold illnesses, maladies such as *pasmo* and *susto*, the sprinkling of Holy Water, the laying on of hands, and psychosomatic cleansings with smoke simply called *limpias*.

Huila not only instructed her on where the most potent curative herbs could be found but also took her to a secret cave not far from Cábora where Mayo curanderas had found a certain kind of clay with unique curative powers. Huila may have also cultivated in Teresista the sense of spiritual power, resilience, and resistance that the Yaqui had expressed for centuries.

Once, when Huila saw that young Teresista was calming and curing her patients with some preternatural gift, she simply said to her disciple, "You may have something powerful I do not."

·ঌ·

Huila began to take her along whenever she collected medicinal herbs in the monte, amid the gorgeous guayacán trees and towering *cardón barbón* and pitahaya cactus. She gradually taught Teresista to identify, collect, and prepare nearly two hundred kinds of medicinal herbs, barks, seeds, roots, and clays, in addition to ground rattlesnake meat and rennet from the fourth stomach of Criollo Corriente cows.

While Teresista was still a teenager, Huila nurtured in her the extraordinary skill of matching curative herbs with certain maladies. She learned to treat what Sonoran Indians called "the wandering sicknesses," respiratory viruses, bacterial infections of the stomach, fungal infections of the skin, yeast infections of the urinary tract, and the venomous stings of spiders, scorpions, snakes, and Gila monsters.

While Teresista quickly learned of the natural healing properties of plants and animal parts, Huila was also opening her up to the supernatural, through metaphors that the Yaqui had shared among themselves since time immemorial.

Once a year, Teresista accompanied her father and Huila to the open-air market in nearby Navajoa, where an old curandero from the neighboring Mayo tribe taught her how to use the red roots of *cocolmeca* from the Sierras to calm menstrual cramps, and the astringent roots of *chuchupate* to quell the sore throats and coughs that accompanied *la gripa*.

The young girl also heard Huila describe the emergence of Teresista's miraculous gifts to the old medicine man there: her capacity to fly in her dreams, as María of Ágreda once did, and to engage with the Virgin of Guadalupe, as Juan de Banderas also did in his visions.

By the time she turned fifteen, Teresista had already garnered the homegrown equivalent of a herbology degree. As a *hittoareo*, or herbalist, she could use plant medicines to cure dozens of wandering sicknesses, but her spiritual powers remained nascent. There was still more to learn from Huila and her cronies about the Yaqui way of becoming a hitebi.

That's when Huila began to divulge her more secretive means

for dealing with the more daunting "staying sicknesses," the psychosomatic illnesses that could cause blindness, paralysis, stuttering, nervous tics, or even tumors. These more problematic afflictions were not only harder to diagnose but took the deeper, more disciplined spiritual power of a faith healer to expel evil from the mind and body of the afflicted.

Over the years, her mentor, Huila, taught her how to switch gears in her curing practices, depending upon her diagnosis of the causal agents: *When the body is hurt by things of this world, heal with herbs. When but when the spirit has been damaged by larger forces, cure with your spiritual charisma.*

Because Huila and Teresista might be accused of being brujas or *hechiceras* if word ever got out of their divinations and incantations, they were pressed to keep such esoteric knowledge to themselves. Late in her short, swift time on this earth, Teresista would only offer these few words about her faith healing:

"When sick people come to me, I can see where they are sick, as if I were looking through a window."

Her window into the hidden heart of the world continued to grow in dimension and in clarity. Just as Teresista's fame as a healer began to eclipse that of her beloved teacher, Huila, her life was almost extinguished forever.

In 1889, a lustful mining engineer named Millán became obsessed with the idea of seducing the sixteen year old, ironically echoing the infatuation that her father, Don Tomás, had developed for her mother. When Teresista rebuffed his advances, he apparently cornered her so that he could rape her.

She screamed, then fell into a series of epileptic seizures that brought everyone in the hacienda running to her aid. She was overcome by short bursts of writhing convulsions that could not be controlled even when a half-dozen men and women attempted to hold her still.

Twelve other seizures followed as she fell unconscious into a coma-like state of cataplexy that triggered narcolepsy, a sleep disorder that lasted for the larger part of three months. It was punctuated by brief moments when Teresista would open her eyes, express her need to eat some sacred clay from the Cábora cave, and attempt to explain the dreams she had been having, before falling back out of contact.

Even Huila's gifts as a healer could not bring Teresista out of a coma, and the older curandera declared to Don Tomás that her cherished disciple was dead.

After they washed Teresista's skin, brushed her knee-length hair, and placed her in a white dress, they put her on a table surrounded by candles and let all the women from the hacienda come in to pray for her wake.

To their chilling astonishment, Teresista suddenly awakened and ordered her caretakers to mix her saliva with the curative clay Huila had found at the sacred cave. She told them to halt their applications of a mustard seed plaster meant to relieve her pain and instead to apply the clay mixed with her saliva as a poultice on her temples.

Suddenly, her pain went away because of her self-prescribed cure.

There, in the midst of her own wake, she sat up, opened her eyes, and asked, "What does this mean?"

Only the curandera Huila could honestly speak:

"My child, you were dead. And I prayed harder than I have ever prayed to the Blessed Virgin to give you back to us. She must have heard me, for you are alive again."

"The Blessed Virgin?" Teresista replied. "Yes, she was here with me, talking to me. She told me the many things that I now must go and do."

Many healers from shamanistic traditions around the world have confessed that they had to "die" before they could gain the capacity to save the lives of others. We have no idea whether the "things that she had to go and do" included only her healing arts or included spiritual and political actions as well. All we know is that she later attempted to achieve all three.

If we assume that in her visions the Virgin urged Teresista to care for the suffering, oppressed, and dispossessed, perhaps Teresista conceded that supporting Indigenous struggles for their rights was one means to those ends. It may be that once you've been declared dead and then come back to life, you have little else to lose by helping others with the little time you have to live the second time around.

⁂

And so it began. Teresista stayed in a liminal state for the next 108 days. Then, suddenly, she announced that the Virgin Mary herself had offered her a *don*, gifting her the spiritual power to heal. The Virgin also mandated that Teresista should devote her life to serving others as a curandera.

The first person in need of healing that they brought to her was a poor Indigenous girl who had suffered back pain and a limp from years of dealing with one of her legs being longer than the other.

Teresista began to rub and stretch the girl's shorter leg while staring into her eyes and telling her that she would soon be able to toss aside her walking stick. The girl planted both of her feet squarely on the ground, left her cane behind her, and walked away without any further pain.

In the coming days and weeks, they would bring her a broken man, a cowpoke crippled by the kick of a mule, and she would immediately see that he could not be healed through herbs. She would talk to him in her trance-like voice and make a paste of her saliva and some sacred clay. Teresista would rub this paste into the man's arm or leg or face until he would moan deeply, then rise up to walk without his cane. Finding that he could lift his dangling arm above his head once more, he smiled at her with all his might, as if this Teresista had realigned his life for good.

As later reported years later, when she lived in a cottage at the corner of State and Brooklyn in the Sonora Town barrio of East LA, "The halt, the blind, the inwardly diseased, paralytics, almost helpless and others with bodies ravaged by consumption, are helped to her doors each day by friends and relatives; and none go there without the belief that by the laying on of her magic hands they will be cured."

I remember just a few images of the time when her specter seemed to hover over me, lightly brushing her fingers over the wound between my right eye and my temple:

At first, I was startled, but her touch was so soothing that I quickly overcame my fear. It was as if her fingers ever so lightly glancing across the skin of my forehead were repairing whatever tissues had formerly connected my eyes to my mind.

After a few minutes, I would smell a mildly sweet fragrance emanating from her fingers, or from my wound; who could say? My sight was impaired, but my capacity to detect scents had been magnified by my accident. I felt so calmed that I fell off to sleep with the sense that someone was kissing my eyelids.

When I awakened once more and touched my own fingers, there was the grit of moistened soil or clay-like paste all around my eyes. I guessed that she had mixed her own saliva with some clay she had gathered from a nearby cave in the desert, so that she could apply a "mud-pack facial" to my wounds.

And then it came to me: In another desert halfway around the world, a healer named Yeshua had often spat on the desert soil to make a muddy paste to smear on the eyes of blind men, women, or girls. Teresista is known to have done the same on many occasions. Is it possible that she had remembered hearing of that spiritual cure for loss of vision in the chapel at Cábora while still a child? Or had she learned it from Huila when she served as an apprentice to that Yaqui healer?

·ⴰ·

Oh, how her healing powers seemed to surge after her resurrection from the dead! Her hair began to grow with the speed of a tropical vine, trailing down her back to her ankles. Her expressions of advice were elegant in their brevity, but confident in their prognoses. Every infirm or crippled soul from all over Sonora sought her out.

And then the dam broke: Strangers swarmed in from the other side of the Great Divide, the Sierra Madre Occidental. Fervor over Teresista spilled out of the mining town of Tomochic, Chihuahua, where a homegrown evangelist and political activist was thirsty for every word he'd heard had come from Teresista's mouth. That Tomochiteco leader, Cruz Chávez, had probably recognized a kindred spirit in Teresista's father, Don Tomás, who had also been critical of the dictatorship of Porfirio Díaz and of the haughty hierarchy of the Catholic Church.

When Cruz came to Cábora to listen to Teresista in the flesh, he realized that he needed no intermediaries from any church—nor any distant saint—to help him reach the grace of God. This little girl with hair flowing down to her feet was fully immersed in the flow of the River of God. Cruz Chávez felt her grace during one of the times he made a pilgrimage to a *romería* gathering in Cábora to celebrate a Saint's Day feast with the Yaqui and Mayo who assembled there. Pretty soon, Cruz was inviting them to join his ranks to Tomochic.

When Cruz Chávez and his Tomochiteco rebels skirmished with the dictator's troops on Thanksgiving Day in 1891, some Yaqui, Mayo, Mountain Pima, and Tarahumara fighters joined them. The insurgents would cry out, "Viva la Virgén y la Santa de Cábora!" as they launched into battle. Their heaven-sent determination was enough to whip the better-equipped soldiers back away from their homes.

For years afterward, Teresista had to explain that she did not instigate, strategically guide, nor secretly lead the Yaqui and other Indigenous rebels in such conflicts with the government, the mines, or the Church:

"I have cured Indians, and they love me for it, but I do not tell them to make revolution. . . . I have had nothing to do with the Yaqui uprisings. They have *always* fought to keep hold of their lands."

Nevertheless, the insurgents realized that they needed help; they could not immediately return to Tomochic because it was occupied by soldiers. Cruz Chávez felt that their only option was to ride their horses over the crest of the Sierra Madre to seek the counsel of Teresista.

By that time, they had designated her as their Matron Saint and had begun to call themselves Teresistas. They had distributed framed sketches and photos of her to pass out among their ranks, and they had hidden her precious handwritten letters to them in clandestine pouches called *suertes* in their shirts, so that her words would be close to their hearts and offer them spiritual protection.

But before Cruz Chávez and his men arrived in Cábora, troops stormed into the Urrea hacienda to arrest Teresista, accusing her of sedition and inciting the Tomochitecos to revolt. At the last minute, Don Tomás dissuaded the troop's captain, Enríquez, from taking Teresista into custody.

He bargained for an alternative: They would go to the Yaqui village of Cocorit, where the Urreas would voluntarily turn Teresista over to authorities for protection there amid all her Yoemem (Yaqui) devotees. If the military force tried to jail or kill her there, they would have to face the wrath of the Yaqui Nation, a wrath that was already legendary.

And so, they went to Cocorit, the place of the fiery, wild chiltepín pepper! When I have visited this Yoemem pueblo on the edge of the Río Yaqui floodplain, I always come away impressed by the creativity, ferocity, and political awareness of its residents. While other Yaqui communities have passion plays for Holy Week in which evil soldiers and pharisees storm into the church on foot to steal the body of Jesus, Cocorit's "sacred actors" literally stampede their horses into a three-walled chapel to kidnap the Christ figure. The Yoemem of Cocorit take the battle between good and evil very seriously.

Long before she had been taken in by the Yaqui curandera Huila, Teresista had been traumatized by seeing many others of this tribe brutally treated by authorities. Perhaps she remembered seeing that Yaqui girl hanging from a tree years before, and that is what kindled in Teresista the strongest urge to defend the Yoemem at all costs:

> I never led the Yaqui into battle, but I sympathized with them. My father employed them on the hacienda and I knew and loved them. I have seen the many wrongs. Before my eyes children not three years old have been lynched, hanged from trees . . . by the order of the military commander of the Sonora District to keep the Yaquis down. . . . Do you know why this tribe fights the forces of such a government? They are the bravest and most persecuted people on earth.

On Christmas Day of 1891, Chávez and the Teresistas from Tomochic bushwhacked the federal troops in the sierra, killing their captain, Enríquez. Then they rode down to pray for thanks in Teresista's own chapel on the hacienda.

When President Porfirio Díaz heard that his men had been defeated, he was furious. He commanded that additional troops scour the sierra in pursuit of Chávez, but he allowed Don Tomás, his daughter, and his sons to return to Cábora, where they could move about freely at the ranch, but always under surveillance.

·~·

When word got out in the *zona serrana* of Sonora and Chihuahua that Teresista was safe and the guerrilla fighters remained undefeated, religious fanaticism and revolutionary fervor spread like wildfire. Other Indigenous uprisings soon followed, each cadre of rebels feeling that they were protected from bullets and lances by their spiritual alliance with Teresista.

These Teresistas carried her picture in amulets hung over their hearts; they tattooed her name on their wrists; they chanted her name for protection as they moved from one hideout to the next. They sent word of her healing powers to their kin who had emigrated to California, Arizona, and New Mexico, so that they, too, could be fortified and freshened in their newly adopted homes north of the border.

The outcasts who found themselves as "refugees at home" in a money-hungry republic that had much they needed to heal or repel if they were to resist their greedy gringo neighbors.

In 1891, the Mayo Indians of far southern Sonora attacked the dictator's troops in Navajoa. The Yaqui militia then stood its ground against land grabbers, swindlers, and other intruders. And soon, rebels carried banners with Teresista's image all the way to Nogales, Palomas, El Paso-Juarez, and Ojinaga-Presidio. They clandestinely recruited troops and purchased more weapons in these border towns, smuggling them across the line at night.

All this did not sit well with Porfirio Díaz, the tough-skinned general, capitalist, and president who was then in the tenth year of his presidency. He was a wealthy Catholic who was firmly against the Spiritist movement in Mexico's northern frontier, for it was one that his antagonist (and later successor) Francisco Madero had embraced.

Ironically, the most powerful man in Mexico feared the growing praise for Teresista given by his enemies, for they believed that a genuinely holy but humble individual like Teresista had a direct connection to the Creator, one that could both bypass and undermine the hierarchy of priests and politicians.

The next year, Teresista and her father were forced to go into exile in the United States, riding a brand-new railroad line up from Guaymas, Sonora, to the border towns of Ambos Nogales on July 5, 1892.

·𝔖·

Why Nogales? Her Yaqui protectors had kept outposts in southern Arizona for centuries and by then were the second-most populous tribe in southern Arizona. They had hideaways guarded by their militias that could accommodate Teresista and her father.

But arriving along with them was one of the primary promoters of Spiritism and revolution in the Mexican northwest: Lauro Aguirre, an engineer and surveyor who knew Chihuahua and Sonora like the back of his hand.

Aguirre was born at the bottom of the Barranca del Cobre in the Tarahumara village of Batopilas. He had grown up and worked throughout the mining country of the Sierra Madre Occidental, receiving a decent education along the way. He had personally seen the abuse that Indigenous miners endured in mountain towns like Tomochic, Chihuahua. Early in 1892, Lauro had begun coaching Tomochic's populist leaders like Cruz Chávez, secretly encouraging them to revolt against the mining companies and the government.

But that same year, he would turn his attention in another direction: to become the primary coach, promoter, guardian, and propagandist for this young woman whose story needed to be told to the entire world. It felt less like a job and more like a sacred duty, one that would occupy most of his time and all of his conscience for many years.

·𝔖·

In September of 1892—less than three months since Teresista had gone into exile—President Díaz ordered his federal troops to destroy Tomochic and kill all the insurgents aligned with Teresista and Lauro. The Díaz military officers believed they could accomplish their task in days. But they met with the ferocious resistance from those who carried pictures of Teresista over their hearts and shouted her name with every charge. It took hundreds of troops and weeks of fighting for them to accomplish their massacre of four hundred Tomochiteco men.

Not a single male adult or teenage resident of Tomochic survived the slaughter, including the local leader, Cruz Chávez, who was one of the last to survive, only to be shot with six of his lifelong friends before a firing squad. But when military officers scoured the Chávez home for evidence that Cruz Chávez and Teresista Urrea were in cahoots in planning a more pervasive revolt, they only found a letter to Cruz from the mystic healer that set out a completely different narrative. To their chagrin, Teresista had recommended these virtues:

"Tolerance and love for one's neighbors, aid for the destitute, mercy by the victors, and succor for the dying. Charity is the best road to God."

Back in Nogales, Aguirre's journalistic and pamphleteering skills ensured that Teresista's fame continued to spread rapidly on both sides of the borderline. The Saint of Cábora would become the poster child for the international Spiritist movement. More than that, Teresista was implicitly regarded as the visionary who would spiritually guide a Holy War against President Díaz even though much of the printed rhetoric attributed to her came from Aguirre's mind and pen.

Some critics have accused Aguirre of treating Teresista like an attention-attracting puppet, putting political words in the mouth of a charismatic woman who largely spoke of spiritual concerns both in public and in private.

But even when Teresista was free of Lauro's loose transcriptions of her words, she still demonstrated her deep support for Indigenous communities and Mexican railroad workers whether they were in Mexico or the United States.

One time when she was in Los Angeles without Aguirre anywhere in sight, she led a crowd of irate Spanish-speaking women in a march. They sought support for a wildcat strike of railroad workers who were part of the Unión Federal Mexicana. While the women and the railroad workers lost that brief battle, they later formed the first labor union in the United States led by Mexican railroad workers. It led to a larger collaboration across languages, races, and cultures that sought to protect laborers from police violence, scab worker recruitment, and horribly low wages.

Teresista—not Lauro—was the catalyst for the unity in that march. Most of her spoken words came from her own heart, not from some ventriloquist.

That said, Teresista was sympathetic to her protector and promoter, and Aguirre was immensely successful in forming a hybrid image of her as both a saintly mystic and revolutionary.

There was some remarkable symbiosis between them that ended up attracting as many as four to five hundred people who came for inspiration and comfort from her healing hands nearly every day. All in all, her hands probably touched more than fifty thousand ill, infirm, or indisposed individuals during the years of her spiritual healing, as documented by Lauro and others. Who knows how many more were healed in her earlier, more private years as a curandera?

By the mid-1880s, Teresista's healing powers and Lauro's myth making had created a rage from San Francisco to New York City. She began to be called Santa Teresa, the Fanatical Miracle Healer while also being treated as if she were a warrior herself.

There is some truth to that, for she and Lauro were in on the planning of the armed Yaqui uprising at the Nogales Custom House in August of 1896. The Yaqui warriors who were killed on the border that day had letters from Lauro and amulets of Teresista on their bodies at the time of their deaths.

That "coincidence" enraged President Porfirio Díaz, who repeatedly called for their extradition to Mexico between 1896 and the last days of 1905. At the same time, Díaz's spies and soldiers secretly plotted to take her down. Nevertheless, Teresista somehow escaped all attempts to capture or assassinate her.

Although she anchored herself in a stance as a pacifist for the rest of her days, she was still perceived as having an “apocalyptic but dangerous gift,” as Alex Nava—who grew up near Nogales—once put it.

Her gift was ultimately dangerous to her own health. Being at the center of such conflict and controversy had exhausted her. Her flowing locks ceased to grow, and her skin no longer glowed. Her healing powers slowly began to fail Teresista in the last months prior to her untimely death in January 1906. She succumbed to sorrow and fatigue in Clifton, Arizona, at the age of thirty-two.

Teresista had looked deeply into the heart of the lives around her. But that had left her weary of the huge disparities, horrific brutalities, and woeful indignities that Indigenous peoples had suffered as their lands, lives, and liberties were taken from them.

It should come as no surprise that the other women in her extended family of Urreas would decide to carry on her healing practices. To this day, some of her descendants proudly call themselves curanderas or spiritual healers.

As for Lauro Aguirre, he continued to seed discontent through his writings. He was a key strategist for a group of insurgents that surreptitiously planned armed uprisings against the Porfiriato in Mexico, involving a growing number of Teresistas in his plots.

Lauro increasingly aligned himself with the Flores Magón brothers and their Partido Liberal Mexicano. He was present at secret meetings that planned simultaneous attacks on several border towns. These raids were successful enough to drive President Díaz into undertaking unprecedented actions against activists on both sides of the border.

Lauro somehow escaped sentencing and extradition several times, based on “insufficient evidence” of sedition. President Díaz was, however, ultimately successful in getting US spies and officials to track down and jail Lauro's comrade Ricardo Flores Magón in Los Angeles.

Remarkably, the first wave of FBI detectives—led by Thomas Furlong—spent their initial months on the job planning a raid of the hideout where Ricardo and friends were sequestered in August of 1907. Several charges were followed by temporary releases, but Furlong and the FBI assured that new charges and sentences followed. Finally, in May of 1909, a judge found Ricardo and two allies guilty of violating the US Neutrality Act. Furlong—the first successful spy for the FBI—escorted them off to Yuma Territorial Prison in Arizona for fifteen months of penance.

The time in prison nearly broke Ricardo, who had to be transferred from a jail cell to a hospital for much of his sentence. But while Magón was imprisoned, the Partido Liberal Mexicano spread like a tsunami, with some of Aguirre's recycled tracts fanning the flames.

Díaz was angry that he had never been able to shake Aguirre's biting criticism. To the day he was unseated as president in May of 1911, Díaz remained hell bent on abducting Aguirre so that he could be shot before a firing squad in Mexico.

There were many reasons that the Mexican Revolution took down President Díaz after his decades as supreme commander. And yet, the possibility that revolutionary zeal might spill over into the United States worried the likes of the Roosevelts, the Rockefellers, and the Harrimans. Their days of land grabs and economic imperialism in Mexico were nearly over. Their infamy south of the border was largely due to the brilliant coverage by Aguirre and his cronies of the American millionaires' carte blanche given to them by Díaz to acquire as much land and minerals as they could manage.

Lauro Aguirre—the Spiritist and confidante of Teresista—was one of those independent journalists who had set the stage. It was this Chihuahuan journalist who first seeded these stories in alternative news media throughout the Mexican Republic as well as in the mainstream media of the United States.

After requesting and receiving protection by the US government as political refugees, Lauro Aguirre and his family remained north of the border in El Paso. It was there that he published an anarchist broadside, *La Reforma Social*, one that continued to espouse the revolutionary polemics of Ricardo and Enrique Flores Magón.

Although they were not directly involved in the last set of events that ignited the Mexican Revolution, Aguirre and the Flores Magón brothers were gratified by their success of inspiring the Cananea copper mine strike in Sonora and the Acayacuan Rebellion in Veracruz the same year. These incursions are regarded as the first flashpoints that brought on the Mexican Revolution, an internecine conflict that lasted from 1910 to 1920. It unseated Porfirio Díaz after thirty-five years of power, one the longest dictatorships in the history of Latin America. During the Porfiriato, the gap in wealth between rich and poor—in particular, for poor Indigenous families—widened like no other time in Mexican history.

For the most part, Lauro Aguirre's revolutionary zeal has not been given the same regard as that of the Flores Magón brothers, Pancho Villa, or Emiliano Zapata. He wrote mostly ephemera: broadsides, eight-page daily rags, and smuggled letters read by no more than a handful of people after the Revolution began. His fame as a writer so quickly waned after 1910 that it was the hyperbolic Ricardo Flores Magón—not Lauro—who became widely known as "the intellectual author of the Mexican Revolution."

On the insistence of his wife, who was exhausted by his prolonged absences, numerous affairs, risky behavior, and meager income, Lauro gave up all writing by 1920. Instead, he worked for a while as a designer in print shops and tobacconist in smoke shops. Later, he returned to his first career as a civil engineer and helped finesse land transfers in Sonora and Baja California.

Somehow, Lauro lived twice as long as Teresista lived, dying in

El Paso on a cold January day in 1925. His wife, Toma, immediately burned all his papers, hoping to save her family members from any more persecution like what they had suffered for decades.

In contrast, it was Teresista's transcendent spirit—not some political or military power—that propelled her devotees into one of the most game-changing revolutions ever known in the Americas. When the Mexican Revolution erupted in 1910, many of those who fought along the northern edges of Mexico still carried cameos and suertes of La Santa Niña of Cábora into the battlefields.

The poor *campesinos* of the deserts and sierras always had sufficient reason to revolt, but she offered hope that their wounds could heal and their lives could change for the better. She did not gift them any pistols, bombs, or knives, only healing prayers, mud, spittle, and apocalyptic visions. It was if she had given them the spiritual stamina to resist the underlying illness of greed that was overtaking the modern world.

More than a century after Teresista's death in 1906, I accompanied a half-dozen Yaqui leaders and historians to an often-overlooked stretch of the Santa Cruz River Valley northwest of Ambos Nogales on the border.

Three centuries earlier, a Spanish cartographer noted that there had been an Indigenous pueblo there called Raum, now spelled Rahum. A century ago, it was marked on maps simply as Bosque—a closed canopy woodland of mesquite trees—at or near a site called Palo Parado. It was very likely one of the northernmost Yaqui outposts at the time when Jesuit missionaries first came into what we now call Arizona.

There, in the remnants of that mesquite bosque along the Santa Cruz River, oral history claims that Teresista was hidden and protected by Yaqui bodyguards who were guarding her against intrusions by the spies and mercenary troops of Porfirio Díaz.

It was the perfect kind of peaceful sanctuary where Teresista and her father could hide while Lauro Aguirre promoted her charisma in newspapers and pamphlets he printed and sent on trains from Nogales, Sonora, to all parts of the border states.

Could that mesquite bosque that lies within a mile of Palo Parado—"the Place of Where the Stand of Trees Stop Any Passage"—be the the sanctuary where Teresista rested, just before her Yaqui guards help her escape assassins? Could it be the same place that the contemporary Yoemem now call E'eusiwa'apo, or Hideout? Was it where the northernmost Yoemem aggregated and rested in Arizona after their pilgrimage up the Yaqui Trail from their eight sacred pueblos in southern Sonora?

An elderly Yaqui man with our group thought about that question for a while as we stood in the cool shade of a towering mesquite tree on a hundred-degree day. After a minute or two, he quietly whispered to me this confirmation:

"Our word for a mesquite bosque like this and for a sanctuary, refuge, or hideout is one and the same."

CHAPTER NINE

Dust

Woody Guthrie and Tim Z. Hernandez

THEY CALLED him Woody Guthrie, the Folkiest of the Folksingers, the Rowdiest of the Rounders, and the Dustiest of the Dust Bowlers. He was widely known as a Dust Bowl refugee, but not in the way you might think an Okie would be.

Never did he farm back in Oklahoma, and in those desultory labor camps in California he worked as a journalist and songster, not as a short-hoed farmworker. Still, he lived, breathed, and sang the life of the kind of refugee that was torn from his roots:

My brothers and my sisters are stranded on this road
A hot and dusty road that a million feet have trod
Rich man took my home and drove me from my door
And I ain't got no home in this world anymore.

Woodrow Wilson Guthrie was born in the summer of 1912, five years after Oklahoma became a state. In that same decade, three crude oil discoveries put Woody's birthplace of Okemah and the county of Okfuskee on the map in the Sooner State. The boom town grew from just one thousand souls at statehood to four thousand by the onset of the Depression in 1929.

While still in diapers, Woody and his siblings were plopped down on the dry ground amid rampant boomerism and turbulent weather. The latter alone generated relentless uncertainty and sometimes sheer chaos, as temperatures could soar as high as 115 degrees, then drop to 17 below in a matter of hours or days.

Oklahoma Territory was not quite a true desert, but it could be scorching hot and parching dry. To get into the Union, Oklahoma had declared itself a "dry state" in its constitution. Of course, there wasn't much water to be had there anyway, so farmers and oilmen turned to clandestine bootlegging to quench their thirst. During drought years, annual rainfall trickled down to twenty-two inches, so they had even more reason to drink moonshine. When no rain arrived for over a month at a time, even children were given a sip of hooch to slake and soothe their chaffed throats, calm them down, and tide them over until the next rainy season.

Sometimes without notice, a gully buster could storm in, dumping nine inches in buckets of rain during a single day. That was enough to drown any turkey or a drunk or any other critter that had its head tossed back and mouth wide open.

Such downpours became less frequent as Woody grew up. As he once put it in his song "The Talkin' Dust Bowl Blues," "one day, my gal fainted in the rain, so I throwed a bucket o' dirt in her face just to bring her back again."

In the first decade of Woody's youth, the Goodland Artificial Rain Company competed against the Swisher Rain Company to see which could dupe the most Okies gullible enough to pay for their dubious services. About that time, Woody decided he might be better off singing for rain than paying for Swisher or Goodland for its delivery. To accompany his warbling voice, he took up the guitar, which he later admitted had become such a dangerous weapon that it could "kill Fascists."

Woody came to believe that there was a good chance that anything he wished for or dreamed of might eventually happen. For him, dreaming and prophesying were better ways to live than believing nothing would ever happen at all. He was not alone. Okies of his era were natural-born weathercocks, bounders, cloud arousers, temporizers, go-getters, chameleons, and flexitarians. Woody evolved to be all of these and more: a rake and a rambler, a roughrider, a high plains drifter, and a weary hobo.

Nonetheless, disaster, depression, drought, and desertification devastated the Great Plains where Woody had cut his teeth. The Guthrie family was plagued by fires at home for generations, including one that destroyed their home in Okemeh when Woody was four. When he was six, his older sister Clara died when she set her clothes on fire in a fight with her mother, Nora Belle. Then, when Woody was fifteen, Nora's Huntington's chorea disease had created erratic behavior, causing her to throw a kerosene lantern on his father, Charley, scarring him. She was moved to a sterile place that had a belated understanding of her genetic affliction: the Oklahoma Hospital of the Insane. As Nora Guthrie's bizarre spells became more frequent and severe, Woody lamented that "my mother's nerves gave way like an overloaded bridge."

Nora Belle died on June 13, 1930, a day before Woody's eighteenth birthday. It was the loss of his sister to fire and the loss of his mother to Huntington's chorea that broke up his family and turned Woody into a refugee, not the Dust Bowl itself.

Before those losses, he was on the same upwardly mobile trajectory that his father had first taken. But when his beloved mother was pushed out onto the margins of society then into the ground, Woody never fully came back into the fold. His heart was broken but still beating, and yet his brain became infected with the mindset of an outcast.

To get him out of his blue funk, Woody's father, Charley, his Uncle Jeff, and older brother Roy decided that a change of scenery might do some good. In 1931, they drove an old Model T truck almost six hundred miles from Pampa, Texas, in the Panhandle, south to Big Bend. It was in the thick of a lingering drought, and all the water in the Río Grande had disappeared into the sand. Starving cows went belly-up, and after they died, they turned into tough sacks of leather with strands of tasajo beef jerky hidden inside. Nevertheless, the

Guthrie mob was hell-bent on relocating a lost mine of silver, gold, and mercury-rich cinnabar that had been cursorily claimed by Woody and Roy's grandfather.

Trouble was Grandpa Guthrie never made a good map, a detailed set of directions, or a fully legal claim on his discovery. His descendants decided the onus was on them to rediscover it and prove it up.

That motherlode of ore had stayed hidden off Rough Run Creek not far from Terlingua, Texas, the cinnabar capital of the entire universe for the few decades before Woody's birth. The Guthries scurried around in the rocks like squirrels searching for the stack of rocks grandaddy had left behind, but they never found a lick of the material riches they sought.

And yet, it was there that Woody was gifted another sort of treasure that stayed with him the rest of his life: the capacity to sing, hoot, and holler out where canyon walls echoed the crazy rhythms of his own words as if he were in a recording studio. That wild adventure opened Woody's mind and heart to kinds of richness other than the material. As he told his sweetheart Helen the Hell Cat at that time:

"They's more kinds of gold than you can poke yer tongue at: Rivery gold, mount'ny gold; sandy, rotten, windblown desert gold; canyon gold; cliff-rim gold," and on and on.

Big Bend did indeed have golden sunsets, golden mesas, golden buttes, and golden-haired beauties. It was also inhabited by a *capirotada*-like mélange of outcasts: Mexican bootleggers of sotol and mezcal; candelilla wax extractors; chino grass harvesters; Black, Seminole, Kickapoo, Mescalero, and Lipan Apache cowboys; as well as Corriente cattle ranchers of Scottish and Irish clans. All these ethnicities camped and cowboyed, homesteaded and harvested, whored about and wandered around in the wildest, craggiest, thorniest, driest stretches of both sides of the border.

They would all rendezvous for all-night dances at the Sam Nail Ranch a few miles away from their own paltry camp, dive into a cattle tank to wash off the grit, then commence to play guitar, fiddle, piano, and harmonica 'til the wee hours of the morning. Woody came to love playing music at these all-night chicken scratch dances, where everyone danced a bit, then sipped some Mexican sotol or maize moonshine until they fell over and slept right on the dance floor.

He loved the refreshing rawness of his contact with the rich and varied lives of the Indians all around him. Perhaps it was because his own kin had married into the Creek and Cherokee communities in Oklahoma over the decades when it was still called Indian Territory.

Some had married for love, others for oil.

Woody quickly developed empathy for the plight of oppressed, repressed, and depressed. He slowly began to distance himself from the values of his father, Charley, who back in Oklahoma had allegedly engaged in cultish Ku Klux Klan rites. A year before Woody's birth, some historians claim that Charley was present if not engaged in the racist lynching of a Black woman named Laura and her thirteen-year-old son Lawrence on the Canadian River Bridge. Her second child was left to die on the roadside near the bridge.

Woody later wrote that his father, Charley, had told him the whole lurid story, which had haunted him for years. He also wrote a song about it called "Don't Kill My Baby and My Son" and a poem called "High Balladee," drawing on the horrible photos of the incident that were sold in Okemah while he was growing up:

> *A nickel post card I buy off your rack,*
> *To show you what happens if you're black and fight back,*
> *A lady and two boys hanging down by their necks*
> *From the rusty iron rigs of my Canadian Bridge.*

⁂

By the time Woody was done with his time in Big Bend, he was both alert and curious about the cultural mélange he had stumbled into:

> Born and raised amongst Indians and Mexicans, back in Oklahoma, my eye was quick to guess and to judge the crowd [in Big Bend]. They could have all been of nearly any tribe from Colorado, New Mexico, Arizona, Utah, Oklahoma, or Texas. Hopi. Apache. Seminole. Cherokee. Ute. The Creek. The Osage. Or any of the tribes.
>
> The four whites around our truck, Papa, Eddie, and myself, could hardly be seen [among so many red-, black-, and browned-skinned people present.] The wide eyes of the young girls in the crowd sparkled with a light that asked questions. The older ones in the crowd asked older questions. Where are you from? Why did you come here? How many blisters do you have on your hands? Do you know how to take care of yourself out lost in the cactus hills? Can you wade through a muddy flood, and can you swim a high river with a blanket roll? What do you want from us? Are you going to help my people? Are you going to hurt my people? Are you here to carry more of us away to die on the daggery road, to die in the crops? Did you drive your truck down here to load our silver and mercury all in it, to blast down our mountains, and to leave us robbed and hungry like coyotes?

Woody could see that his own father's quest for wealth, status, and stability had not made him any happier nor any more secure. As Woody later confessed, "I wasn't in the class that John Steinbeck called 'the Okies' because my dad to start with was worth thirty-five or forty-thousand dollars, and he had everything hunky-dory. Then he started to have bad luck."

By the time his family had left Okemah and Pampa, there wasn't a place left that he had to call home. The song that he and his cousin Jack wrote, "Oklahoma Hills," tied a nostalgic knot on that part of his life, for he never returned to live for any length of time in Okemah. His lament and farewell became his only Western Swing classic that has stood the test of time:

Many a month has come and gone
Since I wandered from my home
In those Oklahoma hills where I was born.
Many a page of life has turned,
Many a lesson I have learned;
Well, I feel like in those hills I still belong.

For a while, he sang on street corners, preached the Good News, painted signs for a few bucks each, and drew cartoons for tips from passersby. He soon reckoned that those pursuits would not pan out as ways to make a decent living. With little else to lose, Woody promptly followed the Okie exodus out of the Dust Bowl, weaving through southern New Mexico and Arizona deserts before seeking better fortune in California's Sugar Bowl and Peach Bowl.

After putting "So Long, It's Been Good to Know Yuh" to music with his Corn Cob Trio in 1935, Woody left his first wife and children to become a drifter, wandering farther away from his home and family than he had ever gone.

·✧·

One winter, Woody took to drifting way beyond Oklahoma and the Texas Panhandle, beginning with hitchhiking, and sauntering down into southern New Mexico through Alamogordo. From there to Las Cruces, Woody crossed White Sands on foot. He later conceded that part of the journey "was one of the hardest times I'd ever had," for the songwriter's adventure had shapeshifted into a hobo's harsh nightmare: "The valley highway turned into a dry, bare stretch of low-lying hills, too little to be mountains, and too hilly to be flat desert.... You could see the road ahead shining like a string of tinfoil flattened out, and then you'd lose sight of it again and walk for hours and hours, without ever coming to the part you'd been looking at ahead for so long... Blister on your feet, shoes hot as a horse's hide."

At last, he thumbed a ride to Las Cruces, then another one that took him part of the way toward Deming. But then he had to walk along the highway until past midnight without catching another ride or finding a town.

Beginning again before dawn the next morning, he walked for five more hours until he stowed away on a fast-moving freight train. It took him over the Continental Divide for the first time in his life. From the tiny railroad town of Lordsburg, New Mexico, he rode out of the Chihuahuan Desert on the rails during one of the coldest nights of the year, huddled together with a young Black boy in the coal bin to keep from freezing.

The next morning, the two survivors awakened as the train rolled to a stop in the railyards next to Barrio Libre of Tucson, Arizona, in the heart of the Sonoran Desert. It was the same railyard where a Yaqui gandydancer, singer, and poet named Refugio Savala worked at that time, not far from Lalo Guerrero's boyhood home in Barrio Viejo on Meyer Street. Music was in the air in that part of Tucson, but in languages and rhythms Woody hardly knew.

In *Bound for Glory*, Woody conceded that he found no immediate glory on the far side of the Great Divide. His arrival at the railroad yards in Tucson occurred on a bitterly chilly winter morning at the height of the Depression in 1937. He and his African American sidekick were covered with coal soot from head to foot.

As Woody and his companion hit the ground, the other hobos piling out from boxcars warned all the newcomers about the peculiar perils of the Old Pueblo: "Tucson's a bitch. Boys, Tucson's a bitch." "'Tain't no town, 'tain't no city. Not fer guys like you an' me. You'll find out soon enough."

Soon enough, Woody noticed that every time a hobo knocked on the door of a Tucson adobe home to ask for work, a biscuit, or bread, the door was slammed shut and latched tight. Ever since the onset of the Depression, Tucsonans had been living close to the bone themselves, with little to nibble on. Hardly any food was coming in on the rails in the middle of the winter, and local crops had failed.

Used to panhandling in small towns, Woody was shocked that no one in Tucson appeared able to spare a dime, a piece of stale bread, or even a corn tortilla:

> This was a strange town, with a funny feeling hanging over it, a feeling like there were lots of people in it—the Mexican workers, the white workers, and the travelers of all skins and colors of eyes—caught hungry, hunting for work to do. I was too proud to go out like the other man and knock at the doors [but then] I kept getting weaker and emptier. I got so nervous that I commenced shaking and could not hold myself still. I could smell a piece of bacon or corncake frying at a half a mile away. . . . I kept shaking and looking blanker and blanker. My brain didn't work as good as usual. I couldn't think.

Woody was at last completing his rite of initiation as a true Dust Bowl refugee, although he still never felt worthy of using that moniker for himself. His *Dust Bowl Ballads* was the first concept album and perhaps the only string of eleven songs on the same theme ever recorded on 78 rpm vinyl. It chronicled his journey out of the desert.

Oddly, his often-covered classic "Pretty Boy Floyd" never made it onto the initial three-disc set, perhaps due to its length or because it lionized a socialist-leaning outlaw. But the strength of the *Dust Bowl Ballads* was his empathy for the hard times of Okie farmworkers who resettled in California, but at immense costs to their sanity and families. Nonetheless, it was in California that Woody's singin' and pickin', hootin' and hollerin' finally hit pay dirt.

Once Woody arrived on the West Coast, he did indeed hang around the many "jungle camps" of farmworkers, but only to listen to stories and sing his own in the bottomlands where the migrants would gather at the river:

> [One] camp was called Hooversville, and if such a bad place as this was named after my name, I believe I'd commit suicide before morning. People take old rusty buckets, beat them out flat, and nail them onto a frame of rickety boards—and that's

> a plumb good house in Hooversville. It is garbage-to-garbage and water-to-water [to where] 400 people hungry and dirty are bogged down in the shack town called Hooversville.
>
> There are flies crawling over babies' faces. There are little pot bellies by the hundreds swelled up with the gas that is caused by malnutrition. There you'll see the torn holes in the flour sack dresses that the kids wear. Red, fevered skin is showing through these clothes like the blistered hide of the several hundred thousand Okies that crawled and walked and marched across twelve hundred miles of red-hot desert to get from Oklahoma's trash pile to California's green pretty places.

Woody frequented those jungle camps not to get paid as farm laborer but as reporter for a left-leaning rag called the *People's World*. He had tried then backed out of being a honkytonk musician sitting in with the Maddox Brothers and their sister, Rose. When drunken rowdies began to throw beer bottles at him while he was on stage in bars, he wisely conceded that he wouldn't be living long like that.

He soon took refuge in the sanctity of a radio studio, where he was offered good money for singing and joking on KFVD in Los Angeles every morning at 8:00 a.m. He began to hang less with the down-and-out Okies themselves, and more with cultural creatives like actor Will Geer, novelist John Steinbeck, and a hot young singer with the birth name of Maxine Crissman.

Maxine was a voluptuous young vocalist nicknamed Lefty Lou of Old Mizzou. Together, they released the first vinyl record version of his clever complaint about California, "Do Re Mi," in 1940. The duo didn't last all that long, but that record launched Guthrie's hardly-ever-very-commercial career while establishing a beloved place for him in popular culture.

And yet, even with a few radio and record hits and some high-falutin' friends, Woody never abandoned his extraordinary rapport and empathy with the downtrodden. He kept one foot in and one foot out of proletariat life, weaving between rags and riches for decades.

Whether he landed for the night in a flophouse or in a fancy hotel, Woody remained a voice crying out in the wilderness. He was like a John the Baptist coming out of the desert to wash the people in the River Jordan. Like other prophets, he sang, spoke, or wrote as if some kind of revelation had overtaken them.

Gradually, Woody became cocksure that if he preached fanatically enough, prayed deeply enough, or sang loudly enough, his vision of the world would eventually and inexorably overtake and remake the society that had oppressed so many around him.

If the desert, the Dust Bowl, and the Depression were the cauldrons that shaped who Woody became, his innate capacity for artistry allowed him rise just enough above the steam and smoke. Woody's gifted way with words helped him deeply describe any scene he stumbled upon. At the same time, he could mythologize any farm labor camp, massacre of miners, or plane wreck, somehow making its story universal and transcendent.

Taking the abundant dust generated by unprecedented droughts and farm foreclosures, Woody mixed his own spit and wit into it to make a metaphorical clay that he shaped into enduring vessels. Through the darkest and driest of times, Woody's songs held hope like a pottery jar holds water.

Should there be any doubt that penning a simple song can somehow have lasting impact on society at large, think of how many millions of American youths have been subconsciously inoculated with the words, "This land was made for you and me."

It was an anthem stunningly different in its values and earthiness from jingoistic ditties like "America the Beautiful" and "The Star-Spangled Banner." In fact, Woody intentionally wrote it as a critical counterpoint to Irving Berlin's strident "God Bless America."

Woody's four-line verses have become the unofficial plainsong for those Americans who don't believe that God is always on the side of *our* troops against all others. To this day, more US citizens can remember and sing the seven unexpurgated verses of "This Land Is Your Land" more than they can its saccharine-sweet patriotic competitors.

It may have been possible for his friends to lure Woody away from a political rally, but they could not take the rally out of Woody. By the time Guthrie had taken up the life of a wandering minstrel, he had mastered a way of making searingly sarcastic and satirical songs acceptable to the salt of the earth, who often thought of them as dancin' and drinkin' songs, not ones of "high-falutin' preachin' and politikin'."

Even after his Huntington's chorea made Woody's melodies more sing-songy like so many nursery rhymes, Woody still seemed preternaturally capable of getting to the gist of any social injustice he stumbled upon. Looking back, he humbly conceded that he had been accidentally air-dropped at the right time into the right place:

"I just happened to be in the Dust Bowl. I mean, it wasn't something that I particularly wanted or craved, but since I was there and the dust was there, I thought, well, I'll write a little song about it."

Even as his inherited affliction became more apparent to family and friends, he did not stop penning a song or two more about the Dust Bowl; he ended up gifting us with a whole bowlful of them. The same is true with protest songs supporting the rights of farmworkers, miners, and factory workers.

In 1941, he told a journalist from the *Daily Worker* that his work was "aimed at restoring the right amount of land and the right amount of houses and the right amount of groceries to the right amount of working folks."

As Woody had to repeatedly explain to others, he was compelled to write song after song to vanquish fatalism, to evict cynicism, to demolish low self-esteem, and to prevent the loss of hope.

I hate a song that makes you think that you are not any good.
I hate a song that makes you think that you are just born to lose.
Bound to lose.

No good to nobody. No good for nothing. Because you are too old or too young or too fat or too slim or too ugly or too this or too that.
Songs that run you down or poke fun at you on account of your bad luck or hard traveling.
I am out to fight those songs to my very last breath of air and my last drop of blood.
I am out to sing songs that will prove to you that this is your world and that if it has hit you pretty hard and knocked you for a dozen loops, no matter what color, what size you are, how you are built,
I am out to sing the songs that make you take pride in yourself and in your work.

Back when Woody was barely nineteen, he spent time in the desert with some Spanish-speaking vaqueros on their way back to Mexico through the twin border towns of Presidio, Texas, and Ojinaga, Chihuahua. It seems that he wrote of this memorable encounter with migrants in his notebook at the time:

"Rosalita called out first to the cowboy and his horse, 'Adiós, Jesús!' Carlos was louder, 'Jesús, amigo, adiós!'"

Seventeen years later, the names of his Mexican compañeros who had headed back across the border must have stirred in his memory as he read a ninety-word dispatch released on January 28, 1948. It carried the headline "32 Are Killed in California Plane Crash."

Woody read on, trying to imagine the disaster in palpable, personal terms.

Of the thirty-two killed in Los Gatos Canyon in western Fresno County, twenty-eight were Mexican deportees whose charred bodies "were mangled beyond recognition." They were undocumented workers being flown back to the Mexican border. Although the Anglo flight crew members were named, mourned, and buried in separate graves in their hometowns, none of the names of the farmworkers killed in the crash were included in any English-speaking newspapers covering "the worst aviation accident in California history."

Woody was shocked to read a short newspaper account that revealed only the names of four Anglo Americans who had died in a terrible plane crash in Fresno County, California, without mentioning a single name of the twenty-eight Mexican farmworkers who were killed while being deported on that same plane:

Who are all these friends, all scattered like dry leaves?
The radio says, "They are just deportees."

When he tried to evoke some possible Spanish names to fill in the blanks, Jesus and Rosalita from down by Presidio along the Big Bend must have popped into his head:

Goodbye to my Juan, goodbye Rosalita,
Adiós mis amigos, Jesús y María,
You won't have a name when you ride the big airplane
All they will call you will be deportees.

.ɷ.

Woody's handwritten poem stayed in a shoe box for years until it was included in a volume of lyrics of American "protest music," even though Guthrie himself had never offered a tune to any of his friends to go with the lyrics.

Instead, a young folk singer from Arizona named Martin Hoffman came up with a melody for Woody's "Deportee" poem years later. Martin had the chance to sing it to Woody's close friend Pete Seeger, who loved it. When Seeger's version was recorded—attributing it to the team of Guthrie and Hoffman—dozens of other artists began to sing it, first in English, then in Spanish as well.

By 1966, brothers Luis and Danny Valdez began to sing their Spanish translation of Woody's poem to crowds of farmworkers rallied together by Dolores Huerta and César Chávez. The Valdez brothers' Banda Calavera sang for their Teatro Campesino, recording just one of forty-some versions of "Plane Wreck at Los Gatos (Deportee)" that have reached the American air waves.

The short poem that Woody never personally recited nor sang anywhere in public somehow became the most popular song of lament for Spanish-speaking farmworkers ever to emerge from the American earth. It is perhaps his most widely covered song, with versions by bestselling artists such as Byrds, Dolly Parton, Johnny Rodriguez, Odetta, Nana Mouskouri, and Joni Mitchell. It was probably the last great song Woody would write during his career.

But within a year of the Valdez brothers taking the Spanish translation on the road to give voice to migrant farmworkers' *lucha*, Woody's own capacity for speaking and singing had dramatically deteriorated.

The very degenerative disease that had crippled and killed his own mother had begun to disrupt Woody's own behavior as early as 1952. It had gotten completely out of control by the mid-1960s, for he would forget where he lived and disappear for days before someone recognized him sleeping in a park or a Skid Row alley.

The timing of the onset of his illness was ironic, for it hit him hard just as a resurgence of interest in his artistic and political work began to surge. By the time Woody was belatedly diagnosed with an incurable, inheritable malady called Huntington's disease, the psychoneurotic consequences from it were immense.

Woody—the insatiable drifter, incurable rambler, and restless radical—would spend the last third of his life bedridden, hospitalized, and increasingly unable to sing his way completely through any of his own tunes. He died of his prolonged illness in 1967 at the age of fifty-five, leaving more than a thousand unnervingly poignant songs behind him.

Despite the acclaim that "Deportee" continued to receive after his death, Woody would never glimpse the impact it had generated and would never know the real names of those who were *scattered like dry leaves.*

·ஜ·

Those near-forgotten Spanish names continued to remain hidden from view for decades longer. At some point, it was simply assumed that anyone who had personally known those killed in Los Gatos Canyon had also passed, leaving little or no glowing embers to rekindle.

That assumption was faulty, as poet and oral historian Tim Z. Hernandez soon confirmed. Tim took on years of work to crack the code of this mystery and daylight the names of those who had been forgotten by history.

Hernandez found a way to take a one-sided story of a tragic event that had devastated dozens of families on both sides of the border and make the narrative whole. His work generated a kind of belated healing for many of the survivors of those who had been scattered like dry leaves.

Over the decades since Woody's illness and death, many have tried to pair his work with the likes of Leadbelly, Cisco Houston, Pete Seeger, Joan Baez, Bob Dylan, or even that of Arlo, Woody's son. But in Woody's wake, only Tim Z. Hernandez was tenacious, courageous, and compassionate enough to let the dust from the 1948 plane wreck settle so that families could at last see what had been kept out of view for decades.

Tim Z. Hernandez understood dust. He grew up in it, swallowed it, cleaned it out of nostrils and ears, and wrote poems about it. Tim's debut novel was entitled *Breathing, In Dust*.

Tim is the grandson of a Dust Bowl–era farmworker not all that unlike those who died in that devastating crash at Los Gatos Canyon. As he mourned in his poem, "Variations on *This Land*,"

This land is my grandfather's land
whipped to suffer his color in the cumin air,
to erase that he ever loved, the way only a brown boy
can love Brownsville, beneath oil derricks
and sugarcane horizons, and fields
of afterthought, a cluster of cancerous
lovers in the wake of red dust . . .

In talking with Tim on one of his trips through the desert from El Paso to Tucson, I realized that much of his work as a poet, novelist, and oral archivist gravitated toward revealing the hidden side of some stories that had been told in a one-sided way for decades.

In doing so, Hernandez had found a way to move those affected by physical tragedies and racist behaviors toward places of pride and dignity about their families' contributions to American history. When told carefully and considerately, those full-bodied stories could help close wounds that had been festering for years.

When you hear Tim himself tell how he tracked down so many dry leaves that had scattered over the decades, you inevitably wish that Woody could have heard the answers that Tim found to Guthrie's nagging question.

Tim's poetics and ethics, his craft as performance artist, and his uncanny luck on wild goose chases have forever changed how people will hear Woody's second most popular song.

It was Tim who brought the widows and descendants of those twenty-eight "once nameless" farmworkers together to affirm the names that were finally placed on a memorial in Fresno County Holy Cross Cemetery. And it is Tim who continues to record the stories from those who had been lost as a gesture of healing.

At last, a kind of spiritual and social justice has emerged from bringing together the two sides of that unspeakable tragedy. What Woody began, Tim has brought closure to in a manner just as poetic, empathetic, and prophetic.

In doing so, Tim Z. Hernandez deserves the same stature as a national treasure as that which Americans of all races have given to Woody, the Folkiest of the Folksingers, the Rowdiest of the Rounders, and the Dustiest of the Dust Bowlers. Maybe someday, Tim Z. Hernandez will be remembered as the most Resonant of Razafirme Poets, the Dustiest of the Atzlán Descendants, the Cheekiest of Chicano Activists, the most Open-Eared of Latinx Oral Historians, and the Two-Sidedest of all Desert Borderland Storytellers.

Not only does Woody live on in Tim's work but so do the lives and loves of twenty-eight Mexican farmworkers who might have otherwise been lost to history.

CHAPTER TEN

Steinbeck and Ricketts

Broken Men Breaking Through

JOHN STEINBECK must have deeply identified with the ornate box turtle he'd seen persevere after narrowly escaping being run over by a truck. It is possible he witnessed such an incident in the fall of 1937, after coming back from Europe and driving across the country on his way to California.

He left no note of it in his journals, only in his novel *The Grapes of Wrath*. Had he watched as it was flung off a highway, as it righted itself and then continued on its journey, just as he was doing?

There was something about its tenacity—its perspicacity—that Steinbeck not only admired but aspired to emulate in his own life:

"The turtle had jerked into its shell, but now it hurried on, for the highway was burning hot. And now a light truck approached, and as it came near, the driver saw the turtle and swerved to hit it. His front wheel struck the edge of the shell, flipped the turtle like a tiddlywink, spun it like a coin, and rolled it off the highway."

By the time John Steinbeck was thirty-four, his writing began to get him into serious trouble, tossing him out of the fast lane and back into the margins of America's mainstream society. Up until that time, his novel *Tortilla Flat* had won him some praise from newspaper critics and even media attention and a movie contract. By June of 1936, he had won his first significant book award, the California Literature Medal, also for *Tortilla Flat*.

And yet, by 1936 (after finishing *Of Mice and Men*) he began two years of journalistic field research on farm labor unions and migrant labor camps for Okies. His sympathetic interview with a striker had begun to trigger a backlash from some of his father's old friends and colleagues in the Salinas Valley and beyond. They were California's agribusiness oligarchs and politicians who did not take to him always siding with the down and out in the valley: Filipinos, Chinese, Mexicans, and that nebulous term for Dust Bowl refugees, "Okies."

In 1935, Steinbeck had been befriended by Tom Collins, the first FSA administrator to set up some of the eighteen federal migratory labor camps in California, from Brawley, Bakersfield, and Visalia, all the way to Yuba City. These camps were established to provide "safe harbors" for over 300,000 Dust Bowl refugees, and perhaps as many as a half million of them. They joined the 1.3 million migrant laborers that came to California in jalopy caravans looking for work between 1910 and 1950.

Until Collins established these federally subsidized facilities, these "harvest hobos," "fruit tramps," "drifting derelicts," and "bindlestiffs" mostly lived in roadside camps, under trees along streams, and in wildcat "Hoovervilles" between 1910 and 1950. (It was in a farmworker camp at Visalia in the San Joaquin Valley where Reies Tijerina would later receive his apocalyptic vision about agrarian land rights for migrant workers, a decade after Steinbeck and Collins had gone there together.)

Collins allowed Steinbeck to stay with farmworkers at Arvin Camp—nicknamed Weedpatch—which sheltered some of the most desperate, down-and-out "Okie" migrants who had failed at becoming gainfully employed year-round in California's cotton fields. Collins was adept at helping find jobs for many of the migrants who stayed at Weedpatch. Under Collins's wing, Steinbeck had conducted dozens of interviews with Weedpatch farmworkers after hours. He had gotten a brief gig working undercover in the fields to get a feel for rhythms of the harvest, calling himself Migrant John while keeping a low profile whenever crew bosses came around.

Collins—a brilliant and generous man who had trained for priesthood—not only mentored Steinbeck but offered him dozens of farm labor reports from his files as background reading for the novel he was writing. Steinbeck had already read some of them in San Francisco and was impressed by them well before he stayed at Arvin with Collins or briefly met with report author Sanora Babb.

The corporate farmers in central California became concerned that Steinbeck and Sanora Babb—like Tom Collins and his successor, Fred Ross, in FSA's Resettlement Administration—were so empathetic and absorbed by the plight of the Okie and Arkie farmworkers that they were no longer being "objective." They would have preferred that the young upstart from the Salinas Valley would stick to writing lighter, more entertaining novels filled with humorous characters and local color rather than following up on his prounion diatribe, *In Dubious Battle*. In particular, they wanted him to write about the Salinas Valley like he did in 1933. As Steinbeck commented later:

"I was born to it and my father was. Our bodies came from this soil, our bones came . . . from the limestone of our own mountains and our blood is distilled from the juices of this earth. I tell you now that my country—a hundred miles long and about fifty wide—is unique in the world."

Regretfully, they came to believe that Steinbeck was venturing too far into muckraking reportage that did not tell *their* story but someone else's. Their fears were confirmed when the *San Francisco News* released his seven-part series daily from October 5 to 12 in 1936. You can see why when you read the first paragraph of his first article in the series called *Harvest Gypsies*:

> The squatters camps are located all over California. Let us see what a typical one is like. It is located on the banks of a river, near an irrigation ditch, or on a side road where a spring of water is available. From a distance, it looks like a city dump,

> and well it may, for the city dumps were the sources for the material of which it is built. You see a litter of dirty rags and scrap iron, of houses built of weeds, of flattened cans or of paper. It is only on close approach that it can be seen that these are homes.

And in the midst of that squalor were the Okies and Arkies, hoboes, and other harvest gypsies, mostly climate refugees from the Dust Bowl afflicting six states in the southern Great Plains. They had hoped that farm work in California would raise them out of their poverty and fill their stomachs. But that is not what Steinbeck witnessed, nor what he reported, for many were hungry to the point of starvation.

"Here, in the faces of the husband and his wife, you begin to see . . . not worry, but absolute terror of the starvation that crowds in against the borders of the camp."

This was not the bucolic scene that California boosters and agricultural moguls had hoped to promote to the rest of America. The Associated Farmers of California (AFC)—which had rallied the state's most influential antilabor politicians between 1934 and 1939—were not amused by Steinbeck's portrayal of their farms.

They would rather hide the disparities between the executives of the state's biggest agricultural corporations and the laborers who harvested the fruit for wine and the grain for our daily bread. They wrote letters of rebuttal to the *San Francisco News*, but "the horse had already left the barn." Few newspaper readers ever take time to read letters to the editor from those who are unhappy about their portrayal.

Undaunted by their criticism, Steinbeck spent even more time in 1937 visiting other migrant farmworker camps in the Central Valley. Tom and John also spent a two-week period together in February 1938 trying to save and resettle four to five thousand drifters and tramps whose tent camps were being washed away by torrential rains and flash floods in the Visalia–Nipomo Dunes area. They would literally fall into the mud from exhaustion, the conditions were so logistically challenging.

Steinbeck also became fast friends with Fred Ross, who took over the management of the FSA's Weedpatch Camp near Bakersfield. He not only welcomed Steinbeck to interact with migrants there but also introduced him to the work of photographer Dorothea Lange, singer Woody Guthrie, actor Will Geer, organizer Luke Hinman, and scholar-activist Carey McWilliams. They were all working in parallel at the time, but met one another later on. It was also Fred Ross who later coached César Chávez and Dolores Huerta on farmworker organizing with the lessons he had learned from Hinman and McWilliams.

Inspired by such stunning talent, Steinbeck became further emboldened. He refined his earlier journalistic pieces on migrant farmers called *Harvest Gypsies* to bring their plight before larger and larger audiences. It later became a book-length narrative, *Their Blood Is Strong*, which echoed Lange's powerful black-and-white portraits of women in the farm labor work force, published in 1938.

It was clear by that time to Steinbeck and Lange that Okies were not some stereotypical "poor white trash" from Oklahoma, but included Blacks and Cherokee and Choctaw, Filipinos and Mexicans fleeing from a half-dozen states in the Southwest.

Steinbeck became convinced that their exodus was not simply triggered by a decade-long drought. He and his father had both worked in sugar beet mills in the Salinas Valley and knew who was in cahoots with whom. Banks, big mills, tractor suppliers, and agribusiness firms were undermining small farmers and farmworkers. But he saw that the story went further than that: They were also accelerating soil erosion, damaging the economies of rural communities, degrading food-producing landscapes, draining aquifers and rivers, and forcing wildlife to flee from the woodlots and streambanks where they had formerly been sheltered.

Steinbeck both read about and saw the systemic collapse of

small-farm-based communities in both the Great Plains and California. He reckoned that society as a whole would suffer further as the land was made poorer and the water was controlled by just a few.

Through interstitial parables stitched into a larger narrative that spoke to what was happening to turtles and the land itself, Steinbeck found a way to juxtapose the damage done to the environment in both Oklahoma and California with the damage done to the diverse communities whose livelihoods had depended on the fruits of the land. He swept that nondual sensibility into his next blockbuster, *The Grapes of Wrath*, released on April 5, 1939, just five months before World War II broke loose.

By that time, it was clear that the Associated Farmers of California (AFC) had declared war on Steinbeck, for he became their primary target for character assassination. As his epic narrative sold 430,000 copies in its first year, the Associated Farmers became more and more belligerent.

Their secondary target was Carey McWilliams, Collins's colleague who had been appointed to head California's Division of Immigration and Housing. McWilliams's book *Factories in the Field* was also published in 1939, and was just as offensive to California's agricultural oligarchy.

As Steinbeck later conceded, "The Associated Farmers have begun an hysterical personal attack on me in both the papers and a whispering campaign. [They claim] I'm a Jew, a pervert, a drunk, and a dope fiend."

Steinbeck wrote to his longtime friend and agent, Elizabeth Otis, lamenting that "The Associated Farmers are really working up a campaign [inundating his family with hate mail]. I made powerful enemies with the Grapes. They will not kill me, I think, but they will destroy me, if and when they can."

He was instructed by the Santa Cruz County sheriff to carry a gun for self-protection and never to check into a hotel in a California farm town by himself without a friend nearby who could keep tabs on him.

If his notoriety among his neighbors in the Salinas Valley was not troubling enough for him, the continuing surge of sales for *The Grapes of Wrath* through early 1940 also riled up conservatives in Oklahoma. They claimed that Okies categorically hated their portrayal in the book. They noted that Sallisaw—the town Steinbeck had chosen in their state as their point of departure for the Okie exodus to California—was far too humid to suffer from many Dust Bowl–era farm foreclosures.

They also doubted that the horrendous levels of soil erosion during the Dust Bowl was in any way aggravated by large tractors and the deep-reaching blades of their *bukker* plows, the so-called "plow that broke the Plains," as Pare Lorentz depicted in his stunning film documentary named with the same phrase. They claimed that the way they farmed had *nothing* at all to do with either the lack of rain or the billowing dust clouds that moved eastward all way to Washington, DC.

Oklahoma politicians went berserk when they learned that nine days before Steinbeck's masterpiece was released to the public, his agent had sent one of the first copies to Eleanor Roosevelt, who devoured it immediately. It prompted her to schedule "White House" visits to farm labor camps.

While visiting these camps, Mrs. Roosevelt confirmed for herself that there was validity to Steinbeck's descriptions. She had already encouraged her husband, Franklin Delano, to pass the 1935 Wagner Act—also known as the National Labor Relations Act—which gave farmworkers the legal right to organize after most of the two hundred farm labor strikes in the previous year had ended in failure.

The first lady was so deeply entranced by the book that she was emboldened to do further work on her own to help farmworkers and small farmers. Heartened by her promise to move farm labor reforms through Congress, Steinbeck himself sent telegrams to the USDA's Farm Service Agency urging it not to shut down its farm labor camps.

His capacity to pull strings in Washington further incensed Steinbeck's detractors, including Oklahoma congressman Lyle Boren, who famously told the House of Representatives that *The Grapes of Wrath* was "a lie, a black, infernal creation of a twisted, distorted mind."

That hate speech prompted several conservative congressmen in several states to brand Steinbeck as a communist. They sought to ban *The Grapes of Wrath* from public libraries and schools. They secretly urged the FBI's J. Edgar Hoover to begin undercover investigations of Steinbeck, McWilliams, Guthrie, and their cronies. Those frivolous but irritating investigations persisted for two decades.

Of course, Steinbeck knew that his narratives were far different than any communist propaganda, both in rhetoric and content, but especially in morals. He was deeply concerned about the health and well-being of Americans themselves, as well as that of their lands and waters. But as he demonstrated in writing *In Dubious Battle*, he was also wary himself of "communist agitators" unnecessarily manipulating messages as they organized farmworkers against the California oligarchs.

Nothing in his articles or books bought into Marx's reductionist view that the materialistic struggles between classes for control of land, commodities, and power were sufficient to explain what was plaguing America. Instead, he believed that something larger was out of kilter in how Americans viewed themselves as well as their ethical and spiritual commitment to the land. He listened, watched, and bore witness to the forty-seven thousand farmworkers who chose to be involved in more than thirty major strikes in California between 1931 and 1940.

By simply accompanying the farmworkers and giving voice to some of their many stories that were later read in his books by millions of Americans, Steinbeck exposed a bleeding sore in America that needed to be healed. He was not the doctor but one of the first responders who arrived on the scene.

Nevertheless, he felt increasingly misunderstood by most

everyone around him. His already fraught relationship with his wife, Carol, became irreparably frayed. In late December of 1939—just as the film versions of *The Grapes of Wrath* and *Of Mice and Men* were being prepared for release in New York City—Carol informed John that she was pregnant. He insisted that she have an abortion, but Carol developed an infection during the operation that led to a hysterectomy. There is no doubt that Carol felt deeply scarred, as both slipped into the darkness of winter solstice and psychic isolation from one another.

Whatever triggered it, something cracked in Steinbeck in the early months of 1940, and he swore that he would never write another novel again.

When Steinbeck himself flipped like a tiddlywink, he not only spun off the paved road to success he'd been traveling but he went offshore and into the unpopulated reaches of Mexico.

John and Carol had been going down to Mexico since 1935 and had loved it. They were both close to the marine ecologist in Monterrey named Ed Ricketts, whom John had met in 1930. Carol had worked for him as an assistant in his Pacific Biological Laboratories. Ed had taken other friends and family down the shore of Baja California several times, and John had dreamed of going down that road to Ensenada just with Ed. And now, as both Ed's and John's relationships with their wives were in shambles, they dreamed of getting away to Mexico together.

The dream kept morphing, as their mutual friend Joel Hedgepeth later recalled:

> The expedition to the Gulf of California began as a plan for John Steinbeck to accompany Ed on one of his annual trips to the coast south of Ensenada. Then John talked on buying a truck, and perhaps renting some fishing boat out of San Felipe [on the other side of the peninsula, in the Sea of Cortés]. Then it was to be a drive to Guaymas [on the southern coast of Sonora]. . . . And so on. Probably it was John who suggested

> they charter a boat in Monterrey and go all the way by sea. This would not only be doing something for Ed; it would [also] enable Steinbeck to escape for a while from the publicity over *The Grapes of Wrath.*

For an expedition that would last from March 11 to April 20, they chartered a fine boat large enough for seven passengers, including six men (all mentioned in Steinbeck's subsequent book, *The Log from the Sea of Cortez*) and one woman, Carol (who is never mentioned at all in *The Log*). As songwriter John Prine once described a similar adventure a half century later, it was perhaps an effort at "Trying to save our marriage and perhaps catch a few fish. Whatever seemed easier."

They were two broken men trying to stitch their lives back together on the eve of America's participation in World War II. And yet, rather than succumb to anxiety, depression, or anger as this crisis approached, Ricketts and Steinbeck stepped away from the political scene altogether. They sought out a refuge where they could rethink their lives, a marine sanctuary where they could immerse themselves in other-than-human lives, slowing down to listen to and watch what was happening outside the human sphere.

They took time out from work and worry in a way that allowed them to break out of the mold that their friend Robinson Jeffers warned them against:

"The whole human race spends too much emotion on itself. The happiest and freest man is the scientist investigating nature or the artist admiring it, the person who is interested in things that are not human. Or if he is interested in human beings, let him regard them objectively as a small part of the great music."

Perhaps it was only because they were so brokenhearted at that moment that they had the chance to "break through" to another realm of consciousness, one that had been latent but not fully expressed in the work of either of them up until the moment they set sail.

They opted to be silent publicly in order go deeper into "the great music" of nature itself rather than joining the war cries in the cities. In doing so, they discovered what Dr. Barbara Holmes, a mystic and scholar of African American contemplative spirituality, calls "the sacred refuge."

Like all good trips, something quite unusual and perhaps unanticipated happened along the way. As "Doc" Ricketts and "Jon" Steinbeck (as "Doc" often spelled Steinbeck's first name) explained in the introduction to *Sea of Cortez: A Leisurely Journal of Travel and Research*: "We have a book to write about the Gulf of California. We could do one of several things about its design. But we have decided to let it form itself: its boundaries a boat and a sea; its duration six weeks' charter time; its subject everything we could see or even imagine."

What formed or emerged through constant dialogue between two trusting friends became one of the most vivid, life-affirming books in American letters. *The Sea of Cortez* was published in December 1941, when the world needed it most: just two days before the Japanese attack on Pearl Harbor that forced the United States out of neutrality and into the horrors of World War II.

Whether heeded or not, that fresh way of looking at the world offered Americans that contemplative refuge they sorely needed at that moment. America would need the tenacity and perspicacity of an ornate box turtle flung off course to "right the ship" and return of course after a bloody war and the detonation of the first two atomic bombs.

But in that tranquil but all-too-brief period between March of 1940 and December of 1941, the extraordinary friendship and creative dialogue between Jon and Doc kicked the literary quality of nature writing up about three full notches toward heaven.

Somehow, the disciplines of field biology and literary artisanry, protracted observation of the tiniest details of the aqueous world and reflections on the loftiest aspirations of humankind, merged into one voice that chanted in harmony with all other voices in the pluriverse. The beauty and mystical achievement of their coauthored book can be witnessed on nearly every page, but felt most powerfully in one long sea-of-consciousness soliloquy, rendered here as three small paragraphs:

> Our own interest lay in relationships of animal to animal. If one observes in this relational sense, it seems apparent that species are only commas in sentence, that each species is at once a point and the base of a pyramid, that all life is relational to the point where Einsteinian relativity seems to emerge. And then not only the meaning but the feeling about species grows murky.
>
> One merges into another, groups melt into ecological groups until that time when what we know as life meets and enters what we think of as non-life: barnacle and rock, rock and earth, earth and tree, tree and rain and air. And the units nestle into the whole and are inseparable from it. . . .
>
> And it is a strange thing that most of the feeling we call religious, most of the mystical outcrying which is one of the most prized and used and desired reactions of our species, is really the understanding and the attempt to say that man is related to the whole thing, related inextricably to all reality, known and unknowable. This is a simple thing to say, but the profound feeling of it made a Jesus, a Saint Augustine, a Saint Francis, a Roger Bacon, a Charles Darwin, and an Einstein. Each of them in his own tempo and with his own voice discovered and reaffirmed that all things are one thing and that one thing is all things—plankton, a shimmering phosphorescence on the sea and the spinning planets and an expanding universe, all bound together by an elastic string of time. It is advisable to look from the tidepool to the stars and then back to the tidepool again.

Less than a month after the Steinbeck's returned from the Sea of Cortés to California, he was honored with both the Pulitzer Prize and National Book Award for *The Grapes of Wrath*. And yet years later, Steinbeck confessed to his third wife, Elaine, that *The Sea of Cortez* remained his favorite of all the books upon which he had worked.

Three decades after *The Sea of Cortez* was published, I had a dream in which three cultural creatives of the Pacific coast—John Steinbeck, Doc Ricketts, and poet Robinson Jeffers, who were in fact all good friends—kept changing forms, shifting from being crusty old men to crustaceans. In the dream, which then became a poem that garnered a national student poetry award three years later, the crusty old men of the Monterey Peninsula became one voice, "Reading Legends of Pacific Crustaceans":

The crusty old man of the tidepools
Now floats beyond reach out at sea
Cracking cities against his chest like stones
Licking, loving, tonguing their insides

The bristly old growth on his face
The ancient kelp forest seen in his eyes
Reflect his wrinkled body letting loose
Then contracting
Wherever spring tides are awash with spawn

This man weaves his net out of seaweed
The hurls it out into the tumultuous sea
Catching nothing that the fish peddlers ask for
But wriggling riches he spills out for all of us

Which is why we must meet him in forgotten grottos
And dive into caves popped open by moons
Where anemones pulse and everything else
Becomes for us so shimmeringly clear:

We are fueled by salt water,
We are drunk on it, we are drugged by it
And the undertow that is dragging us out
Is a pull far stronger than mental will.

After initially reading *The Excerpts of Sea of Cortez* in my late teens, it became clear to me that I wanted a life in which I pursued *the practice* of both field biology and literary expression. The risk, of course, was I could not possibly excel at either as much as Ricketts excelled at being a mystical marine biologist, and as much as Steinbeck excelled at being a literary voice for social justice. Both of them had likened the tide pool communities of the Pacific coast to human communities in rural and urban areas, so for them, there was no either/or dualism that forced one to be attentive *either* to human needs or to nature's sanctity.

But as I grew older, I realized that I did not need to be "both of them" in spirit or practice but could enjoy collaborations with others that allowed us to collectively break *through* the barriers believed to divide nature from spirit or science from art.

I was not surprised to see other cultural creatives whom I knew and admired choose to collaborate across the boundaries of natural sciences and literary or visual artistry: Cormac McCarthy and Roger Payne; Robert Hass and Edward O. Wilson; Ann Zwinger and Beatrice Willard; Peter Matthiessen and George Schaller; Wes Jackson and Wendell Berry; Robin Kimmerer, Elizabeth Gilbert, and Richard Powers; or Steve Hopp and Barbara Kingsolver.

While I have personally been blessed and boosted in energy by collaborating with at least two dozen other cultural creatives over the years, I still look upon the Doc Ricketts and Jon Steinbeck friendship as the prototypical relationship for achieving nondualistic, nonteleological thinking.

The two of them challenged one another to do so on the verge of a war triggered by *us versus them* dualistic thinking that truly threatened the entire planet. Perhaps we cannot attribute to them the leap in linking environmental conservation to social justice that we saw emerge globally after the first Earth Day in 1970, but neither can we imagine a post–Earth Day world without the mystical/earthy voices of Steinbeck and Ricketts. From an impulse that they followed though four thousand nautical miles on their entire six-week trip to the Sea of Cortés and back home to California, we now have a road map that reaches from the tide pools along the desert coast of western Mexico clear to the stars above us.

It may escape many of their readers, but the expedition and writings by Steinbeck and Ricketts set the foundation both for the establishment of nine protected areas in the Sea of Cortés, including a World Heritage Site for its islands and the waters immediately around them. As one of the few seas in the world almost completely surrounded by deserts, it is also the richest in marine and coastal biodiversity, resources from which thousands of Indigenous and Mexican fishers still make a living. Ricketts's pioneering collection, identification, and biogeographic placement of tidepool species in the sea formed the basis of the current tally of more than five thousand species recorded in the sea, many of them found no place else in the world.

We should be grateful that those two joyous but heartbroken characters converged in a way that illustrates for all of us how to navigate a future that is fraught with higher sea levels and ever more daunting human challenges.

CHAPTER ELEVEN

Reies López Tijerina and Arturo Sandoval

ON THE autumnal equinox of 1993, as temperatures reached above 105 degrees in central Arizona for ten straight days, I ran through the landscape that Reies López Tijerina had once called "the Valley of Peace" and "Paradise." It was where his quest for land reform in the desert borderlands began. It is where his vision for returning homelands to Hispanic and Indigenous families scaled up from 160 acres of desert to 3 million acres in six southwestern states.

But what I saw forty years after Tijerina—the Land Grant Prophet—had staked his claim in the desert was nothing short of dismal. As we ran south past Sunland Gin Road after leaving the sprawling farm town called Casa Grande, we came close to the abandoned site of his commune. Although he had intended to build paradise there, it was obvious that his dream for that land never bore fruit at all. It blew away.

I was running in the vicinity of the Valle de Paz with an Akimel O'odham friend, Adrian Hendricks, on the first day of a 180-mile pilgrimage across the desert. (Thirty years later, Adrian is still running enormously long distances through the desert, but now goes by the Piman name of Jivik Siiki.) The destination was the multicultural Fiesta de San Francisco de Asís in Magdalena, Sonora. Seven hours after we were blessed at dawn on the Gila River floodplain near Sacaton, we were just miles away from entering the Tohono O'odham Reservation, where we would find a place to sleep at White Horse Pass.

My journal notes indicate that in the last few miles of the twenty-two miles that we had already run before hitting the rez, we saw a desultory wasteland that was all that was left around Tijerina's utopian community in the Valle de Paz:

"To the north of the boundary line with the rez the scene seemed so frayed and impoverished, with wells gone dry, denuded lands, abandoned bunkers with broken skylight windows, and gutted chassis of Ramblers and Edsels. It seemed as if all the junked cars and trailers that had ridden into the West after the Dust Bowl had come to a stop there. They were just waiting for a fiery another blast of wind to come along and send them on their way once more."

And yet, it was while living in that desert wasteland that Tijerina received the greatest of the visions that propelled his life and work, almost thirty years after the first of his visions came to him in his sleep.

In 1926, at the age of four, Reies López Tijerina began having his visions, and something of this nascent prophetic capacity kept with him until he died at the age of eighty-nine in 2015. The first one came with the onset of the Great Depression, when his family of "Texican" migrant farmworkers had hit rock bottom.

They were all hungry and thirsty, every one of them. They had no fixed abode and simply camped or stayed in migrant farmworker shacks off to the side of cotton fields and pecan orchards, between the barns and the rusty array of farm equipment and dead trucks.

Landless. Homeless.

One night, all they had to share for dinner was half a cup of tea made from the bark of pecan trees. The parents urged their children to go to sleep early as a means to mute the hunger that had plagued them for days.

Their little boy—already weary and sweat-drenched from a day in the fields—descended into a sleep so deep that his parents feared that he was dying of hunger. They were so concerned that they dispatched Reies's older brother Anselmo to go to the "big house" of the landowner to ask if they would call for a doctor.

Reies survived. In fact, the next day, the boy seemed preternaturally alive. As soon as Reies awakened and sat up, he was bubbling over with excitement:

"Jesus took me by the hand and showed me these big green pastures, a garden full of flowers, beautiful places. And then he pulled me along in one of those little red wagons—yes, a red one! I never had one before, but now Jesus was pulling me along in one."

Over the years that followed, Tijerina told that story many times, as an indication that he was chosen by Jesus to ride with him through the heavens and the earth.

Reies became convinced by the time he was a young adult that he had a special place in God's plan, to work as the right-hand man for Jesus. He began to read significance into little "signs" in the landscape that Jesus offered that no one else could see. He was cocksure that his calling was to help his people break free of servitude to wander through the desert until they reached their Promised Land, just as Moses had done for the Jews enslaved in Egypt.

By the time he turned twenty-nine, Reies was indeed leading a small group of devoted followers into the desert as Moses had done. But this was the rough-and-tumble Sonoran Desert just outside of Casa Grande, Arizona. Casa Grande was named for what the local O'odham tribes called Siwañ Wa'a Ki, a temple-like ceremonial structure that the prehistoric Hohokam had built and then abandoned not far from the Gila River.

Although that river had run wild up through the nineteenth century, its year-round flows ceased when dams were built upstream. But then, Anglo farmers switched to pumping groundwater to irrigate their crops in the Casa Grande Valley, and the water in the aquifer dropped below the root depths of cottonwoods and willows and mesquites, killing the lush thickets that Akimel O'odham elder George Webb also used to call "Paradise." Even the oldest mesquite trees along the Gila River near Siwañ Wa'a Ki in the valley all died, were cut for firewood, and became a graveyard of tree stumps, a fallen paradise.

Ironically, Tijerina had inadvertently placed his utopian commune in between the ruins of the ceremonial temple of the collapsed Hohokam culture to the north and a failed Jesuit mission of Santa Catalina Kuitoakbagum to the south. The latter place of worship, which had been placed on the most remote reaches of evangelization—called the Rim of Christendom in the desert at that time—had been attacked and destroyed by five hundred angry O'odham warriors in May of 1757 and never resettled.

Let us just say the Valley of Peace was not considered prime real estate by anyone, but Tijerina's vision for the place did not allow him to read any of those historic signs on the land. Tijerina simply called it "the wildest place I could find where we wouldn't be bothered," or at least for the $1,400 that his devotees could scrape together by surrendering their life savings. They had just enough capital to purchase the land, but virtually no funds left over to build residences or infrastructure to support them.

It did not seem to matter to Reies that twelve poor families of more than thirty Mexican Americans had given up all personal earnings and inheritances to join him. He was now their prophet, calling himself Iratéo, the Wrath of God.

Iratéo forced the men he called the Heralds of Peace to wear long white robes and the women to wear head scarves and long, heavy dresses in the desert heat as if they were Arabs, Berbers, or Anabaptist pilgrims. There are rumors that he was tough on the other men, and too close for comfort with the women, for his religious fervor spilled into fanatical control over his devotees. Their antiquated apparel triggered the ridicule and scorn of local teenagers in Casa Grande, who bullied the Valle de Paz students in their school, looted their homes, stomped on their rooves, and set fire to the few wooden frame buildings they had above ground. After getting no response from law enforcement to halt the harassment from local hoodlums, Tijerina refused to let the children in his commune go to public schools.

In his autobiography, *Mi Lucha por la Tierra*, Reies confessed that "Only in the first few months [of 1956] did we enjoy ourselves with the peace and liberty we sought. It was the Anglos who began to cause us difficulties. The Pima [O'odham] Indians, natives of these lands, never caused us any difficulties, nor did the Blacks, much less the Mexicans."

Perhaps it was the strangeness and insularity of Iratéo's utopian community that generated such animosity in the Anglo community of cotton farmers and ranchers around them. Every time they went into Casa Grande or Toltec for supplies, they were showered with racist insults and called "dirty Mexicans who lived like rats in holes."

The "holes" their detractors were referring to were what Iratéo himself called *fosas*, a Spanish term that could refer to pits, cavities, ditches, or graves.

All the "dwellings" were subterranean hovels scraped out of the powdery silt and alkaline caliche crusts characteristic of that stretch of desert. Using steel and wooden uprights at the corners of each excavated hole, they placed the salvaged hoods, trunk covers, and car tops over the posts and used sheets of tin or layers of palm fronds to keep the hard-packed dirt in the walls from collapsing.

The fosas were barely six feet deep, just enough for most men to stand up in without hitting their head on a ceiling of recycled metal, and most were only about ten feet long.

While these subterranean "suites" could keep the children and pregnant women in his commune sheltered from the wind and direct exposure to the desert sun, the dwellings were like ovens during the summer, magnifying the brutal heat aboveground.

Even when they cooled off inside, there was another persistent danger: Nocturnally active reptiles such as sidewinders, Western diamondbacks, and coachwhips loved to slither down into the underground hovels. It is said that one rattlesnake landed at the head of the bed where Tijerina's wife, Mary Escobar, lay just after she had given birth to their daughter.

Reies rolled the mother and newborn out of the way and swiftly killed the rattlesnake, claiming he was ridding the world of its evil. He threw the writhing snake out of their fosa before it could scare or do any harm to the baby girl that he then named Ira de Alláh. He claimed that her name also meant Wrath of God, but was derived from Muslim scriptures.

And yet, over the remaining months that she spent as Iratéo's wife in the Valley of Peace, Mary Escobar realized that the evil serpents had not been vanquished. Reies's wife tallied up eighty-seven snakes that invaded the homes of the congregation before they were killed. Evil continued to arrive in the Valle de Paz at a steady pace.

If that were not enough stress on Mary, the mother of the baby that Iratéo had himself delivered, the self-proclaimed prophet disappeared to Visalia, California, within ten days of the birth. He took leave from his family to rustle up more funds and recruit more members for his congregation in the Valley of Peace.

While he was gone, a cloud-busting thunderstorm let loose with a downpour that might have even frightened the prophets Elijah and Noah, for it caused sheet flooding across the desert floor and inundation of every one of the congregation's homes.

The next morning, Tijerina received a call from his second-in-command, Guadalupe Júaregui, who was the bearer of bad news:

"Your wife is living under a tree . . . because the subterranean home is full of water."

She was found shivering, huddled under a tarp with her three adolescents and the new baby.

One of the survivors announced to Tijerina that the Valle de Paz had become the Valle de Lagrimas and that his family could no longer tolerate it. Others were deciding whether to flee. Hearing of the tragedy, Tijerina shed his own tears that he could not be there to help his wife, his family, or his other followers. He realized that he had left them without food and cash.

Tijerina became overwhelmed by sorrow and guilt, and for once admitted his own mistakes and flaws. He must have realized that his utopian community had already sunk into the mud, and that he could not right the ship. He moaned out loud to God, just as Job might had done:

"When will I encounter the mission of my life?"

It was as if Reies were a four-year-old again, asking Jesus to pull his little red wagon out of the mud, or to gift him a new one:

"The news split my soul. . . . That night I could not sleep [in Visalia]. Alone, I retired to meditate. All night, I stayed outside the house. [It was during] that night I had a vision."

Yes, the same night that he learned that the Valley of Peace was toast—soggy toast—Tijerina took flight and escaped into a hallucinatory reverie that changed the course of his life and mission. He later called it his Moment of Revelation, his Super Dream or Gran Visión.

At first, it was a vision that seemed hard for him to decipher. Reies dreamed that three angels descended from heaven, picked him up off the ground, and lifted him up onto a cloud. The cloud carried Reies along with the angels through the heavens until they came to a dark wood, a shady forest in the mountains so unlike the desert where he had been struggling to survive.

There he entered something akin to a *camposanto* or *panteón*—a graveyard or holy resting place—where there were pretty horses that were frozen and unable to move. Frozen assets.

But when he and the angels mounted one particularly pretty horse, it stirred out of its narcolepsy and took flight. It transported him into a beautiful *kin-dom* where waiting crowds broke into applause, cheering for his arrival.

It was there that Reies said he met "the One," an elder clothed in white robes who welcomed him. He let Reies sit for a bit in his throne, then gifted him with a key that would unlock the solutions to the world's woes and wretched weaknesses.

"Was it *God*? You sat in *his* throne?" His astonished listeners asked. He was quiet for a moment, his intense brown eyes twinkling.

"Who else could it be?" Call the One YHWH, Allah, Elohim, Adonis, or the Creator and Benefactor of All Things, the name alone didn't matter. He had let Reies sit on his throne, so obviously he found favor with Reies.

·~·

That dream had changed everything. Well, almost. When he returned the next day from Visalia to the Valle de Paz, Tijerina was more confident, almost laser focused. He told his heralds of peace that in trying to decipher the dream, he had a hunch that the beautiful kingdom with the forests, mountains, and horses was in northern New Mexico.

Reies had evangelized up and down the valleys in the Río Arriba near Tierra Amarilla when he was an itinerant preacher in the 1940s and early 1950s. He admired the Hispanos he had met up there and was envious of their deep, place-based agrarian traditions that he had not grown up with in south Texas. He decided that he should take his family and a few friends up to Fruita, Colorado, to work picking apples and other fruit until they had some funds again, but then take five of the most trusted heralds of peace with him to Tierra Amarilla.

Within a few years, Tijerina's renewed relationship with Hispanics in the Río Arriba headwaters near Tierra Amarilla would put him in the national news and would put the little town below yellow-streaked cliffs on the map in a big way.

·~·

But first, the heralds of peace chose to listen to the locals about what those mythic horses—those frozen assets—might mean to *them*. As Reies asked him questions, a Hispanic elder named Zebedeo Martínez unfolded the sorry history of land grabs in his region. Zebedeo was angered by the loss of the *communes* or working landscapes held in common by the corporate community.

Since the time of the Spanish land grants, long before New Mexico became a state in the United States, la familia Martínez were among those who referred to themselves as the *herederos de la merced*. In other words, they were the legitimate heirs to the communal portion of the land grants called *tierras realengas*.

The Treaty of Guadalupe Hidalgo had paved the way for the transfer of millions of square miles of Mexican lands to the United States beginning in 1848. It was supposed to guarantee the right of former Mexican citizens to the lands they had inherited as families or as communities. But as the Martínez clan told Tijerina and his crew, their rights were gradually compromised and eroded by legal actions that favored Anglos with ties to state or federal politicians.

The Martínez clan claimed—with good proof—that these lands had been illegally taken from them by carpetbagger politicians and land swindlers beginning in the second half of the nineteenth century, during the Lincoln County Wars. Those armed conflicts had brought notoriety to the likes of Billy the Kid and *Ben Hur* writer Lew Wallace but had done little to resolve land disputes farther north in the Río Arriba.

Estimates vary, but within the six southwestern states, four of them forming the border with Mexico, as much as seventeen million acres of Spanish-era land holdings of rural communities went up for grabs. Few of the old Indigenous or Hispanic families could retain their land holdings, and most of them plummeted into poverty. When Tijerina realized what a huge social injustice this was—affecting hundreds of thousands of la Raza over the previous century—he identified the "secular" mission he had been seeking that might be elevated by his remarkable oratorical skills.

But before he could do that and permanently settle in New Mexico, he had some mopping up to do back in Arizona. The families remaining in the Valle de Paz were in full disarray, dealing with accusations against Tijerina and other male elders forming the heralds of peace.

On top of that, he and his henchmen were arrested twice for petty theft charges, one for stealing truck tires from an Anglo neighbor and another for taking government property from a National Forest Service facility in Arizona.

If that were not enough, Reies got caught trying to break one of his brothers, Margarito Tijerina, out of a Pinal County prison. Reies was arrested while waiting in his Ford sedan outside the prison, after an O'odham Indian alerted the jail guards that Margarito would be sawing through the bars of his cell as part of a jail break engineered by Reies.

Tijerina served ninety days in jail for the first offenses, then was released just in time for the second set of charges to hit. He refused to tolerate being incarcerated again.

And so, Tijerina went on the lam, spending the next seven years as a fugitive from the law and an exile from the land he loved. While these were difficult times for him and his estranged family, some observers say it toughened him up and sharpened his focus.

After a stint in Mexico doing archival research on Spanish land grants and the Treaty of Guadalupe Hidalgo, he had convinced himself that he had at last found the "key" he'd been granted by the One. He would spend the rest of his life helping Hispanic communities in the Río Arriba regain title to the land that had slipped through their hands in the nineteenth and early twentieth centuries.

We now know—thanks to the remarkable rapport that historian Ramon Gutiérrez struck up with Tijerina and his family—that Reies did not ever abandon his self-proclaimed role as a spiritual prophet for more secular pursuits. Instead, he insisted he was merely responding to a God-given call to return sacred homelands to their rightful stewards who had become the dispossessed. He would use the second half of his life to gain wide support for this "political cause" among other civil rights activists, but he was doing it for religious reasons.

From then on, Reies Tijerina was a man with a singular mission: the struggle to restore land rights through nothing less than an agrarian revolt.

As Tijerina boasted many times, the Alianza's goal was nothing less than "to unite la Raza against the Anglo and take our land back by force, if necessary."

After his life as a fugitive had been largely forgotten, Tijerina barnstormed the northern counties of New Mexico and the southernmost reaches of Colorado doing stump speeches. He gained appointments with governors, senators, judges, and legal historians. He went on speaking tours, and he organized marches, demonstrations, and rallies.

Those of my friends who heard Tijerina speak during this era had never heard an agrarian activist with so much fire and brimstone in his appeals. His storytelling about the blatant robbery of Indigenous and Hispano homelands was nothing short of electrifying.

When he incorporated the Federal Alliance of Land Grant Heirs—the Alianza Federal de Mercedes para Herederos—five thousand rural dwellers joined the cause immediately after hearing that Tijerina would help them recuperate all the royal land grants or tierras realengas their ancestors had cared for.

As many of ten thousand others from all parts of the United States paid membership fees to support Tijerina's land sovereignty movement for "Indo-Hispanos" and other cultures. At last, Tijerina had something of a decent budget to sustain his travel and pamphleteering.

Inspired by Tijerina, alliance members throughout the Río Arriba began to post eviction notices on fences of rangelands on Forest Service or private lands then being grazed by livestock owned by Anglo ranchers. The Corporation of Abiquiu members sent letters to Forest Service officials and other authorities announcing that they were ready to "perform their property claims" and remove livestock, equipment, and vehicles belonging to interlopers.

As fictionalized later in John Nichol's *Milagro Beanfield War*, angry agrarian activists blew up an irrigation ditch in bottomlands being managed by wealthy land developer Kenneth Heron, who appears to have had a history of buying lands out from under elderly couples who had not resolved issues with delinquent taxes.

Some agrarian reform advocates were burning down barns, sabotaging gas tanks with sugar, slashing the tires of trucks and tractors, slaughtering livestock, and torching hay bales in pastures that their ancestors had formerly tended. The FBI agents and district attorneys recorded dozens of incidents of clandestine sabotage and tried in vain to link all of them back to Tijerina.

At the same time, Tijerina was speaking out nationally—on radio, television, and in civil rights marches—to obtain the support and endorsement of activists held in high regard across America. He met with Black leaders such as Martin Luther King Jr., Coretta Scott King, Elijah Muhammad, and Ralph Abernathy; with brown leaders such as Corky Gonzales, César Chávez, and José Angel Gutiérrez; and with Indigenous leaders of a dozen tribes, including Hopi prophet Thomas Banyaca and Tuscarora activist Mad Bear Anderson.

While few of those high-profile activists had much extra time to crosswalk their concerns and strategies with activists of other races, they welcomed Tijerina to do so when he sought them out. It was the beginnings of a unified front of peoples of color. Tijerina invested considerable time in such exchanges, if only to elevate his own visibility.

His oratory and resolve had begun to gain Tijerina monikers like the King of Adobe, the New Mexican Moses, El Tigre, and King Tiger on a national scale. But who would stay with him and who would turn against him would radically change on June 5, 1967.

It was called the Summer of Love, but in northern New Mexico in 1967, violence and hatred flared up to obscure the love fests happening in hippie communes nearby. June 5 was the hot summer day when "los Tijerinas" occupied the modest Río Arriba County courthouse in Tierra Amarilla to exert their constitutional right to perform a citizen's arrest of district attorney Alfonso Sánchez. In their minds, Sánchez had violated their rights to assemble and to petition the government to address their grievances.

The Tierra Amarilla courthouse occupation became a turning point in the history of land sovereignty in the United States. One activist proclaimed that it was "the first act of armed insurrection in the Chicano advance toward independence."

Another observer, Raza Unida's founder, José Angel Gutiérrez, no doubt angered some other activists by his blunt comparison: "He did what Malcom X and the Black Panthers only talked about. He waged war against the state of New Mexico and the United States government . . . He literally took possession and control of illegally occupied land in New Mexico."

The telling of Tijerina's story often goes into slow motion with the finely detailed firsthand accounts of every event surrounding the Tierra Amarilla courthouse conflict by Peter Nabokov and other radical journalists. In less than an hour, twenty armed protesters entered the Río Arriba County courthouse, attempting to capture Sánchez, who happened not to be present at the moment; but in the chaos, three others in the courthouse, the jailer, a state police officer, and a deputy sheriff, were badly injured. Others were beaten, tied up, or kidnapped.

That brief incident triggered the largest and one of the longest manhunts in American history, lasting months and involving dozens of raids by state police, county sheriffs, the National Guard, and the Federal Bureau of Investigation (which had been monitoring Tijerina's "communist" activities since 1956). They brought in helicopters, tanks, all-terrain vehicles, and planes. The sky was buzzing with activity; roadblocks were placed on every highway. More than 450 men and women were sent out to scour a 2,500-square-mile area in New Mexico and Colorado for the insurrectionists.

While some of the perpetrators were caught and held within the first three days, six others slipped away. Tijerina was a fugitive once more, remaining undetected for five days, until he surrendered the Monday after the raid when police in Albuquerque detected him sleeping in his car and woke him up. Others were still fugitives and remained on the lam after Tijerina was jailed.

The manhunt in New Mexico consistently made as much national news as the Six-Day War between Israel and Arab forces from Jordan, Syria, and Egypt, which happened at the same time halfway around the world. Some journalists portrayed Tijerina as a prominent civil rights leader who had been harassed by the FBI and nearly martyred, just as Martin Luther King Jr. was a year later. Others portrayed him as a communist agent, a con man, a deranged insurgent, or a domestic terrorist that was threatening law and order in the West.

The month after Tijerina's arrest, two women once active in the Student Nonviolent Coordinating Committee in the South moved to New Mexico to publish the civil rights newspaper *El Grito del Norte*, the Cry of the North.

Disgusted by the mainstream coverage Tijerina had received, Chicana writer Betita Martínez and lawyer Beverly Axelrod carefully followed the trials of Tijerina and his codefendants, and then continued to bolster Chicano civil rights land reform in northern New Mexico for many more years.

Without a doubt, these events and the hope they inspired in northern New Mexico emboldened the next generation of Chicano and Indo-Hispano activists to do what Reies López Tijerina could not simply do: broaden, deepen, and sustain the promotion of agrarian land rights and rural prosperity in the historic communities of the dispossessed.

The list of activists who built on the Alianza's work—whether condoning its initial tactics or not—reads like the who's who of individuals who have made a tangible difference in northern New Mexico and southern Colorado.

That cadre includes Maria Varela, Juan Estevan Arrellano, Ernie Atencio, Alvin Warren, Paula Garcia, Devon Peña, Eduardo Lavadie, Antonio and Molly Manzanares, Shirley Romero Otero, Sylvia Rodriguez, and Arturo Sandoval. Some of these individuals who were living in or near Tierra Amarilla helped to spark the return of the first two hundred acres of land grant parcels to the Hispanic community by a private party.

But not all these individuals focused their life work exclusively on Spanish land grants as Tijerina did; they found ways to advance the management of common lands and acequia systems while promoting community-based strategies for economic development, food security, and traditional management and use of forest and rangeland resources.

At the national level, New Mexicans formed a Land Grant Forum that successfully lobbied their congressional delegation to pass a bill in the US House to establish a federal Land Claims Commission. When the Senate did not pass a similar bill, New Mexico's senators obtained an appropriation for a Government Accounting Office study of the issue in 1995. That study recorded all court decisions regarding the return of 295 Spanish and Mexican land grants—including those to Indian nations—but conceded that there was no clear legal path to uphold all "non-Indian claims" because of records that had been historically lost or because of legal precedents that ruled against certain parcels being repatriated.

At the state level, the New Mexico State Legislature then established a Land Grant Commission to oversee and respond to community concerns about contested land grants and voluntary transfers of titles. It recognized the status of local boards of trustees to govern thirty-five community land grants in the state.

About the same time, the Land Rights Council in southern Colorado, founded by Shirley Otero in 1977, filed a lawsuit to regain rights for a thousand Hispano and Indigenous heirs who had foraged and hunted in the million-acre Sangre de Cristo land grant dubiously awarded to the Beaubien family in 1843.

After twenty-one years of legal battles, the Colorado Supreme Court decided in favor of 143 plaintiffs on behalf of their heirs or herederos in 2002, and in November 2018 their rights were upheld in a final court decision. This landmark case will likely guide the future of other adjudication of the kind that Tijerina could have only hoped for while he was still alive.

If there was any flaw in Tijerina's logic, it was that land access alone would help Indo-Hispanos prosper in the rural landscapes of the border states that had been their homeland for centuries. Restoring livelihoods in crippled rural economies would be just as important, as Corky Gonzalez noted in his Plan Espiritual de Aztlán that emerged out of the Chicano youth moment he fostered at a conference in Denver in March of 1969, the same week that Reies, his brother Cristóbal, and three others were jailed for violations of federal laws.

But if any activist of that era exemplified Chicano youth engagement in social and environmental justice, it was a young New Mexican named Arturo Sandoval, who had been going to meetings about the communal management of Mercedes land grants since he was in high school. The impassioned speeches of elderly Hispanics in the Río Arriba won him over and set him on a trajectory different than others in his family.

I first ran into Arturo when we were both engaged in planning and promoting the first Earth Day to be held in April of 1970. We both worked part time out of the Environmental Action headquarters in Washington, DC, that coordinated events across America.

•ও•

When the first celebration of Earth Day was being planned for April 1970, few people of color were on the front lines of the environmental justice movement. Although twenty million people of all races, creeds, and cultures came out to renew their relationship with Mother Earth, the national organizing team in Washington, DC, included only one person from an ethnic or racial minority.

Fortunately, that was Arturo, then a twenty-two year old, already deeply engaged in multicultural activism in Albuquerque. He had demonstrated enough "street smarts" to be able to reach out to la Raza in several Western states as early as possible. That allowed the national organizing team to foster a more inclusive rollout of environmental teach-ins, rallies, and marches slated for that landmark day in the history of the environmental movement.

More than five decades after that first Earth Day, Arturo continued with his work as a pioneer in environmental justice, food justice, and social justice. His initiatives have tangibly benefited Indigenous, Mexicanos, and Nuevo Mexicanos in both rural and urban communities throughout the Southwest.

As a seventeen-year-old Arab American intern at Earth Day headquarters in the early months of 1970, I felt that Arturo's presence was a breath of fresh air. I witnessed a heavy bias toward Ivy League and Stanford graduates on the leadership team, but Arturo—with his black hair, mustache, and quizzical smile—reminded me more of the street activists I'd grown up around. And we both wondered—Arturo as a Hispanic American and me as an Arab American—whether this new movement would be making room for as many of those who looked like our darker-skinned cousins as it would for educated white guys. Indeed, Arturo was already attentive to the Chicano or Indo-Hispano movement before he left his hometown of Española to attend the University of New Mexico in the late 1960s. It was in the early 1960s, however, that he attended his first gathering about land rights in Anton Chico; that is what may have set him on his life path.

As he told me with a twinkle of amusement in his eyes, "I changed from a nice, polite, risk-averse Catholic boy who had been leaning toward a sedate lifestyle and came out as a Chicano activist. I'm sure that made some of my family members uneasy at the time. But I found the counterculture movement was a fantastic opening out of our worldview that looked beyond the constraints of the oppressive religious orthodoxy of that era."

Sandoval then played a special role in making environmental concerns credible to minority populations. He had been so articulate about his values as a college student at the University of New Mexico that he assumed a leadership role in the United Mexican American Students (UMAS) coalition, helping with a wildcat strike on campus organized exclusively by students themselves.

Felipe González, who met Sandoval around 1968, remembers him as "very dynamic . . . with a strongly developed awareness of issues in relationship to the Chicano and Chicana people."

Within two years, Earth Day coordinator Denis Hayes enlisted Arturo to join him in the nonprofit offices of Environmental Teach-In, Inc., where he and I met in late January or February of 1970.

"I truly felt I shared a lot of social justice and peacemaking values with the rest of the staff," Arturo recalled. "The good thing about the participants in the counterculture at that time was that they modeled the behaviors they wanted to see changed in America; they didn't just talk about them. They truly wanted to live in harmony with all races and cultures and with Mother Earth as well."

Both Arturo and I were struck by the fact that the youthful Earth Day organizers selected a place for their offices in a Black neighborhood in Washington, DC, near DuPont Circle. It was in a street scene that the staffs of other environmental nonprofits considered to be tough, if not dangerous.

"But I loved to take breaks from my 10-hour-a-day work and listen to the African drumming circles in the park below us. . . . I guess I felt somewhat isolated from my own people at the time—my first long stay away from New Mexico—so I did a lot of outreach for Earth Day with Chicano groups in the West, not just Albuquerque, but LA, San Francisco, Denver, and metro areas in Texas and Arizona."

Sandoval admitted to me that at times, Earth Day was a tough sell to people of color in urban areas.

"Their initial response to the Earth Day concept was bemusement or even indifference. They were immersed in their own critically important, day-to-day, hand-to-mouth issues. . . . Their communities were under a lot of socioeconomic pressure."

Nevertheless, Arturo jumped into the Earth Day dance with both feet, assuming that land rights and the banning of agrichemicals that were killing his farm-working neighbors were as important to Earth Day as wildlife conservation and wilderness preservation.

A half century later, Earth Day cofounder Denis Hayes remains convinced that Sandoval played a unique role in making environmental concerns credible to minority populations: "Arturo had obvious credibility talking about the daily showers of pesticides falling on Chicano field workers and the nitrate poisoning in their drinking water."

Speaking to Arturo in his office at the Center of Southwest Culture in Albuquerque five decades after that first Earth Day, he agreed: "I simply saw my work with the Earth Day team as an extension of my civil rights and peace activism on behalf of la Raza."

During the last two weeks immediately prior to the April 22, 1970, celebration, Arturo headed back to Albuquerque to organize the largest Earth Day rally of Native and Mexican Americans in his home state and maybe in the nation. The multicultural Earth Day protest march that he led along the banks of the Río Grande can rightly be called the first successful environmental justice initiative led by people of color in the United States.

He sought to close a foul-smelling solid waste treatment plant in the South Barelas barrio immediately south of downtown. It had become an eyesore imposed upon one of the oldest settlements in the valley, without any consultation or consent from its Spanish-speaking residents.

Arturo and a local mariachi band led a multicultural protest march of nearly five hundred participants down along the banks of the Río Grande to the site for the demonstration at a location not far from where the National Hispanic Cultural Center stands today.

An old friend of Arturo's, Steve Cotton, reminded me that the entire Earth Day organizing team explicitly chose to focus national media attention for the evening news on Arturo's march and rally. But when the networks claimed they could not get film footage from Albuquerque to New York in time for the evening news, Arturo refused to give them even a soundbite. Finally, ABC and CBS agreed to cover the event on the prime-time news if Arturo would schedule his speech a half hour earlier than planned.

At the last minute, a deal was reached. The two biggest television networks at that time covered the rally, embarrassing the waste facilities planners and operators who had previously ignored community concerns. Their efforts ultimately led to the relocation of the waste treatment facility. Earth Day activism had led to one of the first environmental justice wins for inner-city minorities.

In his seventh decade as an activist, Sandoval continues to guide the Center of Southwest Culture in Albuquerque, which builds capacity among Hispanic and Indigenous communities. The center's programs help dozens of rural communities produce and market affordable organic foods as means to reduce health issues otherwise caused by pesticides and herbicides. Its food security and rural livelihood programs benefit dozens of Indigenous and Latinx communities throughout New Mexico.

Arturo, who turned seventy-six in 2024, insists that the environmental movement ushered in by Earth Day still needs a wider range of voices to help it overcome the deeply imperialistic and colonial history that still underlies most social and environmental justice issues in New Mexico and elsewhere.

"The path forward for the environmental movement is in aligning it with the current values and strategies of activism in México and the rest of Latin America. We once took our leads from the activists on the West Coast or East Coast. Now the axis has changed, and we will be enriched more by interactions with our Spanish- and Indigenous-speaking sisters and brothers to the south in Las Americas than with anyone else."

With that prophecy, Arturo smiled one of those smiles so warm it could melt the snow in the Sandia Mountains. He ended with this:

"Today I am the most in love that I've ever been with this place and its people. I even cowrote a musical about our landscape here, our Tierra Sagrada. I have hope that the human species can still get our relationships right with one another and with the earth. . . . The seedpods of human potential are always waiting to germinate."

CHAPTER TWELVE

Boycott

César Chávez, Dolores Huerta, and Fred Ross

TO THOSE who drive their cars and trucks past crews of farmworkers harvesting asparagus, chiles, lettuce, onions, or tomatoes in the searing heat of the desert borderlands, those migrant laborers toiling and sweating out in the fields may appear to be *people without history*.

As Antoine de Saint-Exupéry once described nomads in another desert halfway around the world,

"But one never knows where to find them. The wind blows them away. They have no roots, and that make their lives very difficult."

I have seen the same thin, young women of sixteen or seventeen years of age—weary and thirsty for potable water—standing around a cooler full of ice, waiting for a drink in a Dixie cup. They are often covered from head to toe in light fabric, their faces shrouded by a mosquito-proof veil, looking like Berber women in their hijabs somewhere in the Sahara.

I might spot their buses one week near Caborca, Sonora, where they cut the early, shoulder-season crop of asparagus; then the next week in Yuma, Arizona, hauling bushel baskets of onions to flatbeds; and the next, across the Colorado River near Calexico, packing melons.

I try my best not to generalize about them but to remember specific individuals: Alejandro, Benito, Carolina, Casimiro, Cornelio, Evangelina, or Rosa Maria. . . . I also force myself to remember what *la lucha* was all about for them in those days: an hourly wage that averaged 85 cents; a life expectancy of less than fifty-five years for the average farmworker; the nagging problems caused by inadequate housing, pesticide exposure, contaminated water and food; and frequent abuse by foremen and bosses.

I first met some of these workers one dawn as work in the field began. They came in like a mirage in the desert, but by noon they were gone to who knows where, to work someplace else on the four-hundred-acre farm, or to recover from dehydration and heat stress in the shade of some eucalyptus and salt cedars. The next day, I looked everywhere, but did not see a one of them.

A coworker told me that they had been given a chance for steadier wage work on another larger, irrigated farm that he didn't know by name. Later that week, I caught a glimpse of them just for a moment as they boarded a bus and left the same quick mart where I had stopped to get more water. They were out of sight in moments, with no easy way to trace them even if they accidentally left something or someone behind.

·ର·

How many American consumers today can put any names to the faces, hands, and hearts of those who harvested what they eat: the grapes, grapefruit, garlic, artichokes, or berries?

When I was in my twenties, picking strawberries or pruning apple trees for daily wages to get out of debt, most of the men and women I worked with were known to us only by nicknames: Alfa-Beta, Flaco, La China, El Gigante, El Gordito, La Jefa, La Morena, or La Princessa.

While I can't recall all their full names anymore, I can remember their blistered, chapped, and soiled hands, with blood smears from stinging cuts still oozing out the tips of their fingers. Even when wearing gloves, the rips and tears and slices from all manner of knives would ruin any kind of fabric or leather, exposing their hands to innumerable insults.

Forty years later, I do not know how many of those workers persisted as field laborers, nor for how long. I do know that my mentor

Carolina was among the lucky ones who "escaped" the fields to live for years in a comfortable home, but still less than ten miles away from the closest fields where she used to labor.

I do not know (but doubt) whether those blistered hands were ever sufficiently paid for the work they did, or for the pain they suffered while holding short-handled hoes, sickles, scythes, or shovels under scorching conditions of late spring and summer.

The three things I do know for sure are these: that the threesome of César Chávez, Dolores Huerta, and Fred Ross Sr. listened to the voices of such farmworkers; that by doing so they tangibly changed the lives of migrant laborers for the better; and that *los de La Raza siempre tienen raices*.

Yes, that might have been one of the few things that Antoine de Saint-Exupéry might have gotten wrong: migratory farmworkers and desert nomads still have roots, and those roots are what have gifted them the tenacity and perspicacity to survive.

Just a handful of modern American writers and photographers—Sanora Babb, David Bacon, George Ballis, Tim Hernandez, Dorothea Lange, Carey McWilliams, Paul Taylor, Luis Urrea, Luis Valdéz, Alfredo Vea Jr., Rubén Martínez, Angus Wright—have helped us trace the migrant workers back to those roots, to imagine the origins of those sunburned faces, battered hands, and weary hearts.

Otherwise, few of us could have ever glimpsed the roots and the rising shoots of those living at the edges of the croplands that supply most of us with our food.

The chroniclers aside, it was César Chávez, Dolores Huerta, and Fred Ross who said, *Basta!* They could no longer let so much pain and suffering rain down on those they knew who lived and toiled on those edges, those who are among the most marginalized by our society, those who live in the bleakest of places, and those who are seldom offered a crumb from America's most prosperous cities.

Despite all the challenges they have faced, it has been these underdogs growing up in the hinterlands—César and Dolores included—who have become the true trailblazers of social action and innovation. They have done more for social justice than many or most activists who live amid the creaturely comforts of the New Yorks, Chicagos, San Franciscos, or Houstons, buffered from the day-to-day realities of las Razas.

In the farm workforce of the desert borderlands states, there are now immigrants and refugees from more than thirty-two other countries—in addition to Chicanos and Blacks from the South—who face the daily perils of sunburn, thirst, muscle pain, and injuries from runaway farm equipment, just so that we may be fed.

In this case, it was the hands of those who grew up most marginalized in the rural stretches of the West that found ways to band together to struggle against injustice and leverage palpable change during the darkest of times.

Regarding la lucha, César Chávez once noted that "The rich have money—and the poor have time. We don't have to win this year or next year or even the year after that. We'll just keep slugging away, day after day. We will never give up. We have nothing else to do with our lives except to continue this non-violent fight."

As Dolores Huerta once put it, "Being poor and not having anything just gives an incredible strength to people. [In particular], the farm workers seem to be able to see around the corner. . . . *Son tan dispuestos a sufrir*. And they take whatever they have to take because they have no escape hatch."

One of those times was in the 1960s, when there was a dire need to deal with the mistreatment of laborers in the world's largest agricultural industry, the Sunbelt salad bowl that encompasses more than ten million acres from southern and central California, across the Colorado River into Arizona, and down the Río Grande of New Mexico and Texas.

CHAPTER TWELVE

By 1960, the living and working conditions of those who harvest our crops were particularly concerning, especially around the dusty, tumbleweed-edged farm towns in the arid West.

There, Spanish-speaking "Chicanos"—now among those known as Latinxs—came to dominate the migrant workforce after World War II. And yet, as their children came of age, a few who had been put down most of their lives rose up in defiance of the conditions their parents had labored under. They did so after realizing that they had little to risk by challenging the norms of agribusiness, because they had so little to begin with.

Bob Dylan succinctly summarized their plight:

"When you ain't got nothin', you got nothin' to lose."

And so they went on strike. They also went on hunger strikes, fasting till they fainted. When they recovered, they marched into capital cities en masse. They led boycotts. They were with French longshoremen, who dumped tons of grapes in the waters of their harbors rather than ignore the plight of farmworkers.

For fostering produce boycotts, they were beaten and then fired. And so, they formed unions, collectives, and credit unions. They fought bureaucrats and oligarchs to get a place at the negotiation table. They passed new laws. They sang and prayed in the face of their adversaries. They gradually changed the world as they had known it when they were younger.

I am speaking of those farmworkers who cut cotton, clipped off clusters of grapes, picked oranges, sorted onions, and broke off asparagus stems year after year, from age eight onward.

I am referring to farmworkers whose necks, faces, and forearms were burnt by the desert sun, whose shoulders and legs were bruised by hours of dumping buckets and bags full of produce.

I am recalling those whose hands were blistered by gripping the rough-hewn tools loaned to them by farmers who never knew their names or aspirations.

Yes, they were raised on the margins, but they moved up and over dozens of obstacles placed in the paths of their lives. They did so not only to survive but to assure others of their kith and kin that they could gain tangible relief from such disparities and inequities.

·ꝗ·

Long before Dolores Huerta and César Chávez joined forces with Fred Ross in central California to change the history of farmworkers in America, their nascent spirits were forged in the steaming cauldron of the desert Southwest. Their journeys toward social justice began in landscapes that were harshly arid and hellaciously racist. They dealt with grinding poverty well before they became adults and well before they joined together to form one of the most memorable agrarian movements in the history of the Americas.

Huerta and Chávez both grew up where farmworkers as well as miners garnered meager labor rights and negligible bargaining power. During their childhoods, each of them was exposed to the heat and hate endemic to the Sunbelt in the era following World War II, when one of the most massive migrations in human history took place. While they were still infants, their families suffered from the sorts of disparity, poverty, and tragedy that Chávez and Huerta later endeavored to vanquish.

Fred Ross Sr. grew up in safer, more comfortable conditions in San Francisco and Echo Park, but by age twenty-two he had thrown himself in with a group of unionists and socialists that had begun "making good trouble" in Southern California. In 1935, at the "ripe old age" of twenty-five, Fred became the coordinator of the federally funded programs at the Arvin Migratory Camp for farmworkers, located near Bakersfield.

There, through the late 1930s and early 1940s, Fred was the primary organizer helping the Dust Bowl refugees in very camps that John Steinbeck wrote of in *The Grapes of Wrath*.

There, he first heard Woody Guthrie and his guitar improvising songs about the plight of Okie and Mexican farmworkers.

There, he helped thousands of migrant farmworkers form camp councils and enact self-governance, giving them a place at the table where decisions were being made that directly affected their lives.

Over the decades, Ross became known as the most influential grassroots organizer of the twentieth century, not only mentoring Chávez and Dolores Huerta but also spearheading the election of the first Latinx member of LA City Council, fighting for the release of Japanese American farmers from internment camps during World War II, and helping Blacks, Asians, and Chicanos to end school segregation in California.

It was June of 1952 when Fred Ross first knocked on the door of a modest, narrow house on Scharf Street where a number of Chicanos were gathered, some wearing their zoot suits and talking in pachuco slang. At that time, San Jose's east side was darkly deemed the Sal Si Puedes (get out if you can) barrio.

The man who came to the door was the twenty-five-year-old named César Chávez, a former farmworker who was struggling to support his wife, Helen, and their children while working at a nearby lumberyard.

César laughed about their first encounter many times over the next few decades of his friendship with Fred:

"The first time I met Fred Ross, he was about the last person I wanted to see."

But together with Dolores Huerta, César and Fred somehow changed the course of agrarian history in America. Years later, Chávez realized what a gift that meeting had been:

"He started talking—and [it] changed my life. . . . Fred did such a good job of explaining how poor people could build power that I could even taste it."

Fred Ross met Huerta in the mid-1950s and immediately saw the incredible charisma and brilliance that she brought to anything she attempted. But if you trace the journey of Dolores "Lola" Fernández (Huerta) back to its beginnings, it looked nothing like the verdant valleys and rolling hills around where they first met in Stockton, California.

Lola was born out on the high, dry plains near Cimarron, New Mexico, in 1930. That's where expansive cinnamon-colored plains spread out between deep slot canyons and lofty mountain ranges. Both the landscape and the social strata were steeped with plenty of ups and downs.

When Lola was born, her parents, Alicia and Juan, lived in a Phelps-Dodge mining camp called Dawson, on the edge of a multi-tiered barranca where coal could be easily extracted. Alicia's ancestors had been in New Mexico since the 1600s, but they still had to move to wherever the work would allow them to survive.

Juan was the son of Mexican immigrants who had worked in the "killing" fields and mines. In the era of her grandparents and parents, Dawson was a thriving boomtown populated by Mexican, Greek, Cretan, and Italian immigrants who slaved away underground for most of the day, only to surface before dusk just in time to purchase food and drink for dinner from the company canteen. As Merle Travis famously sang, they owed their souls to that company store.

Lola's young mother, Alicia, was sooner or later was forced to say, Basta! She already had enough of both her husband, Juan, and the poverty of Dawson; Alicia had already set her sights on greater expectations. So Alicia packed up her sorrows and her children in a small coupe and fled. She did not look back, for she could sense that Dawson was already doomed to become a ghost town.

There are indeed ghosts in that area, displaced spirits of those who died in two terrible mining disasters there. I felt their presence one July when I visited the twelve-mile stretch of mountains between Dawson and Cimarron, New Mexico. Past tragedies remained palpable, as if lingering in the air there.

Dawson's first disaster was the second worst in US history, when an underground explosion of dynamite killed 263 miners and shook the earth for miles around in 1913. Then, just a decade later, another calamity devastated Dawson. Phelps-Dodge crew bosses were trying to rush ahead with some work at their Stag Canyon Mine when a trolley car derailed, sending off sparks that ignited coal dust and triggered another explosion.

The second time, Phelps-Dodge lost "only" 123 of its men beneath the rockslides and collapsed tunnels.

How odd that she was named Dolores, from the Latin and Spanish words for pain, grief, and sorrow. She was born into them. During the three years of toddling around Dawson before she fled its sorrows, they must have called her Lola to deflect attention from so many *dolores* all around them. Even as a toddler, Lola must have met many workers who had been physically crippled and emotionally crushed by one or the other of the mining disasters.

The walking wounded were omnipresent, as were the souls or ghosts of those who had lost their lives.

It appeared that Alicia could no longer bear to raise Dolores and her brothers under such dire conditions. That may be why she went as far west as she could during the Depression, working as a migrant harvester up and down the California coast. After learning the terrain, Alicia decided to settle with her kids in Stockton, California, piecing together a new life where her father, Herculeano, could help her care for Lola and her two brothers.

What Alicia may not have anticipated was that Stockton itself had become a hotbed of racism, xenophobia, and social tensions just before her family took sanctuary there. Mexicans, Filipinos, Japanese, and Chinese workers were being bullied and subjugated by the old-time farming and wine-making families of the San Joaquin Valley.

Racial violence had erupted around 1930, beginning with the Watsonville riots that targeted poor Filipinos. It quickly spilled over into Stockton, Gilroy, and other central California farm towns.

Racially motivated beatings, burnings, and shootings took the lives of men of Filipino, Mexican, Chinese, African, and Japanese descent at the very moment that Dolores and family arrived in the

San Joaquin Valley in late 1933. Interracial acrimony and civil unrest were rampant in the Stockton vicinity through 1936.

Although her entrepreneurial mother, Alicia, quickly moved up the social ladder in Stockton, Lola still had to suffer all manner of ethnic slurs and indignities as a teenager, simply because of her accent and the color of her skin.

But there was a rainbow of skin colors in Stockton, as Lola later recalled: "There were Chinese, Latinos, Native Americans, Blacks, Japanese, Italians, and others. We were all rather poor, but it was an integrated community [and] the teachers treated all of us equally mean."

Later in life, Huerta did remember being treated with prejudice, suspicion, and scorn, as if she were a second-class citizen in her high school. A teacher accused her of stealing another student's work, unconvinced that Lola could do such good work on her own.

"The rich kids always got special treatment in our high school, so I think that's when I first started being aware of injustices that happen."

Toughened by such experiences, Lola went out to prove that teacher wrong many times over, gaining the respect of her peers and mentors in doing so. She was so emboldened by speaking truth to power that her grandfather used to call her Siete Lenguas (Seven Tongues) for her verbal dexterity and loquacity.

By the time Lola graduated high school, she had soared past nearly all her peers in expressions of creativity, compassion, and charisma. In fact, Lola was such a good student that she won second place in a national Girl Scouts school competition. But her school's officials would not accept that a Mexican American girl should be supported for a trip to be a winner of an essay contest.

Her mother, Alicia, had worked hard to provide music lessons for Lola, who swiftly mastered violin, piano, *baile folklorico*, and modern dance. As a teenager, she began to dream of a career as a dancer, but part-time jobs in fruit packing sheds kept her from pursuing that aspiration.

Instead, Lola danced up and down picket lines, revving up the energy of the otherwise disheartened.

·ಌ·

Perhaps Lola never became a full-time farmworker because others quickly spotted her organizing skills and interest in political change, talents that could benefit her neighbors and community. Although she had married and become a teacher and mother, Dolores soon turned to a career of activism and political advocacy that occupied her for another six decades.

Perhaps it was inspired by Lola's reconnection with her father back in New Mexico, where he had become a union organizer and state legislator.

Her father, Juan, once called out a fellow legislator as a dirty scab on the House floor, and then took a punch at him. Whatever Juan Fernández contributed to her sensibilities, Dolores seemed to have some precocious if not preternatural capacity to recognize and deftly respond to social injustices. Her words had a punch to them reminiscent of her father's fist.

·ಌ·

It was this expressiveness that caught the attention of Fred Ross, the firebrand organizer from the Community Services Organization, who had already begun to mentor another gifted young Chicano organizer named César Chávez.

Dolores did not think much of either of them at first, although they ended up working as a triad for fifty years. Upon first contact with community organizers Fred Ross and Saul Alinsky, Huerta suspected that Ross was a communist rabble-rouser. "So I went to the FBI and had him checked out," she once drolly recalled.

But it did not take long before Lola was won over by the way the organizers that Ross mentored had convinced law enforcers to change their racist practices, had built community health clinics for the poor, and had gotten promising young Chicanos elected to council positions and school boards.

After that, it didn't take much for Ross to convince her that her

God-given skills were needed in Stockton, where she became the key organizer in Stockton for the Community Services Organization. She worked on several social justice and health issues at the city council and state legislature, finding her calling:

"This was, of course, something I been looking for all my life. If organizing could make all this happen, then this was definitely something that I wanted to be part of. I think women are particularly good negotiators and organizers because we have a lot of patience, and no ego trips to overcome. Women are more tenacious and that helps a great deal. It unnerves the growers to negotiate with us. Growers can't swear back at us. . . . And then we bring in the *ethical* questions."

Huerta soon met Ross's other prodigy, a Chicano who had become the CSO's executive director in East LA. But she initially found this Chávez to be disappointing because he was so understated. His family called him Manzie when he was a kid because he loved to drink manzanilla (chamomile) tea. He was quiet and calmer than most of the ruffians around him.

In fact, César was so reserved and soft-spoken that it took months before she had a fulfilling conversation with him, simply because he seemed low key compared to any other activist she had ever met:

"I found César to be very shy. The first two or three years I knew him, it was difficult to have a conversation with him. . . . He wouldn't talk to anybody except when he was organizing. But then I heard him speak one time at a board meeting and I was really impressed."

César must have been impressed too, as Dolores subtly suggested:

> Well, after this big voter registration drive in 1960 where we registered 150,000 people, César got this bright idea to send me to Sacramento. So I went to Sacramento and we got all these

> bills passed. I headed up the legislative program in 1961 when we'd fought for old-age pensions for the noncitizens, for the *viejitos*. I lobbied the welfare bill through so parents could stay in the home. César and I worked to get the right to register voters, door to door, and the right for people to take their driver's license exams in Spanish, and disability insurance for farmworkers, and the right for people to get surplus commodities. And of course, we were the ones that ended the Bracero Program.

Gradually, they became fully committed to work together on behalf of la Causa, even though they constantly challenged and bickered with one another for another two decades.

"César and I have a lot of personal fights," Lola once confided in Margo Garcia, "usually over strategy or personalities. I don't think César himself understands why he fights with me. . . . You know, César has fired me fifteen times, and I must have quit about ten times. Then, we'll call each other up and then get back to work."

César found Lola to be absolutely fearless, physically and emotionally. He liked that in her, but he worried that she was so bombastic at times that she would be eventually beaten as he had been.

His worry was ultimately borne out. In September 1988, a baton-swinging San Francisco policeman attacked the fifty-eight-year-old activist at a peaceful and legal protest, breaking two of her ribs and rupturing her spleen. She was back to work in weeks, and she joined in a lawsuit against the police, in which she was eventually granted $825,000 as a settlement for her injuries.

César's early years in the Yuma desert were as austere as Dolores's infancy in Dawson, but the desert cauldron that cooked him up ran twenty to thirty degrees hotter than either Dawson or Stockton.

César Chávez had been born three years earlier than Dolores, in 1927. His extended family aggregated in the extremely arid reaches of the North Gila Valley not far from where the Colorado River passes through Yuma. During his childhood, Yuma's blistering summer often topped the charts as the hottest in all the United States.

César was named for his grandfather Cesario or Papa Chayo, who had crossed the Río Grande from Chihuahua, Mexico, to escape servitude and punishment by wealthy hacendados. Papa Chayo had worked his way westward as a miner, muleskinner, and farmhand before he scraped together enough money to buy a small farm along the Colorado River.

That farm was the beloved patch of fields and tree crops where Papa Chayo's grandchildren all grew up. And that's where Manzie grew up drinking cups of manzanilla tea and quietly speaking in a manner that had a calming effect on most of his family members.

By the time he could walk and talk, Manzie was already called to help his father, Librado, work the irrigation ditches, hoe the sandy loam of the Colorado floodplain, and sow the maize and chiles his family used to subsist on. As an adolescent, Manzie also hung around and helped out at the family's little store, pool hall, and garage.

Manzie was hardly two years of age when the stock market crashed. It triggered the Great Depression, although the ripple effects of that global economic collapse did not hit his family until 1932. By then, their regular customers at the store, garage, and pool hall were so impoverished that they asked the Chávez family for credit to buy food, goods, and services until they got back on their feet. The Chávez family relented for a while, but soon had to shoulder too much debt themselves for their small businesses to stay solvent.

When the Dust Bowl drought hit them in 1933, their crops failed and their indebted customers vanished from sight. The Chávez farm teetered on the edge of bankruptcy for another few years until Librado was refused a New Deal loan from a local bank.

César later learned how a crooked neighbor swindled Librado out of their remaining assets: "My father [initially] qualified for a loan, but the guy living next to us wanted to get our land . . . [he] was the president of the bank, and also of the soil conservation district, so the loan was blocked."

He learned the hard way how farming families became landless.

By 1938, the entire Chávez family was evicted, losing all the farm and ranch lands they once had in the valley where Papa Chayo had first settled decades before. Manzie watched helplessly as bulldozers leveled their homestead:

"[They came with] a monstrous thing, knocking down trees. We left everything behind. Left chickens and cows and horses and all the implements. Things belonging to my father's family and my mother's as well. Everything. If we'd stayed there, possibly I would have been a grower. God writes in exceedingly crooked lines."

At eleven years of age, Manzie had few choices other than to join his now landless father, mother, and four siblings to work as migrant farmworkers in Southern California.

The scar of losing their own farm and becoming wage laborers for other, far wealthier farmers lingered like a stigmata over César's heart for the rest of his life.

"Maybe that's when the rebellion started," he later confessed, matter-of-factly. The farmworker rebellion. *La huelga.*

Like Lola, César had been forced to leave his birthplace and was set adrift to labor in the fields of others, to survive by the sweat of their brows. They could not descend much lower than laboring below sea level in the Imperial Valley of Southern California near the edges of the Salton Sea, America's analog to Galilee.

For César and his family, as it was for Lola and hers, they had dropped so low on the economic ladder that the only way left to go was up.

Worse yet, César attended at least thirty-six schools during the years his father took his entire family to work harvesting crops in the deserts of Southern California. As the new kid on the block, he learned to survive through his scrappiness and cunning.

When César and his wife Helen moved to San Jose's Mayfair district, he was poor and without a car, riding a bike to harvest apricots in orchards nearby. He was kidded for being the only young man of his age in Mayfair still riding around on a bicycle rather than spending time fixing up hot rods. While his family still called him Manzie, his friends in Sal Si Puedes called him Cé-Cé (for his initials) or the Bicicleta Kid. As we shall hear later, it was during this time that a younger Luis Valdez first encountered Chávez without fully understanding they were kin.

By 1961, César was lobbying Dolores, as well as several of his old friends and fellow farmworkers, to meet with him in East LA to start a new union. They were receptive but couldn't immediately drop everything in their life to work for no pay.

But César persisted. In December 1962, Chávez went to Sacramento to see the social justice policy work Dolores was doing for Fred Ross through the CSO.

He pleaded with Dolores to leave the Community Service Organization to be a cofounder in what first became known as the National Farm Workers Association in a small "headquarters" office César had rented in Delano. It would later be called the United Farm Workers.

For a while, Dolores continued to draw a paycheck from the CSO but would drive up to Delano on long weekends to work with César and his wife, Helen. Dolores and her children would sleep on the floor of the Chávez back room until the union had a large enough budget to offer her a modest salary.

She was soon taking on multiple roles in the fledgling organization but found her own sweet spot as vice president in 1964 as they began to plan the Delano grape strike of 1965. From then on, she became César's coleader, working the lines of sometimes unconfident strikers, giving them pep talks with enough love, humor, and hope to persist at their difficult task.

She was admired by so many that for the first decades she was the only woman elected to the leadership team of the new union.

The Chicanos began to call her Nuestra Adelita—making an analogy with a Chihuahuan woman hero during the Mexican Revolution—or Soldadera en Huelga, the Woman Soldier on Strike. Dolores became the raconteur and cheerleader on the picket line:

"Don't be a marshmallow! Come, walk the street with us into history!"

And they indeed walked right into the evening TV news, the legislatures, the courts, and history books.

·ଋ·

As a thirteen-year-old in 1965, I remember being so thrilled by their courage during the March to Delano and the longer grape strike that I convinced my mother and some of my aunts to forgo adding green grapes from California to their Jell-o salads!

A few years later, when picking strawberries for part of one summer near the Michigan-Indiana border, I spotted a UFW poster on a bulletin board announcing an event that had recently occurred, and I put it up in my bedroom. That's also where I picked up my first vinyl copy of the UFW's Teatro Campesino album, *Huelga in General*.

I was surely not the only American intrigued by what the UFW was accomplishing with so little financial resources. Attorney General Bobby Kennedy flew out to Delano to see Chávez while he was still fasting and to chastise a local sheriff for his cruel overreach in trying to break up the strike.

Writer Peter Matthiessen dropped everything to go work with the union for a few months. And famed Chicano musician Lalo Guerrero would write at home the "Corrido de Delano," then call his distant kin—Danny and Luis Valdez—while they were on the road with Teatro Campesino so they could take down the fresh lyrics to memorize and sing the next day.

·⁂·

The 1965 strike brought the key grape growers to the table to negotiate new contracts. But when the contracts expired, other growers in California did a sleight of hand trick to stiff Chávez and Huerta. Benefiting from a special agreement made behind closed doors, lettuce growers signed a contract with the International Brotherhood of Teamsters rather than with the UFW.

When César Chávez heard of the dirty dealings, he immediately went on a hunger strike against the other union. Soon a hasty and imperfect agreement was signed to return the jurisdiction over iceberg lettuce workers to the UFW.

Unfortunately, the agreement collapsed by August 1970, and seven thousand lettuce pickers went on strike in the Salinas Valley alone, in the largest farmworker strike in US history. Shipments of head lettuce in the United States ground to a halt, and the price of fresh lettuce nationwide doubled within weeks. The lettuce growers who had tried to do an end run around the UFW lost a half million dollars a day during the salad bowl strike, the equivalent of nearly four million dollars a day in 2024.

A California district court forbade Chávez, Huerta, and the UFW to do any more picketing and striking, an order they ignored. Defying the court ruling, the UFW called for a nationwide strike of all lettuce until their demands were met.

Violence broke out, a UFW office was bombed, and for the first time ever Chávez was jailed. He remained imprisoned for nineteen days, but when released, he immediately called for another strike against a half-dozen other lettuce growers. The strikes went on for three more months until the first days of spring in 1973, when the Teamsters and UFW signed another temporary agreement over their rights to negotiate for different sets of workers.

Again, the agreements failed when the Teamsters reneged on all former agreements and violence escalated. At least seventy picketing farmworkers were physically attacked, firebombs were thrown into the picket lines, and one UFW member was shot to death in August 1973. As its members feared for their lives, the UFW fell under such financial and legal stress that many felt it could never recover. Some of his detractors and enemies gloated that Chávez, Huerta, and Ross were all washed up.

This was indeed a messy, dangerous time to be involved in boycotts, strikes, or even negotiations with growers, government agencies, and other unions. Over a single decade, at least four thousand United Farm Worker members were jailed for picketing, and hundreds were hospitalized.

Instead of more rural rallies, mass picketing, or highly publicized boycotts, Huerta, Chávez, and Ross chose a less perilous path. Their next move was a quiet, 110-mile march with just a couple hundred UFW leaders from San Francisco to Modesto, where the Gallo winery and headquarters were located. It began on February 22, 1975.

As they slowly and solemnly moved down the highway, one carload after another joined them in their *caminata*, walking side by side in small groups. By the time they reached Modesto seven days later, Huerta, Chávez, and Ross had attracted another fifteen thousand supporters to share in their struggle.

The change in tone appealed not only to Governor Brown but to the California legislature as well. He worked with Dolores Huerta to write and then lobby for the Agricultural Labor Relations Act of

1975, a bill that would give farmworkers in California the right to organize for better compensation and working conditions. Within two months, they reached broad agreement on farm labor reform, and both the California Senate and State Assembly passed the bill in less than seventy days after the Modesto march.

That landmark agrarian labor legislation was signed into law by Brown in June of 1975 and implemented two months later. With two more years, the UFW and the Teamsters signed a broad but lasting agreement of jurisdiction of farm worker contracts. Exactly three years after the Modesto march, the UFW finally declared victory in 1977 and within the year ended all boycotts of iceberg lettuce, table grapes, and wine grapes for good.

That was a quarter century after Fred Ross had first knocked on the front door of the Chávez home in the Sal Si Puedes barrio, offering to mentor him in "organizing." It was not too long before César faced personal losses that devastated him, first the death of his mother in December 1991, and then, nine months later, the death of his finest mentor, Fred Ross. César gave the eulogies at their funeral; as usual, short, sweet, but with a few words that expressed all the love he felt for them.

Perhaps because of those losses, César decided to go with his brother Richard—who had become the life partner of Dolores—back to the part of Chihuahua where Papa Chayo was born to search for their family roots. They confirmed some oral history in their family they had never spoken about publicly: Part of their ancestry was from Raramuri or Tarahumara Indian farmers who had become virtual slaves to wealthy hacendados.

Not only had Papa Chayo fled to avoid a certain death as a young man in the Sierra but hundreds of other Raramuri had to do so as well. That journey back into the past convinced César, Richard, and Dolores that they had to do something to honor Papa Chayo and the land he had farmed in the hyper-arid desert of the Yuma Valley.

Soon after that trip to Mexico, César returned to Yuma but not simply to revisit the farm where his life began. Ironically, he went to defend himself and the UFW against a libel suit initiated by a large agribusiness corporation, one that had taken over Papa Chayo's farm and consolidated it into a larger operation.

Bruce Church, a conservative Republican, claimed that the union had libeled him and his organization. Furthermore, Church claimed that the UFW had threatened supermarkets to get them to stop selling his Red Coach lettuce. His lawyers asserted that the UFW had interfered in his sales of lettuce in a manner that was illegal.

Initially, a jury found the UFW culpable and ordered it to pay $5.4 million in damages, which would have made the union go bankrupt, forcing its demise. Chávez appealed the decision, and the case went back to trial on narrower grounds. The case dragged on from one year to the next, until lawyers requested an appeal in courts against the settlement, and César was ordered by the judge to testify in a Yuma court in 1993.

The stakes in this case could not have been higher for the UFW or to the Chávez family members personally.

While dealing with lawyers and judges in Arizona, Chávez stayed (as he almost always did) with a farmworker's family rather than putting a hotel room on his UFW tab. The family lived in San Luis del Río Colorado, not far from where Papa Chayo had first settled. It was near the stretch of the Colorado River where Cucupá and Quechan Indians had farmed for centuries, including Salvador Palma, the friend of Francisco Garcés. It was where Joaquín Murrieta, his wife, and brothers crossed into California for the Gold Rush.

At last, the gray-haired Chicano once called Manzie was back near the border, the desert, and the river where he had spent his childhood. To his old friends there, César seemed particularly weary and reflective about the long, strange journey he had undertaken over the course of his life. By that time, he was sixty-six years old and had been an unrelenting organizer for more than forty years.

On April 22 of that year, César began another fast for spiritual reasons. He appeared so fragile and fatigued that his family and friends pleaded with him to terminate that ritual, but perhaps their pleas came too late. César Chávez died during the night and was declared dead the next morning, April 23, 1993.

His body was flown to Bakersfield for an autopsy, where his body was placed in a coffin that his brother Richard had built for him. For the funeral procession in Delano later that week, 120 of his friends took turns serving as pallbearers in front of the fifty thousand people that came to César's memorial. It was the largest funeral for any union organizer in American history.

As Tim Z. Hernandez remembers that spring day from his boyhood in the San Joaquin Valley in 1993:

> Everyone's head is tightly wrapped around the news that César Chávez is dead. . . . When we finally reach Delano, bodies are lined up into one infinite snake and it's flowing through the streets and between cracks and over fences. From our parking lot on a low bluff, the main road through town looks like a mudslide of adobe brown, an amoeba shifting and growing. . . . In the bowels of the amoeba, people are shouting into bullhorns, ordering the crowd back into formation. But the crowd is singing, clapping, and stomping along, and shows no signs of order. Zeta and Jesús and I join in. Someone shouts out, "*¡Sí se puede!*" and we all begin to shout, "*¡Sí se puede!*" The chant carries us.

Since Chávez and Ross passed from the scene within six months of one another, Dolores was left to try to hold the union together in a new era. She began to do just that after the Chávez funeral, but despite her seniority and brilliance as a policy strategist, she was bypassed as the next president of the UFW. Within the next decade, she was slowly pushed out of the way by younger leaders. Huerta resigned in 2002 to spearhead the Dolores Huerta Foundation, which has continued to fight to the present day to gain social justice for many marginalized ethnicities.

At the age of eighty-nine, the beloved but at times bombastic Lola Huerta was arrested and placed in handcuffs during a protest in Fresno County, California, over the lack of adequate pay for caregivers who assist the elderly and disabled. Despite the many injuries and traumas she suffered over the three decades after Ross and Chávez died, Dr. Dolores Huerta continued her public speaking at events like her acceptance of at least eight honorary degrees and a Presidential Medal of Freedom.

Perhaps the most touching decoration she has received is the Order of the Aztec Eagle, the highest honor a foreign national can receive from the government of the Republic of Mexico. The Mexican president cited her fifty years of service helping the Mexican community in the United States fight for equal pay, dignity in the workplace, and fair employment practices in border states.

Should anyone presume that her brilliance might dim within our lifetimes, they should remember that her light will continue to shine in the universe through Asteroid 6849 Doloreshuerta, named in her honor by astronomers at the Palomar Observatory.

As of this writing, Lola remains a guiding star for many of us.

CHAPTER THIRTEEN

Huelga en General

Lalo Guerrero and Danny and Luis Valdez

IT WAS fitting that he would write a hit song called "Pancho Claus," for Eduardo "Lalo" Guerrero Murrieta was born in Tucson on Christmas Eve in 1916. His parents, Eduardo Senior and Concepción "Conchita" had eighteen offspring. Only eleven survived to adulthood, and Lalo was one of the lucky ones, for he squeaked through.

"It seemed like every year there was another little white coffin in the living room," Lalo later lamented, referring to the infant deaths of the triplets and twins that Conchita had carried to term.

By the time he turned five, a continent-wide smallpox epidemic had hit Tucson, killing a fifth of all those who contracted the virus over the next year. Tucson was one of the eight American cities most effected by the 1921–1922 smallpox outbreak. When the virus spread to the children in the Guerrero home, his parents feared that Lalo would succumb to the disease and be the next one to go. He survived, but Lalo's appearance and his confidence were badly scarred.

"The first time I saw my face after being so sick, I screamed," Lalo remembered, for the virus left him "pock-marked and ugly" in his own mind. To get under his skin, the boys in his grade school called him Cara de Metate, Face of a Grindstone, or Cacarizo, The One Who Is Pock-Marked or Pitted.

The fever had run its course, but Lalo had already turned inward, unwilling to go out into the street to face the ruffians in the Old Pueblo. He remained reticent and ashamed by his appearance for several years, even though his family moved to a better adobe home at 505 Meyer Street.

There, in what was then called Barrio Libre—now Barrio Viejo—he was teased and taunted by street waifs from his own hood, as well as by their rivals in Barrio Anita a mile to the north. His mother tried to protect and comfort him by taking him to "escape" into musicals and movies that featured great singers and dancers: Al Jolson, Fred Astaire, Ginger Rogers, and Rudy Vallée. The silver screen and all its melodies became his dream world, his sanctuary.

He often fell into a dreamy state where he imagined he was not in Tucson in a one-story adobe with all his many siblings but in a spacious theater or movie set, tap dancing up and down winding stairways with other singers, musicians, and chorus girls. Lalo learned to "escape into the imaginary worlds" that music could conjure up, for it seemed his dreams could become palpable.

At home on Meyer, his mother, Conchita, began teaching him to sing and dance to Mexican and Spanish tunes, clicking castanets and swirling her braids as she performed "La Jota Aragonesa" for him. Conchita, his older brothers, and cousins taught him to play the guitar, "and to love it, and to wrap my heart around it." Then, at age ten, he had taught himself how to play the piano.

Were it not for his Anglo music teacher at Drachman Grammar School, Miss Davis, Lalo—now called Eduardo or Eddie in school—would have never built up the courage to perform outside of their parlor on Meyer before his peers. Miss Davis introduced him to classical music, which he came to love and deeply study.

Lalo worked up the nerve to tell his favorite teacher that he had learned to tap dance from watching movies, so she brought in white gloves, a black hat, and makeup that covered his scars for his career launch at a student assembly at the ripe old age of twelve.

"I was a smash! When I heard the applause, I was hooked." He had found his "dream home."

The shy kid had been rehabilitated by his capacity to sing and dance. Suddenly, he felt comfortable out on the porch of their new home on Meyer Street. Lalo later conceded that he had "spent the happiest years of his life in that house," where "all the kids in the neighborhood used to come to play."

He began to seek out others in the barrio who also loved to play music, including Rudy Arenas, Eddie Matas, the Salaz brothers, and a boy of German and Mexican descent who lived across the tracks, Gilbert Ronstadt. By the age of fifteen, he had learned that his entrancing voice, charming smile, and uproarious sense of humor were enough to make his audience forget or ignore the roughness of his skin and cheeks.

With Manny and Rudy, Eddie Guerrero began to perform as a trio on KGAR radio for an hour every Monday singing pop hits in English like "My Blue Heaven" and "Lazy Bones." But at the same time, Eddie's alter ego, Lalo, was already penning his own *ranchera* and *norteño corridos* in Spanish, some of which he offered to older musicians around town, some that he performed on the "Mexican" radio stations on his own or with musicians his own age.

Very soon, crossing the tracks and crossing the boundaries of race, ethnicity, and class had become Lalo's modus operandi. He was a shape shifter, but, as always, he upheld and enriched the cultural traditions of the Sonoran Desert handed down to him from both his mother and father. Those cultural traditions ran deep in both sides of his family, for his ancestors had personally witnessed some of the most powerful expressions of resistance that had ever taken place in the Mexican Republic.

Ironically, his parents, Eduardo Senior and Concepción, had been wedded on the most important day in borderlands history, right at Ground Zero for an unprecedented explosion of social unrest in Mexico. Even though his father was originally from La Paz, Baja California, and his mother was from Joaquín Murrieta's famous clan in Sonora's Valle de Altar, they had decided to drive up into the mountains to the copper mining town Cananea to take their vows. Little did they know until they arrived in the company town owned by Colonel Greene that they would witness striking miners clashing with both Mexican law enforcers and gunslinging mercenaries called in by Colonel Greene from Bisbee, Arizona. In many ways, the Cananea conflict precipitated the Mexican Revolution on the Guerrero wedding day!

"Mama told me that right in the middle of the ceremony, bullets came flying through the church windows and they had to dive under the pews," Lalo recalled. "When the shooting stopped, they went back up to the altar and they got married and settled down to raise a family."

The newlyweds fled to the United States as war erupted in Mexico, first to Douglas, Arizona, and then to Tucson, but they never abandoned their Sonoran roots. Their house on Meyer became a bilingual, multicultural haven for other Sonoran and Chihuahuan refugees coming north to cross the border to escape both poverty and violence. Among those who stayed with the Guerreros at 505 Meyer for an extended period of time were the parents of Luis and Danny Valdez, whose family also had relatives around Caborca, Sonora, that also had kin who were part of Joaquín Murrieta's clan.

"Lalo was old enough to be an uncle," Danny once explained to me, for his grandmother and Lalo's mother were sisters.

They all grew up singing "El Corrido de Joaquín Murrieta" as if it were both a family anthem *and* a binational anthem:

A los ricos avarientos,	*From greedy rich,*
yo les quito su dinero.	*I took away their money.*
Con los humildes y pobres	*with the humble and the poor,*
yo me quito mi sombrero.	*I took off my hat.*
Ay, que leyes tan injustas	*Oh, what unjust laws*
fue llamarme bandolero . . .	*to label me an outlaw . . .*

Given this background, it is not surprising that over his eight-decade career writing songs, Lalo wrote some of the most potent and passionate songs of social justice that ever came out of the

Chicano movement. Whether paying homage to César Chávez, Ruben Salazár, or Bobby Kennedy, Lalo did not miss a lick.

·~·

After listening to Lalo's songs for two decades, I had the good fortune to spend an entire day side by side with him in front-row seats on a small bus, and then on identical stools out on the desert range of the Jornada del Muerto. The Jornada is a historic pilgrimage route through the hottest stretch of the Chihuahuan Desert, and its legacy was being featured by Denise Chavez at the Border Book Festival in Las Cruces. Denise adored Lalo as much as I did, so she set us up to do four or five stops where there would be fifty chairs and a mike set up in the middle of nowhere. Lalo would sing a few songs, then I would read a short poem or parable about the desert itself.

Lalo was already in his early eighties and seemed a bit shy for a man who had been lauded by presidents and Hollywood stars.

But when I told him that after getting married in my early twenties, my bride and I had lived on Meyer Street—the very place that he sang about in his classic lament, "Barrio Viejo"—he brightened up and became effusive.

"*¡Somos vecinos, pues!* Thanks to my mother, my musical friends, and mentors, those days in the barrio on Meyer were some of the most memorable of my entire career as a performer. Music in the streets. Música norteña, música romantica, and música ranchera! Green corn tamales, blanquillos con chorizo, burritos made with *sobaquera* tortillas the size of pizzas. *¡Ay, caramba!* I can still taste and see; I can still hear those days!"

It was much later that I realized that I had lived in the very same house on Meyer where Lalo and most of his ten surviving siblings had grown up. That realization stopped me in my tracks, right in the middle of Meyer Street on a 110-degree day in Barrio Viejo. I don't think I've ever recovered from that shock of that coincidence, even though there was a fifty-year gap between each of us dwelling there.

What intrigued me most about Lalo's stories that day in the Chihuahuan Desert was his emotional ambivalence about his family moving to Mexico City just as Lalo was going into his senior year of high school in Tucson. He never finished high school (nor did I), felt uprooted from his friends and the Norteño music they loved, and was bullied by Mexico City's chilangos and pachucos who called him a *pocho*, Caló street slang for an Americanized Mexican.

It was the height of the Depression, and Lalo's father was enticed to Mexico City by a Mexican government program to pay their former citizens to return to their homeland to rebuild its workforce and slow the "brain drain." Except for their two older boys who stayed behind to work in Tucson, Lalo's parents took the rest of the family to live in a compound with their uncle's families. Being uprooted was hard for not only Lalo's bruised ego but for his younger siblings.

And yet, that time in the big city was his rite of initiation into a larger, more diverse world of Latino music that constantly blasted out of speakers along every street and in every *mercado* and cantina. Lalo became acquainted with Afro-Cuban and Brazilian rhythms, with the *huapangos*, *sones*, *bambucos*, and *quereques* of Central Mexico. All of these he would later blend into the swing, big band jazz, and rock compositions that would make him famous as a composer. At the same time, three old street musicians in Mexico City showed Lalo how to riff off one another and improvise lyrical stories, making up verses on the spot. He became awed by the complexity and virtuosity of Mexico's greatest living composers, like Augustín Lara and Consuelo Velásquez.

His melodic universe had broken wide open with new influences from so many distinctive Latino cultures. Strangely, he didn't try to exactly imitate the masters; he stitched their styles into a big band sound of swing that crossed all genres and cultures. It would become his life's work to weave them into a single fabric—a crazy quilt—as the father of Chicano music.

He listened intently to the pachucos' Caló slang in the streets of

Mexico City but was still too young and poor to go into the cantinas and clubs with Mexico City's first wave of pachuco entertainers. But at that time, his own compositions still echoed the simpler, sweeter tunes and moods of the desert borderlands, which he longed for. He could not have imagined then that an achingly beautiful homage to Mexico's many musical styles that he composed when he was still a seventeen-year-old—without ever having stepped foot in Mexico—would become a hit all across Mexico.

"Canción Mexicana"—written just a few months before he moved to Mexico City—first became a chartbuster in 1941, when it was recorded by Mexico's most popular vocalist of that era, Lucha Reyes. Although it took Lalo months to understand how his lyrics had gotten into her hands, and why she had been listed as the song's composer, there was a bigger win for him in hearing her sing his song over Mexican radio:

A boy from the north country had written a song that insinuated its way into the heart of Mexico. For all his trauma in being pulled out of Tucson to start at the bottom again in Mexico City, his lyrics had spilled southward over the border to give most Mexicans something to be collectively proud of.

All this from a precociously talented seventeen-year-old pocho.

When he returned to Tucson after months away from the desert in Mexico City, he was eager to try out new rhythms and lyrical innovations from his new repertoire on his friends. They formed a group named Los Carlistas that broke all the racial barriers in Tucson, playing one night in small clubs to an all-Mexican audience, and the next night across the tracks at the swank Arizona Inn or El Conquistador to audiences that were largely Anglo. Then, on Sundays, they would play free concerts at Armory Park, just a few blocks from the railroad tracks that brought a young hobo named Woody Guthrie and his African American sidekick to Armory Park on their first ride west at the height of the Great Depression.

Within short order, the Carlistas sang a song for cowboy star Gene Autry in the Hollywood film *Boots and Saddles*, which began their recording career. Lalo would sing in Spanish on some records with the Carlistas, but then call himself Eddie and sing his compositions in English for another audience.

He moved to San Diego, then Los Angeles during World War II, where he mastered his Caló slang and threaded it into his mixes of American swing, Afro-Cuban, and Mexican rhythms in ways that drove the zoot-suiters wild. They would frantically dance to his big band arrangements, wearing their black balloon-leg pants, their broad-shouldered jackets, and bent-brimmed hats. Lalo was already aware that the whimsical Caló originated not in Chilangolandia but in West Texas, between El Paso, Del Rio, and San Antonio. He would later master it as a lyrical lexicon to put into his swing melodies that the zoot-suiters of East LA would later adopt as the anthem of la Raza.

But the East LA pachucos also affected Lalo and his music in other ways, by bringing in a subtle social conscience, especially after the zoot suit riots of 1943, when Anglo servicemen got into racial conflicts with Mexican Americans who had filled the jobs vacated by GIs going off to war. In June of 1943, the racial tensions spilled over after the August 1942 murder of José Díaz, one of the pachuco partygoers. In its wake, six hundred zoot-suiters and their girlfriends were rounded up by the LA police and temporarily jailed.

That triggered protests for months and slowly moved Lalo into writing lyrics that were more and more explicit about racial disparities. He penned songs like "Himno Chicano," "No Chicanos on TV," "La Tragedia del 29 de Agosto," and "Mexican Mamas, Don't Let Your Children Grow Up to Be Busboys." Four provocative songs he wrote during the pachuco era were later used by Luis Valdez in the play he wrote in 1979 about zoot suit riots, which attracted sellout crowds in both Los Angeles and New York. It was adapted into the 1981 film *Zoot Suit* that made Lalo's songs known to another generation of Chicanos on a national scale.

What most Americans may not know is that Lalo had already been influencing Danny and his brother Luis for years before *Zoot Suit*, not only because of family ties that linked all of them to the Murrieta in northern Sonora but because of their ties with César Chávez.

Both Lalo and Luis Valdez had had a glimpse of César Chávez at dances and other social gatherings long before they threw their hats in with his cause. As Lalo remembered their first encounters:

> When we played [for farmworkers] in the San Joaquin Valley around Bakersfield and Tulare, I noticed one young man who was there for every dance. He'd hang around the bandstand and talk to me at the breaks. He was very intelligent and gave me advice on the dates and places where I would find action in the fields and orchards. For a long time I knew his face, but not his name; he was just one of the guys.
>
> A few years later, everybody in California knew César Chávez. When I first met him, I don't think he had the slightest intention of doing what he did later on. . . . [Then] in the early sixties, César started organizing the workers to improve the situation for the people in the fields. He joined with another hero of our times, Dolores Huerta, to organize the United Farm Workers of America.

Lalo began to casually pen farmworker songs and play them at benefits for the UFW. When Luis Valdez went to Delano to ask Chávez if he and Augustín Lira could involve the farmworkers in street theater for social change, César offhandedly said, "Sure, I know your parents." After Danny left high school, he joined Luis and Augustín on the back of a borrowed flatbed truck, and they were grateful that Lalo allowed them to adapt some songs he had already penned.

Luis had been part of the San Francisco Mime Troupe before he and Augustín decided to form Teatro Campesino, improvising skits that the farmworkers themselves would perform. For their Banda Calavera, Danny also began to write and arrange tunes with Augustín, including "The Migrant's Song" and "El Sol Que Tu Quieres," which they later recorded with Linda Ronstadt.

·✥·

When I asked Luis about the historic roots of many of their songs, he simply referred to their lived experience.

"Our dad, Francisco, and maternal grandfather were strikers in Pixley, California, in 1933, when twelve thousand to eighteen thousand Chicanos and Filipinos had first come together. They protested cotton workers being evicted from company housing in the San Joaquin Valley. They were there in Pixley when two of the strikers—Delfino D'Avila and Dolores Hernández—were killed by vigilantes."

Eight other strikers were wounded after local sheriffs handed out permits to carry concealed weapons to six thousand citizens. Over a ten-year stretch, more than forty-seven thousand farmworkers engaged in at least thirty strikes in the San Joaquin during the 1930s.

> What I'm saying is that when we grew up in Delano and San José, we didn't get any history or resistance in classes that were supposed to cover US history or Mexican history. The references to these historic events in our songs and in my plays are from family history, oral history, lived history.
>
> I briefly worked in the fields at age six. My own paternal grandfather worked in the copper mine in Cananea, where the Mexican Revolution was ignited. Even the connection for me to the stories of Joaquín Murrieta are from my family's history. My maternal grandmother was born in Caborca, Sonora, and my maternal grandfather was from the Valley of Altar. Both grew up within short reach of where the Murrieta clan had remained strong, in smaller towns like Pitiquito and Trincheras.

Luis sighed and began again:

> Back in their time, the Altar Valley had already been depopulated by the Sonoran migration to California for the Gold Rush, and by emigration in general. But those who remained knew each other well. They kept alive the oral histories of the Murrieta brothers who had lived there, from Joaquín's time in the 1840s through their own time as children there. Those are the stories we grew up with, even where we settled in Delano and San José. But the history of the Murrietas and their kin is also engraved like a tattoo across the face of the California landscape.

Luis grew up hearing tales of the boom town of Sonora in Tuolumne County, the largest, most lucrative, and liveliest Mexican settlements along the Gold Country highway. He also heard of the legend of the Yoeme leader Cajeme, who lived at Yaqui Camp during the Gold Rush but returned to Sonora to serve as an Indigenous military leader who fought battles against Mexican governmental attempts to confiscate Yoemem lands in 1882.

Cajeme's name in the Cahitan language of the Yoemem was Kahe'eme, The One Who Does Not Stop to Drink Water, but his Christian name was José María Bonifacio Leyva Pérez, perhaps a descendant of the Leyvas whose dad assisted Juan de Banderas in the 1820s, when they tried to form an Indigenous nation north of Mexico.

These were the role models—heroes more than villains—who moved between the deserts of northern Mexico and the sierra of California. The oral histories that he grew up with captured the imagination of Luis Valdez throughout his songwriting and playwriting career over a half century.

This legacy of social justice and resistance later spilled into the plays and films that Luis and Danny developed for theater and for Hollywood, first *I Am Joaquín*, then *Zoot Suit*, *La Bamba*, and *Bandido!* *Zoot Suit* became the first-ever Chicano full-length Hollywood feature film.

But participatory, improvised street theater—not high-cost films—remained the hallmark of Teatro Campesino and its spinoffs. In the late 1960s, the Valdez brothers drove the Banda Calavera truck gifted to them by the UFW all the way to Chicago, where they performed street theater skits in Chicano barrios in the Windy City. Luis left Teatro Campesino by the end of 1967, but the troupe was honored with an Obie Award for "demonstrating the politics of survival" and with the Los Angeles Drama Critics Award in 1969.

Within two more years, there was an explosion of Chicano street theater troupes throughout the United States, and the movement spread to the rest of Latin America by 1970. It then blended with other artistic expressions of cultural resistance, such as liberation theology and the *volcante* music of Central America that was also inspired by the poetry of Ernesto Cardenal, the Nicaraguan priest, poet, and promoter of primitivist art. As Yolanda Broyles-González later confirmed from surveys across America: "In virtually all centers of Chicana/o population as well as on campuses everywhere, theater groups sprang up that became dedicated to portraying the life, heritage, and problems of Chicanas/os in this country."

Nevertheless, the last word(s) on this movement came from the participants in the Teatro Campesino *actos*, in a manifesto they wrote for themselves:

> Inspire the audience to social action. Illuminate specific points about social problems. Satirize the opposition. Show or hint at a solution. Express what people are feeling . . .
>
> So what's new, right? Plays have been doing that for thousands of years. True, except the major emphasis in the acto is the social vision, as opposed to the individual artist or playwright's vision. Actos are not written. They are created collectively.

CHAPTER FOURTEEN

Sanctuary

Jim Corbett, Ramón Dagoberto Quiñones, and John Fife

MANY OF you may have had an experience like the one I am about to describe: You meet a friend through other friends, and are glad to get to know them, because it seems they have done intriguing if not admirable things in their life before you met them.

And yet, it only slowly—perhaps belatedly—dawns upon you that this individual or group of individuals are making history while you know them, by changing the way Americans think about themselves and their neighbors.

I am not speaking of celebrities, although some of these friends have occasionally been treated that way, but immediately retreated from accepting the notion that they themselves are special. Instead, they regard the people with whom they work as special and deserving of having *their own voices* heard.

They simply go about their daily business not as a *special*-ist but as a *popul*-ist, in service to the larger pueblo within which they belong.

That sort of sums up my on-again, off-again friendships with Jim Corbett and John Fife. The two of them—along with Father Ramón Dagoberto Quiñones, Maria Del Socorro Pardo Viuda De Aguilar, Steve Knapp, Sister Darlene Nicgorski, Phil Willis-Conger, and Demetria Martinez—can be said to be in the front line if not the founding circle of the sanctuary movement.

This international movement brought tens of thousands of refugees into the United States and Canada and held them in churches, synagogues, mosques, and homes across the United States. It also changed government policies and public empathies with regard to political refugees. But as it began in the 1970s and 1980s, it initially seemed less like a movement and more like friends helping friends.

Soon after I moved to Tucson in the mid-1970s, I joined a community garden and goat-milking collective in a vacant lot near the corner of Mountain and Prince. At first, I guessed we'd be largely talking about our seed selections, gardening techniques, and techniques for milking goats without getting the buckets kicked over.

We did talk about all of that, but also much more. I came to realize that many in the group were deeply committed to improving cross-border relations between the United States and our Latin American neighbors, relations that have been plagued by humanitarian problems for decades.

Among the participants were a "Quaker" couple, Jim and Pat Corbett, who lived two miles east of the garden. They were older than the rest of us, but as engaged as any in the group. As seasoned ranchers who had run their family's ranch an hour north of Tucson, they had fundamental knowledge of goat raising and milking that some of the rest of us lacked.

But more intriguing was that Jim had elaborated the philosophy of goat walking, a spiritual practice like walking meditation, except that it included accompanying a small herd of goats into the desert wilderness, drinking little besides goat milk, and eating the same prickly pear fruit, mesquite pods, and wild quelite greens that they did.

Sharing the same diet with his goats, Jim grew out his iconic goatee and gained a determined stubbornness and resolve from his herd that helped him greatly in his later years of trial.

Jim and Pat had a weekly gathering at their house called Los Cabreros Andantes. They cohosted it when he was home, but Jim was often in Baja California Sur helping a small collective improve their herds with milk goats so that they could make high-value cheeses. These cheeses would bring them more income off the same acreage than what could be gained simply by grazing larger herds harder for meat alone.

One time when Jim was away, a fellow gardener whispered that she believed Jim had begun goat walking for political reasons. She claimed that years before, he went "on the hoof" after breaking into a federal draft office to destroy papers in protest of the Vietnam War.

Jim would disappear into the Superstition wilderness for days or weeks while the FBI was searching for him and watching entries and exits to the Corbett Ranch near Florence, Arizona. The more Jim went goat walking, the more he believed it was the perfect antidote to the diseases of Western civilization. (And he looked more like a goat, which may have slowed down any FBI agents who were looking for someone who looked like a Harvard graduate!)

While I hesitated to ask Jim about his time as a fugitive in his own country, we did talk openly about our travels in Mexico, including our visits to the same goat-herding rancherías on the east coast of the Baja California peninsula.

One day, Jim mentioned that he was trimming down on trips to Baja California because he needed to investigate what was happening to Salvadorans and other Central Americans fleeing from gangs and death squads to the south of us. On one of his trips back from Baja, he innocently picked up a hitchhiker on the side of a Mexican highway; the refugee simply told Jim the horrors he had been through, and that was enough to jumpstart Jim's service to refugees. He had then begun going down to "the other Mexican border" with Guatemala, to figure out what routes were being taken up to the northern border by refugees.

Jim had also visited churches, jails, and flophouses to talk to men who had left their homelands as political refugees. Jim cryptically mentioned to me something in passing about the need for an "underground railroad" like escaped slaves had used to get out of the South. But at that time, making such a concept operable in the late twentieth century seemed too immense for me to even take it in.

It was not too immense for Jim's inquiring mind, to be sure.

"How did you even get into the jails in Mexico for visits?" I wondered.

"Well, I went with some of the priests from Nogales who regularly offered communion to the prisoners, some of whom are refugees. They got me a minister's collar and other paraphernalia and told the guards that I was another minister who would be coming along to help with receiving confessions and such."

One of those Nogales priests—a Padre Ramón—has simply begun to call Corbett Padre Jaime. Because Jim hadn't stepped into a Catholic church since he was a boy and didn't know any of the clerical jargon or hand jive, they explained to the guards that Jim was from a rare minor order, La Sociedad de los Amigos.

Later, as Jim got to know the prisoners some, the priest would introduce the Quaker as "*un quakero muy catolico*."

Remembering the incident, Jim laughed out loud, his eyes twinkling.

"Hell, I'm pretty sure I've been called a quack plenty of times, but never a quakero before. I've attended the Pima Friends meetings in Tucson for years, but never formally joined the Society of Friends anyway. My religion—if I have one—has always been broader than any one denomination."

An exceptional priest for the diocese in Nogales, Ramón Dagoberto Quiñones, had been surreptitiously helping political refugees get across the border "from one Nogales (Sonora) to the other (in Arizona)" for some time.

"It's my priestly duty," he explained to others, "to help the persecuted and house the homeless." As Padre Ramón saw it, that was part of any priest's job description, not an add-on to consider under extraordinary circumstances.

Padre Ramón, along with his close colleague Doña Maria del Socorro Pardo de Aguilar, would later be the two Mexican citizens tried in the United States along with Jim, John, and others for human trafficking and other crimes, but they were not at all new to dealing with social justice dilemmas in Mexico. For years, they had been helping refugees get to the border to find holes in the fence to get across to Sacred Heart Catholic Church, where priests and volunteers would help them resettle in the United States.

Ironically, there was nothing "illegal" by Mexican law in what they were doing to assist refugees reach Sacred Heart of Jesus Catholic Church three miles to the north of their own Sanctuario de Nuestra Señora de Guadalupe, one of the most vibrant churches in Nogales, Sonora. Their advice to refugees going north into Arizona was not considered "trafficking" by Mexican law, for they were merely making the outcasts aware of the potential perils to avoid along their journey.

Padre Ramón's own mentor had been key to the resistance movement during the nightmarish Cristero War in Mexico, from 1926 to 1929, a popular uprising against the anti-Catholic government of Plutarco Elia Calles. Later in his career, his mentor became a bishop in Sonora and offered Padre Quiñones a buffer from more conservative officials in the Roman Catholic hierarchy.

This must have been about the time that Jim Corbett and John Fife had a quiet conversation that changed both men's lives. As John recalled their dialogue decades later, Jim approached him:

"John, I don't think we have any choice under the circumstances except to start smuggling refugees safely across the border so they're not captured and imprisoned and deported."

John was thrown off kilter, and snapped back, "*Really?* How do you figure that?"

That's when Jim offered John two landmark moments in history as reference points for the current dilemma at the border.

Jim first made the analogy with nineteenth-century efforts to help Blacks escape from slavery in the southeastern United States. Some churches had consciously chosen to help runaway slaves flee safely across state lines. The churches helped Black leaders like Harriet Tubman find safe havens along underground railroad routes to move fugitives to safer and safer places.

Jim then summarized the first analogy:

"As we read history today, they got it right. They were faithful."

John nodded in agreement.

"Well, yeah, yeah, it's true."

Then Jim pointed to the lack of action by most churches in America in the 1930s and 1940s to protect Jewish and other refugees fleeing the Holocaust in Europe. He said to John, "As we read history now, we call that a complete failure of the church to be faithful."

John said, "Yeah."

And then Jim played his ultimate card, saying, "Well, I don't think we can allow that to happen on our border in our time, can we?"

John was stunned. He simply said, "What do you mean, *we*?"

Jim said, "I mean, *we*."

So John puzzled over this moral dilemma for several sleepless nights, and finally went back to Jim to say this: "Yeah, you're right. I gotta hand in my human being card if I don't sign up with you."

What Jim had noted sunk in, so much so that John had arrived at a turning point for his ethical decision-making around the whole issue.

That's when they started a secretive refugee "travel assistance program" on the border in cooperation with Padre Ramón and Doña Maria, who were running a shelter for Central American refugees in Nogales, Sonora, as means to protect them from Mexican police and immigration.

·❦·

Something new began happening among the members of the goat-walking and gardening group about that time. It seemed everyone was scurrying around acquiring clothes, food, and lodging options for "church visitors" from other countries.

Jim was seldom seen, but when I did see him, there were hints that he had been "goat walking" across the border, from New Mexico westward toward the higher reaches of the Arizona-Sonora border. He casually mentioned that some of the ranchers we both knew along the border had said hi to me.

He also asked if my wife and I were proficient enough in Spanish to help take down formal testimonies of Spanish speakers who wished to legally file for political refugee status in the United States.

> Well, either of you can get some training from our friends in Tucson, or down in Nogales, but the formal trips to help those being held in detention camps might take you as far as El Centro. And you should get to know John Fife's congregation down at Southside Presbyterian Church. Right now, they have a temporary site down near the airport, while they are getting a new church built near one of the Yaqui and O'odham barrios near the expressway in South Tucson. The volunteers at Southside might be able to alert you to when groups are carpooling to take down personal testimonies at various detention centers.

While my partner took off to El Centro to record refugee testimonies, I took our baby son down with me to Southside one Sunday to meet John after a church service. But it was like no other church service I had been to, for it was in multiple languages: Spanish, English, and O'odham *ha-neoki*. The gathering was more like a two-hour dialogue and interplay of different cultures, with gospel music, Mexican folk songs, and full participation of everyone in petitions and prayers.

They were walking the talk, or, as we say along the border, walking the taco.

Not long after that, we received a mid-evening call from a colleague in our garden and goat group.

"Gary, I'm wondering if you could meet me down at the Denny's. We have some distinguished visitors from Guatemala passing through Tucson, and I remembered that you have spent time helping train some Peace Corps volunteers down that way. You might know some people in common."

When I arrived at Denny's, my friend introduced me to three generations of a Guatemalan family: a grandmother in her midfifties; a daughter who had recently lost her husband due to paramilitary incursions into their home village; a toddler; and a newborn baby.

They never told me their last names, nor did they mention whether they had passports and visas, only that that they were hoping to be reunited with the young widow's sister in Los Angeles within a few days. I didn't ask.

Instead, my friend from the community garden asked me a question that would subtly change the course of my life in the borderlands:

Could they possibly stay in your extra room for two or three nights, so that they had time to make travel arrangements with the sister?

They were with us day and night for more than three weeks. They waited until their kin in LA could finally arrange a room for them in a garage behind the house where she had been working as a maid and babysitter. I could palpably feel their trauma as they told me bits of the migration story, weeping or bickering over minor points about their journey.

To this day, I have no idea whether they settled safely and permanently in LA or whether they returned to Guatemala. All I know for sure is the Catholic Padre Ramón, Presbyterian Padre John, and quakero Padre Jaime had built a safety net that successfully harbored refugee family members like them who had no other place to immediately go. And by doing so, some of us "innocent bystanders" were touched by their lives and began to face issues we had previously ignored.

•⁂•

At some point, John and Jim became convinced that there were undercover agents in their midst, and that they were probably being wiretapped by federal agents. About the same time, I was in journal-stuffing parties across town for Earth First!, and we had undercover agents kindly help us put our new journal issues in covers and stitch address labels onto them.

Fortunately, the agents spying on all of us were so inept at clandestine recording that few of the transcripts of their tapes were of much value in court cases. (That would later help Jim Corbett be acquitted of all charges and allow some of the Earth Firsters to be freed on probation after plea agreements.)

But unlike Earth First!–inspired "eco-terrorists"—who were rarely present at our stuffing parties—Jim and John decided to go public about what they were doing on behalf of refugees with no other viable options.

Deliberating how to go public, their inner circle was aware that five churches in Berkeley had already declared themselves a sanctuary for military personnel who opposed the war in Vietnam in 1971. Steve Knapp had drafted a "Sanctuary Covenant" that was endorsed by the Berkeley City Council in November of that year. After the first resolution had passed, nine other resolutions were added to protect other ethnic groups and vulnerable populations from governmental abduction and from hate crimes.

John Fife then pitched the same idea to Tucsonans as means to legitimize their efforts: "Well, maybe we could call the church a sanctuary for Central American refugees because that's what we've been doing; we've been hiding out refugees for some time now, almost a year."

Everyone in their interfaith circle agreed on the strategy, but thought it best if the Southside church made its declaration first:

"Oh yeah," they laughed. "You try that." Only then they would follow.

To be sure, the elaboration of the legal basis for sanctuary and empathy with it took many tragedies and many years before it was publicly accepted. But what may have prompted the immediate need for it in southern Arizona was the July 1980 death of thirteen

Salvadorans in the Sonoran Desert eighty-seven miles west of Tucson, who were among twenty-six refugees abandoned by their coyotes and left without water to die.

On March 24, 1982, the second anniversary of Archbishop Romero's assassination in El Salvador, John Fife held a press conference announcing that Southside would be sheltering four members of a Salvadoran family in the sanctuary of its church. Within a year, some 1,600 Central American refugees would transit through Southside to safe houses around the country.

That was the onset of a continent-wide sanctuary movement that in many ways continues to this day. Four other churches across the nation immediately agreed to offer sanctuary to refuges, and then synagogues, Buddhist temples, and Muslim mosques joined in.

Yes, there were trials *and* tribulations, but there emerged a kind of solidarity among people on both sides of the border that has not been extinguished. It has evolved into what John Fife now calls "an entire ecosystem of support groups for refugees and immigrants in need." One simple gesture by Padre Ramón exemplifies that kind of collective safety net.

When my friend Bill Risner advised Padre Ramón as his lawyer that as a Mexican citizen, he had no legal reason to agree to be tried with the US citizens involved in the sanctuary movement, the priest felt a need to stand together with the other defendants. For him, they were all grounded and bonded in the same "communion of faith," so there was no moral reason that he would evade the same charges that his colleagues were facing, even though the charges were baseless in Mexico. Padre Ramón summarized his ethical commitments this way:

"It is the mission of the church to help the poor and needy, and these charges against me aren't even crimes in Mexico. I believe I had to give witness to my calling, even if it meant risking persecution. This *is* my calling."

·∾·

It has become the calling of many others as well, even after Padre Ramón was found guilty of one count of conspiracy and one misdemeanor and then given five years of probation. By the time he got back to Mexico after that symbolic slap on the hand, there were already others in Nogales, Sonora, who were helping him complete construction on an expansion of El Sanctuario so he could house twice as many refugees.

At last count, there are more than eight hundred other houses of worship that have opened their doors as sanctuaries to protect refugees and other immigrants from being deported. Two hundred religious orders—Christian, Buddhist, and otherwise—have endorsed sanctuary as an ethical responsibility. Rallying around the moral imperative of sanctuary for political and climate refugees, six hundred faith-based and interfaith nonprofits have now offered support to refugees, and 3,300 priests, rabbis, imams, and roshis have lent their names to this cause.

What had begun on back roads in the desert and holes in the border fence engendered an ethical stance by hundreds of thousands of US and Mexican citizens to work together for immigration justice.

Acknowledgments

Before anything else, I wish to acknowledge my debt to Dr. William Carlos Williams, whose 1925 book from New Directions—*In the American Grain*—has enriched and inspired me for years as the first great poetic history of America. Hats off, too, to Eduardo Galeano for further advancing this realm of truly literary history. My deep debt to Stephen Hull, Sonia Dickey, Anna Pohlod, and Don Redpath at the University of New Mexico Press, as well as Enrique Lamadrid and Drew Bryan, for "keeping the faith" cannot be fully expressed; so, too, with my literary agent, Victoria Shoemaker.

If any four scholars got me going on the path that this book has explored, they were Edward "Ned" Spicer, James Griffith, Amadeo Rea, and Thomas E. Sheridan. Throw in the longtime scholarly influence of Bunny Fontana, Susan Shillinglaw, Octaviana Trujillo, Ruben Martínez, Juan Estevan Arrellano, Enrique Madrid, Jack Loeffler, Denise Chávez, Ernesto Camou Healy, Cynthia Radding de Murrieta, Larry Evers, and Rick Brusca, and I have indeed been fortunate. In addition, note my reliance on the wisdom of Miriam Davidson, Manual Monroy, Ernesto Molina, Maria Varela, Antonio Manzanares, Cathy Moser, Robert Valencia, Ernie Atencio, and Felipe Molina, and you understand how lucky I am to live in a circle of people who intensely love and understand the dynamic of desert cultures. More recently, I have been wisely informed by Alberto Mellado Jr., Kelly Lytle Hernandez, Estevan Ancona, Mark Guerreo, Jeff Biggers, Will Kaufman, Ernesto Molina, Devon Peña, Ernie Atencio, Anibel Galindo, Anna M. Nogar, Evelyn Hu-de Harte,

DeJa Walker, Jennifer Koshatka Sema, Mona Polacca, Robert Irwin, Jeff Biggers, Rafael Brewster Folsom, Tim Z. Hernandez, and Teresa Lysight.

I have been honored to have had face time and dialogue—however briefly—with the likes of Lalo Guerrero, Luis and Danny Valdez, Arturo Sandoval, George "Elfie" and Maia Ballis, Tim Z. Hernandez, Luis Urrea, Jim and Pat Corbett, John Fife, and Enrique and Ruby Madrid, all of whom are featured in these interlocking essays. They remain my heroes and spiritual compasses.

Further Reading and Cited Literature

Introduction

Gibson, Carrie. *El Norte: The Epic and Forgotten History of Hispanic North America*. New York: Atlantic Monthly Press, 2019.

Hernández, Kelly Lytle. *Bad Mexicans: Race, Empire and Revolution in the Borderlands*. New York: W. W. Norton, 2022.

Williams, William Carlos. *In the American Grain*. San Francisco: New Directions, 1925.

Resistance

Evers, Larry, and Felipe S. Molina. "The Holy Dividing Line: Inscription and Resistance in Yaqui Culture." *Journal of the Southwest* 34, no. 1 (Spring 1992).

Evers, Larry, and Felipe S. Molina. *Yaqui Deer Songs/Maso Bwikam: A Native American Poetry*. Tucson: University of Arizona Press, 1987.

Folsom, Raphael Brewster. *The Yaquis and Empire*. New Haven, CT: Yale University Press, 2014.

Hu-DeHart, Evelyn. *Missionaries, Miners, and Indians: Spanish Contact with the Yaqui Nation of Northwest Mexico*. Tucson: University of Arizona Press, 1981.

Molina, Felipe, and Herminia Valenzuela, with David L. Shaul. *Yoeme-English/English Yoeme Standard Dictionary*. New York: Hippocrene Books, 1999.

Smith, T. Buckingham. *The Relation of Alvar Nuñez Cabeza de Vaca, 1871*. Ithaca, NY: Cornell University Press, 2009.

Spicer, Edward H. *The Yaquis: A Cultural History*. Tucson: University of Arizona Press, 1980.

Metamorphosis

Adorno, Rolena, and Patrick Pautz. *Álvar Núñez Cabeza de Vaca: His Account, His Life, and the Expedition of Panfilo de Narváez*. Lincoln: University of Nebraska Press, 1999.

Folsom, Raphael Brewster. *The Yaquis and Empire*. New Haven, CT: Yale University Press, 2014.

Herrick, Dennis. *Esteban: The African Slave Who Explored America*. Albuquerque: University of New Mexico Press, 2018.

Krieger, Alex D., and Margery H. Krieger, eds. *We Came Naked and Barefoot: The Journey of Cabeza de Vaca Across America*. Austin: University of Texas Press, 2002.

Lalami, Laiila. *The Moor's Account*. New York: Pantheon, 2014.

Nabhan, Gary Paul. "Hungry for Home: Mostafa al-Azemmouri Discovers a New World of Desert Foods." In *Desert Terroir*. Austin: University of Texas Press, 2012.

Newcomb, W. W., Jr. *The Indians of Texas*. Austin: University of Texas Press, 1961.

Schneider, Paul. *Brutal Journey: Cabeza de Vaca and the Epic Crossing of America*. New York: Henry Holt, 2006.

Valdez, Luis, and Sten Steiner. *Aztlan: An Anthology of Mexican-American Literature*. New York, Vintage Books, 1972.

Volition

Colahan, Clark. *The Vision of Sor María de Ágreda: Writing, Knowledge, and Power*. Tucson: University of Arizona Press, 1994.

Llamas, P. Enrique. *La Madre Ágreda y la Mariología de Vaticano II*. Madrid: Editorial Arca de Alianza, 2006.

Morganthaler, Jefferson. *The River Has Never Divided Us: A Border History of La Junta de los Rios*. Austin: University of Texas Press, 2004.

Nogar, Anna M. *Quill and Cross in the Borderlands: Sor María de Ágreda and the Lady in Blue*. Notre Dame, IN: University of Notre Dame Press, 2018.

Nogar, Anna M., and Enrique R. La Madrid. *Sisters in Blue: or María de Ágreda Comes to New Mexico*. Albuquerque: University of New Mexico Press, 2023.

Abyss

Brown, Alan K. *With Anza to California 1775–1776: The Journal of Pedro Font, OFM*. Norman: University of Oklahoma Press, 2011.

Santiago, Mark. *Massacre at the Yuma Crossing: Spanish Relations with the Quechans*. Tucson: University of Arizona Press, 1988.

Sheridan, Thomas E., and Bill Broyles. "First Europeans to Forty-Niners: 1540–1854." In *Last Water on the Devil's Highway: Cultural and Natural History of Tinaja Altas*, edited by Bill Broyles, Gayle Harrison Hartman, Thomas E. Sheridan, Gary Paul Nabhan, and Mary Charlotte Tuttle. Tucson: University of Arizona Press, 2012.

Indigenous Nationhood

Folsom, Raphael Brewster. *The Yaquis and Empire*. New Haven, CT: Yale University Press, 2014.

Gonzalez, Gregorio. Review of *Are We Not Foreigners Here? Indigenous Nationalism in the US–Mexico Borderlands*, by Jeffrey Schulze. *American Indian Culture and Research Journal* 42, no. 1 (2018).

Hu-Duhart, Evelyn. *Missionaries, Miners and Indians: Spanish Contact with the Yaqui Nations of Northwestern Spain, 1533–1820*. Tucson: University of Arizona Press, 2014.

Hu-Duhart, Evelyn. *Yaqui Resistance and Survival: The Struggle for Land and Autonomy, 1821–1910*. Madison: University of Wisconsin Press, 1984.

McEnroe, Sean F. *From Colony to Nationhood in Mexico: Laying the Foundations, 1560–1840*. Cambridge: Cambridge University Press, 2012.

Spicer, Edward H. *The Yaquis: A Cultural History*. Tucson: University of Arizona Press, 1980.

Race

Irwin, Robert McKee. *Bandits, Captives, Heroines, and Saints: Cultural Icons of Mexico's Northwest Borderlands*. Minneapolis: University of Minnesota Press, 2007.

Irwin, Robert McKee. "The Union of Coyote Iguana and Lola Casanova Set in a Time of Crisis." *Journal of the Southwest* 63, no. 4 (Winter 2024).

Lowell, Susan, and Edith Lowell. "Dining with Lola and Coyote: A Conversation." *Journal of the Southwest* 63, no. 4 (Winter 2024).

Mellado Moreno, Alberto. *Los Comcaac: Una Historia Narativa II*. Hermosillo/Punta Chueca: Nakima Impresos, 2020.

Mellado Moreno, Alberto. "The Oral Histories of Coyote Iguana and Dolores Casanova Among the Comcaac." *Journal of the Southwest* 63, no. 4 (Winter 2024).

Moser-Marlett, Mary Beck, and Roberto Tompson. "Seri History (1904): Two Documents." *Journal of the Southwest* 30, no. 4 (Winter 1998).

Nabhan, Gary Paul. "How Good Is Oral History and What Is It Good For? Upshot of Comcaac Oral Histories of Coyote Iguana and Lola Casanova as Cultural Resistance by a Persistent Indigenous People." *Journal of the Southwest* 63, no. 4 (Winter 2024).

Rebellion

Acosta Figueroa, Alfredo. *Joaquin Murrieta: Hero of the Chicano*. Blythe, CA: International Association of the Descendents of Joaquin Murrieta, 2020.

Acosta Figueroa, Alfredo. *Xicana: Origin and Ethnology*. Blythe, CA: La Cuna de Atzlan Publications, 2023.

Bacon, David. *Communities Without Borders: Images and Voices of the World of Immigration*. Ithaca, NY: ILR Press/Cornell University Press, 2006.

Garza, Humberto. *Demystifying the Murrieta Legend*. San José: Sun House Publishing, 2004.

Garza, Humberto. *Joaquin Murrieta: A Quest for Justice!* San José: Sun House Publishing, 2002.

Irwin, Robert McKee. *Bandits, Captives, Heroines, and Saints: Cultural Icons of Mexico's Northwest Borderlands*. Minneapolis: University of Minnesota Press, 2007.

Sheridan, Thomas E., and Bill Broyles. "First Europeans to Forty-Niners: 1540–1854." In *Last Water on the Devil's Highway: Cultural and Natural History of Tinaja Altas*, edited by Bill Broyles, Gayle Harrison Hartman, Thomas E. Sheridan,

Gary Paul Nabhan, and Mary Charlotte Tuttle. Tucson: University of Arizona Press, 2012.

Valdez, Luis, and Sten Steiner. *Aztlan: An Anthology of Mexican-American Literature*. New York, Vintage Books.

Revolution

Folsom, Raphael Brewster. *The Yaquis and Empire*. New Haven, CT: Yale University Press, 2014.

Griffith, James S. *Folk Saints of the Borderlands: Victims, Bandits and Healers*. Tucson: Río Nuevo Press, 2013.

Hernández, Kelly Lytle. *Bad Mexicans: Race, Empire and Revolution in the Borderlands*. New York: W. W. Norton, 2022.

Holden, William Curry. *Teresita*. Owings Mills, MD: Stemmer House, 1978.

Irwin, Robert McKee. *Bandits, Captives, Heroines, and Saints: Cultural Icons of Mexico's Northwest Borderlands*. Minneapolis: University of Minnesota Press, 2007.

La Madrid, Enrique R. "'El Corrido de Tomochic': Honor, Grace, Gender, and Power in the First Ballad of the Mexican Revolution." *Journal of the Southwest* (1999): 441–60.

Seman, Jennifer Koshatka. *Borderlands Curanderos: The Worlds of Santa Teresa Urrea and Don Pedrito Jaramillo*. Austin: University of Texas Press, 2021.

Taibo, Paco Ignacio II. *Yaquis: Historia de Una Guerra Popular y de Un Genocidio en México*. México: Planeta, 2013.

Urrea, Luis Alberto. *The Hummingbird's Daughter*. New York: Little, Brown and Company, 2019.

Urrea, Luis Alberto. *Queen of America*. New York: Little, Brown and Company, 2011.

Vanderwood, Paul W. *The Power of God Against the Guns of Government: Religious Upheaval at the Turn of the Nineteenth Century*. Palo Alto, CA: Stanford University Press, 1998.

Dust

Guthrie, Woody. *Bound for Glory*. New York: E. P. Dutton, 1943.

Guthrie, Woody. *Seeds of Man*. New York: E. P. Dutton, 1976.

Hernández, Tim Z. *All They Will Call You*. Tucson: University of Arizona Press, 2017.

Hernández, Tim Z. *Breathing, In Dust*. Lubbock: Texas Tech University Press, 2010.

Hernández, Tim Z. *They Call You Back*. Tucson: University of Arizona Press, 2024.

Kaufman, Will. *Mapping Woody Guthrie*. Norman: University of Oklahoma Press, 2019.

Kaufman, Will. *Woody Guthrie, American Radical*. Chicago: University of Illinois Press, 2011.

Tierra o Muerte

Gutiérrez, José Angel. *Tracking King Tiger: Reies López Tijerina, and the FBI*. East Lansing: Michigan State University Press, 2019.

Gutiérrez, Ramón A. *New Mexico's Moses: Reies López Tijerina, and the Religious Origins of the Civil Rights Movement*. Albuquerque: University of New Mexico Press, 2022.

Nabokov, Peter. *Tijerina and the Courthouse Raid*. Berkeley: Ramparts, 1970.

Oropeza, Lorena. *The King of Adobe: Reies López Tijerina, Lost Prophet of the Chicano Movement*. Chapel Hill: University of North Carolina Press, 2019.

Tijerina, Reies López. *They Called Me "King Tiger": My Struggle for the Land and Our Rights*. Houston: Arte Público Press, 2000.

Valdez, Luis, and Stan Steiner. *Aztlan: An Anthology of Mexican-American Literature*. New York: Vintage Books, 1972.

Boycott

Bacon, David. *Communities Without Borders: Images and Voices of the World of Immigration*. Ithaca, NY: ILR Press/Cornell University Press, 2006.

Ferriss, Susan, and Ricardo Sandoval. *The Fight in the Fields: Cesar Chavez and the Farmworkers Movement*. New York: Harcourt Brace, 1977.

García, Margo T. *A Dolores Huerta Reader*. Albuquerque: University of New Mexico Press, 2008.

García, Matt T. *From the Jaws of Victory: The Triumph and Tragedy of Cesar Chavez and the Farmworkers Movement*. Berkeley: University of California Press, 2012.

Jensen, Richard J., and John H. Hammerback. *The Words of César Chávez*. College Station: Texas A&M University Press, 2004.

Matthiessen, Peter. *Sal Si Puedes: Cesar Chavez and the New American Revolution*. Berkeley: University of California Press, 1969.

Valdez, Luis, and Stan Steiner. *Aztlan: An Anthology of Mexican-American Literature*. New York: Vintage Books, 1972.

Huelga en General

Broyles-González, Yolanda. *Teatro Campesino: Theater in the Chicano Movement*. Austin: University of Texas Press, 1994.

Guerrero, Lalo, and Sherilyn Meece Mentes. *Lalo: My Life and Music*. Tucson: University of Arizona Press, 2002.

Loza, Steven. *Barrio Rhythm: Mexican-American Music in Los Angeles*. Chicago: University of Illinois Press, 1993.

Valdez, Luis. *Luis Valdez: Early Works*. Houston: Arte Publico Press, 1994.

Valdez, Luis. *Zoot Suit and Other Plays*. Houston: Arte Publico Press, 1992.

Valdez, Luis, and Michael M. Chemers. *The Theater of the Sphere: The Vibrant Being*. London: Routledge, 2021.

Sanctuary

Bacon, David. *Illegal People: How Globalization Immigration Creates Migration and Criminalizes Immigrants*. Boston: Beacon Press, 2009.

Corbett, James A. *Goatwalking: A Guide to a Peaceable Kingdom*. New York: Viking/Penguin, 1999.

Corbett, James A. *Sanctuary for All Life*. Cascabel Books, 2005.

Davidson, Miriam. *Convictions of the Heart: Jim Corbett and the Sanctuary Movement*. Tucson: University of Arizona Press, 1998.

Slade, Peter, Shea Tuttle, and Jacqueline A. Bussie, eds. *People Get Ready: Twelve Jesus-Haunted Misfits, Malcontents and Dreamers in Pursuit of Justice*. Grand Rapids, MI: Wm. B. Eerdmans, 2023.